THE AQUATIC FRONTIER

A VOLUME IN THE SERIES
Environmental History of the Northeast
EDITED BY
Anthony N. Penna and Richard W. Judd

THE AQUATIC FRONTIER

Oysters and Aquaculture
in the Progressive Era

Samuel P. Hanes

University of Massachusetts Press
AMHERST AND BOSTON

Copyright © 2019 by University of Massachusetts Press
All rights reserved
Printed in the United States of America

ISBN 978-1-62534-413-7 (paper); 412-0 (hardcover)

Designed by Jen Jackowitz
Set in Optima and Minion Pro

Cover design by William Boardman
Cover art by A. Hoen & Co., Lithographer. *Fresh oysters—Thos. J. Myer & Co., Baltimore*, ca. 1870. Courtesy of Library of Congress.

Library of Congress Cataloging-in-Publication Data
Names: Hanes, Samuel P., author.
Title: The aquatic frontier : oysters and aquaculture in the progressive era / Samuel P. Hanes.
Description: Amherst : University of Massachusetts Press, [2019] | Series: Environmental history of the northeast | Includes bibliographical references and index. |
Identifiers: LCCN 2018051549 (print) | LCCN 2018052963 (ebook) | ISBN 9781613766606 (ebook) | ISBN 9781613766613 (ebook) | ISBN 9781625344120 (hardcover) | ISBN 9781625344137 (paperback)
Subjects: LCSH: Oyster culture—United States—Environmental conditions—19th century. | Oyster culture—United States—Environmental conditions—20th century. | Oyster culture—Law and legislation—United States—History—19th century. | Oyster culture—Law and legislation—United States—History—20th century.
Classification: LCC SH365.A3 (ebook) | LCC SH365.A3 H36 2019 (print) | DDC 333.95/541—dc23
LC record available at https://lccn.loc.gov/2018051549

British Library Cataloguing-in-Publication Data
A catalog record for this book is available from the British Library.

Chapter 5 is derived, in part, from Samuel P. Hanes, "Common Property Mapping and the Preservation of Traditional Rights in Chesapeake Bay's Oyster Fishery, 1892–1914," *Journal of Cultural Geography* 30, no. 3 (2013): 307–27 (https://www.tandfonline.com/doi/full/10.1080/08873631.2013.828483).

TO TERESA

CONTENTS

PREFACE IX

Introduction
Inshore Fisheries, Aquaculture, and Complexity in Environmental History 1

Chapter 1
Oyster Management before 1880 21

Chapter 2
Oyster Law Enforcement 45

Chapter 3
Shellfish Commissions 63

Chapter 4
Natural Science 96

Chapter 5
Mapping Natural Beds 133

Chapter 6
Mapping Planters' Property 155

Conclusion
The Challenge of Complexity 180

NOTES 185

INDEX 213

PREFACE

This book started in the cow pastures of central Texas, where I first became interested in understanding why people developed simplified approaches to environmental management. I recall learning how some ranchland managers tried to eliminate the omnipresent scraggly mesquite trees, whereas others cultivated them for their nitrogen-fixing properties. Why did some people try to work with mesquite-country ecology while others attempted to bypass it? I found that I too held simplified views. I always thought of cows as invaders that damaged these grassland ecosystems until I met people who used cows to reprise the role bison once played. Learning these stories about landscape change led me to study geography. Cultural landscapes, places shaped by culture intertwined with nature, are endlessly fascinating objects of study. As I read more on this subject, I started to see a pattern in diverse sources like Carolyn Merchant's *The Death of Nature*, Wendell Berry's *The Unsettling of America*, and Fritjof Capra's *The Turning Point*. These books take a long view of Western culture. They emphasize the way we respond to the challenge of managing highly complex environmental systems. I thought this would be an exciting topic that, though nontraditional, would fit under the big tent of academic geography.

This admittedly vague idea took firmer shape when by chance I read James Scott's *Seeing Like a State* and Samuel Hays's *Conservation and the Gospel of Efficiency* the same month. Scott provided a useful synthesis that seemed to mirror Hays's picture of the first American conservation agencies. I began reading more Progressive Era environmental history and decided this field was an ideal place to apply Scott's framework.

I first considered writing about the Progressive Era oyster fishery simply because I was living in New Jersey at the time. New Jersey was right in the heart of the main oyster-producing region in the United States. The more I read about oysters, the more I wanted to write about them. The first state shellfish commissions seemed like the perfect fit for the sort of investigation I envisioned. I soon discovered, however, that the management agencies I wanted to write about varied a great deal from state to state. To capture the range of these agencies' actions, I realized I had to study the major oyster-producing states from Virginia to Massachusetts.

When I began my research in earnest, I had another surprise. I knew from reading Bonnie McCay's *Oyster Wars and the Public Trust* that oystermen had fought for common property rights, but I was impressed by how elaborate their common property management system was before the Progressive Era. When I brought this up one day, a friend recommended Richard Judd's *Common Lands, Common People*. Judd's book changed the way I conceived of this project. This was not just a story about shellfish commissions facing a complex natural environment; they also confronted a complex *social* system of preexisting oyster conservation. I grew to see this as the defining feature of early oyster management.

Any such study would be impossible without a great deal of help. I am especially indebted to archivists at university special collections (University of Rhode Island, Yale University, Rutgers, University of Maryland, University of Virginia), state libraries, and the National Archives. Staffs at the Connecticut Maritime Museums and the Chesapeake Bay Maritime Museum provided helpful assistance as well. Brian Halley, Rachael DeShano, and Jon Berry at the University of Massachusetts Press offered expert guidance for a novice author. Two external reviewers provided invaluable advice. Bonnie McCay's comments on two early drafts strengthened the theoretical focus of this project. Phaedra Daipha, David Hughes, Tom Rudel, and Kevin St. Martin provided constructive suggestions on an early version of the book. Susan Schrepfer introduced me to the field of environmental history. Richard Judd and Stephen Hornsby encouraged me to write this as a book rather than collection of papers. Kourtney Collum, Frank Drummond, Cyndy Loftin, and Tim Waring helped me work out ideas about complexity in resource management and agricultural systems. A Rutgers University human ecology travel grant made my National Archives research possible. The University of Maine's College of Liberal Arts and Sciences pretenure fellowship provided time off from teaching, which I used to write the final draft. Essential course-release funding was provided by Sustainable Ecological Aquaculture Network (SEANET), a National Science Foundation project. Being a part of SEANET gave me the opportunity to speak with Maine aquaculture farmers and scientists. On a more personal note, the University of Maine Children's Center teachers provided indispensible peace of mind. My wife, Teresa Johnson, kept my depiction of marine policy more realistic. Those who know her may recognize many of her ideas herein; she has made it a better book.

THE AQUATIC FRONTIER

INTRODUCTION

INSHORE FISHERIES, AQUACULTURE, AND COMPLEXITY IN ENVIRONMENTAL HISTORY

This book explores the forms that simplification took in the history of fisheries and aquaculture. It examines why simplification led to unsustainable and inequitable outcomes. Radical reformers wanted to simplify property rights, conservation practices, and ecological relationships, but they failed to do so. What happened instead was a success story. The first government agencies, sometimes against their will, preserved a complex conservation system in the oyster fishery and its aquaculture sector. Recent years have seen many nuanced studies of modernizing and industrializing fisheries. This book adds to them by focusing on simplification and its alternatives in Progressive Era conservation. The challenge of complexity continues to define options for fisheries and aquaculture today.

Oysters never had their Melville. Lacking a *Moby Dick*, oyster history faded from popular memory. The history of American fisheries instead conjures up images of the great sailing ships immortalized by Winslow Homer. Popular books and movies today, such as *The Perfect Storm* and *Cod*, keep these images alive. Romanticized cousins eclipsed the story of the oyster, and so few recall that the oyster fishery once rivaled the North Atlantic finfish fisheries. Oysters were the second largest U.S. fishery in 1880.[1] Some of the world's largest oyster beds lay between Cape Cod and Cape Hatteras.[2] This book explores the fishery from Massachusetts to Virginia, in part because these states accounted for 96 percent of the astonishing seventeen million bushels harvested in 1880.[3] Different states created quite different forms of management, and so a study of any one would necessarily miss much. In addition, regional interactions shaped this fishery and provide another rationale for a larger study. Aquaculture began in New Jersey and New York and expanded from there. Connecticut developed the first truly industrial-scale aquaculture that served as a model for other states. Connecticut and New York also led the way in canning, although Baltimore grew more prominent later. The growth of northern farms and packing houses created the "Southern Trade," or the shipment of oysters from Chesapeake Bay to New York and Connecticut. Oyster management differed in each state: Connecticut had vast aquaculture farms and packing houses, whereas Virginia had few of either and large exports to the North. To understand broader patterns, this book studies the whole region.

The oyster fishery included four groups: tongers, planters, dredgers, and packers. Most oyster fishermen were called "tongers" after their gear because they fished from small boats close to shore with tongs, which were rake-like implements fastened together like a pair of scissors to scoop oysters from shallow water. "Planters" were oyster aquaculture farmers, ranging from the marine equivalent of small farmers to the rich capitalists who harvested thousands of acres with steamships. Tongers were often quite poor and many sold small seed oysters to planters; the two depended on one another but also competed over space in some areas. On larger ships "dredgers" relied on wage labor to pull dredges over oyster beds. The final group, "packers," owned packing houses or canneries.

Oystermen developed conservation practices before 1880, and this mostly forgotten system deserves acknowledgment as an important piece of American environmental history. Conservation included closed seasons, gear restrictions, vessel size limits, and local residency requirements. Unfortunately, these measures proved unable to accommodate increasing demand. Industrialization hammered the fishery on and off shore, as mechanical dredges, canning factories, and railroad connections propelled rising harvests. The oyster fishery differed from other fisheries industrializing at this time, however, in that it had a larger aquaculture sector. Scientists began raising fish species in hatcheries, but only oyster farmers deployed extensive farms in coastal waters in the nineteenth century. Shellfish were easier to farm than finfish, and oysters had been farmed for over two thousand years.[4] Aquaculture farmers moved living oysters and farmed them in shallow water close to shore. Oyster farms spread across the East Coast by the late nineteenth century, and farms in Connecticut grew to a truly industrial scale for the first time. Industrialization wreaked havoc in the wild fishery while aquaculture expanded.

State governments founded new agencies to tackle oyster overfishing. These agencies espoused what Samuel Hays called the "gospel of efficiency."[5] Progressive Era conservation agencies tried to eliminate waste and increase efficiency through the application of objective science to resource management problems. They followed a larger trend, shifting America's political locus from the town-level to more centralized entities and toward public acceptance of a more interventionist government in response to new challenges.[6] Richard Judd and Karl Jacoby show the importance of understanding how these new agencies interacted with rural people and their preexisting norms of resource use.[7] Oyster conservation was no different, and reaction to it divided government agencies. They argue for two distinct gospels of efficiency. One solution radically recast oyster conservation by replacing much, or all, of the capture fishery with privatized aquaculture farms. This solution simplified complex local property rights and elaborate conservation measures, replacing them with the single ownership of marine space. It sought to simplify the ecological system by ending dependence on the intricate ecology in natural oyster reefs and instead creating large-scale oyster farms stocked by hatcheries. Proponents of the simplifying solution felt optimistic about their ability to control social and ecological systems because they misunderstood the complexity of how society and nature worked. Such views led them to see twin interventions as the keys that would unlock progress: privatization and hatcheries. At the other extreme, oyster agencies articulated a different gospel. This second solution attempted to preserve traditional conservation measures and property rights, including more modestly scaled aquaculture farms. This solution sought to protect and retain complex conservation systems and ecological relationships.

By studying this interaction, this book seeks to reframe Progressive Era conservation in terms of the simplification of complex social-ecological systems. A social-ecological system refers to any place where people utilize natural resources. Most resource use simplifies natural systems. Farmers grow radically fewer species per acre than whatever ecosystem they replace. While we simplify natural systems to survive, farms vary widely in their degree of simplification. Monocultures cultivate fewer species than polycultural or agroforestry operations. There are many reasons people choose simpler systems over their more complex counterparts; this book focuses on Progressive Era resource management and asks why environmental reformers in this time period often sought to simplify social-ecological systems.

There are two sides of social-ecological systems and this book devotes most of its space to the social side. It does so mainly because there is already an excellent and widely read book in the field of environmental history illustrating the simplification of a natural system: Nancy Langston's *Forest Dreams, Forest Nightmares*.[8] Langston does not use these terms or explicitly seek to understand the dynamic of system simplification, but one can easily learn those lessons from her book. She shows how the first generation of foresters in the new National Forests of the Blue Mountains faced serious challenges and pressures that mirrored those in the oyster fishery. Foresters needed to come up with management plans for timber harvesting, pest reduction, and fire management, and they needed to do so quickly. Their training in eastern forests proved ill-suited for understanding the drier, highly varied western forests. Foresters needed time they did not have to conduct long-term research.

Without the knowledge they needed, they dove in and crafted plans that simplified the forest. Their interventions worked in the short run but backfired dramatically in the long run, leading to the western "forest health crisis."

The way foresters simplified the fire regime bears careful consideration as it exemplified the broader pattern. When foresters arrived, ponderosa forests had low-temperature ground fires approximately once every ten years. Ground fires burned off flammable material on the ground and killed many small trees. Thick bark protected larger trees. Periodic fires left forests much more open than those in the East. Stopping fires let small trees survive and litter build up on the forest floor. Eventually, fires did start in this altered environment. They burned hotter on the forest floor due to the litter built up, and flames could ascend into the trees by climbing the ladder of branches made available by the small trees. Ponderosa pine needles and upper branches lack the thick bark of the trunk and burn when ignited in these fires. Foresters had inadvertently created the perfect conditions for devastating crown fires. A *High Country News* headline captures the predicament in these forests today: "The West's hottest question: How to burn what's bound to burn."[9] Foresters simplified the fire system by eliminating fire. This worked well for a few decades, but then it backfired and the system no longer functioned as intended. Now forest managers set controlled fires in an attempt to recreate something like the older fire cycle, which is a more complex way to manage fire in the ponderosas. We can summarize the basic dynamic as follows: (1) people oversimply a complex ecological system because they lack knowledge but need control, (2) they obtain short-term success, (3) they encounter deleterious long-term results, and (4) they seek ways to make the system more complex again. This pattern plays out again and again in modern environmental history.

Langston illustrates how this works in a natural system, but people simplify social systems too. The reasons and results are often the same. The GRE (Graduate Record Examinations) is an example familiar to academic readers. It takes an applicant's aptitude for graduate school and boils it down to three numbers. Graduate admissions committees faced with stacks of admissions documents are like Langston's foresters: they must make decisions, they lack time to fully understand everything they might like to know, and they must resort to simplifications. The GRE is useful, and it is useful precisely because a holistic picture is impossible. Graduate admissions committees use many other sources to supplement GRE scores. Using scores alone would be an oversimplification that would lead to unwanted outcomes.

Managers must avoid similar oversimplification in social-ecological systems. The social side of the system in the oyster case was an elaborate suite of common-property management rules developed at the local level before the Progressive Era. These rules and laws sought mainly to preserve access to oysters and in so doing achieved conservation goals as well. The great policy debate of the first Progressive Era agencies was whether to preserve the older management measures, which were under considerable duress, or to wipe the slate clean and introduce new measures. Eliminating common-property rights was analogous to eliminating fire in Langston's case. Common rights evolved over time to fit local conditions and cultures, and without them the oyster system would suffer social deterioration just as surely as the ponderosas faced natural decline. Many thousands of tongers would have lost their livelihoods or shifted from free fishermen to wage laborers on the farms of the wealthy.

One of the most influential books looking at social-ecological system simplification is James Scott's *Seeing Like a State*.[10] Scott looks at cases in which "high modernist" planners attempted to increase control over society and nature by increasing visibility. This drive for legibility led state actors to simplify natural and social systems, as simpler forests and property rights were more visible to the state. Visibility is a prerequisite for control; by making people and nature more visible, the state could control both more thoroughly. These simplifying projects failed because they undermined the complexity that sustained social and natural systems. Scott uses the case of nineteenth-century German forestry as a paradigmatic example. German forestry at the time emphasized maximizing production and eliminating waste by planting trees in even-age rows for easier, more predictable harvesting. Foresters also removed species without monetary value for the state. These measures greatly simplified the forest by reducing the biodiversity and spatial-age diversity. The result was several decades of excellent harvests. However, Germany's forest health crisis followed after this. It was brought on by the removal of beneficial species that played vital, if unseen, roles in the ecosystem. Local people lost out more immediately, as they had traditionally harvested many nontimber species that foresters removed.

Progressive Era oyster agencies advanced two policy solutions that dealt with complexity in opposite ways: preserve it or eliminate it. The literature on Progressive Era natural-resource-management politics documents the split between preservationist and conservationist ideals within early U.S. agencies.[11] Conservationists focused on utilitarian resource use by applying science as a means of eliminating waste and improving efficiency.[12] All oyster agencies offered utilitarian advice, but they preached two gospels of efficiency. This book refers to these perspectives as "modernist" and "populist." Modernist commissioners sought to simplify the social-ecological system. Scott's definition of high modernism epitomizes their actions and statements: "It is best conceived as a strong, one might even say muscle-bound, version of the self-confidence about scientific and technical progress, the expansion of production, the growing satisfaction of human needs, the mastery of nature (including human nature), and, above all, the rational design of social order commensurate with the scientific understanding of natural laws."[13] Modernist shellfish commissioners maintained a faith in natural laws that guided human behavior and wanted legislatures to improve efficiency by applying these social laws. Their thinking on efficiency led them to equate maximizing productivity with the public good. Modernist commissioners argued that privatization was the key to maximizing productivity, and they saw private property, planting, and industrial technology as more advanced.[14]

Modernist commissioners also believed that science would allow them to cultivate oysters in hatcheries in a way that would significantly expand their numbers for planters. They believed applying social laws and scientific advances would lessen conflict by maximizing production. These imagined social laws made privatization and planting seem natural and inevitable, and scientific cultivation promised to end conflict by dramatically increasing oyster production. These modernist plans disproportionately benefited the wealthier sectors of the industry, a pattern that occurred in agricultural science as well.[15] Agricultural historians have focused on the importance of the "organizational synthesis" or "associative state-building" in which the weakness of new state agencies forced government scientists and administrators to form entrepreneurial partnerships with private interest groups.[16]

At the other extreme stood "populist" commissioners. They wanted to increase efficiency as well, but they sought to preserve traditional conservation. Populist commissioners avoided radical change. They were more respectful of oystermen, especially tongers, and their advice was more cautious. Hays emphasizes the progressive fight against waste; populists thought overfishing wasted a natural resource, whereas modernists thought tongers wasted bay space by limiting aquaculture.

Thomas Princen's *Logic of Sufficiency* adds another dimension to the process that Scott describes by exploring how a similar simplification applies to goals.[17] Princen notes that efficiency became the main goal of many progressive reformers, especially in natural resource management. They saw increasing efficiency as synonymous with the public good. The common progressive definition of efficiency was maximizing production per labor spent with the implicit goal of increasing revenues. Tongers on the other hand valued equity and access. Increasing productivity could undermine equity if new technologies or practices changed access to the fishery. Tongers also valued their independence, and so a tonger might well consider himself efficient even if he earned less than his counterpart employed on someone else's oyster farm. One maximized independence and the other income. The question was whose definition should guide management and policy? The choice to define efficiency as maximizing production simplified traditional goals. Princen argues that the ideal of maximizing production caught on, "because it appeared singularly capable of resolving otherwise inherently conflicting interests."[18] The efficiency ideal further required the simplifying assumption that human motivations were rational calculations where individuals sought to maximize a single, and usually monetary, variable. Faith in efficiency's power depends on "a worldview that is at once mechanistic and cornucopian."[19] Efficiency was a common goal in the oyster fishery, but not a universal one. Both populist and modernists oyster commissioners were progressive reformers who wanted to reduce waste and modernize management. The key difference was that modernists often used maximizing production as a rationale for replacing the older management system.

Environmental historians have long explored similar themes. Donald Worster's *Rivers of Empire* offers a most useful exploration of this pattern. Worster examines the relationship between rationalization and resource characteristics, and his book suggests, inadvertently, the importance of oysters as a case study. Worster calls the American West a land of "imperial power" because of the way scarce water resources allow for an "ecological and social regimentation" that is "absolutely dependent on a sharply alienating, intensely managerial relationship with nature."[20] Water managers imposed a simplified, abstract order to manage a difficult and unpredictable environment. A centralized, hierarchical elite who controlled capital and expertise ran western U.S. dam building. Worster explains that this was only possible because the state could centralize control over water. He goes on to associate this type of resource management with the modern capitalist state. He describes this as the barest expression of its tendency and ties water commodification to "instrumental rationality" and the drive to maximize production. He further argues that we need comparative irrigation studies to test his model. This book offers such a comparison by studying a resource whose characteristics created opposite conditions: the great East Coast oyster beds. In comparison to the rivers Worster studied, it was more difficult for one group to bring oysters under their control, which is generally true for marine resources. It proved much harder to exclude people from using oysters, and information on them remained elusive. These characteristics made it difficult for a central technocratic elite to control the fishery. Oysters provide an ideal case study for investigating alternatives to instrumental rationality.

Worster's argument comes from his engagement with Karl Wittfogel's *Oriental Despotism* and the Frankfurt School.[21] Wittfogel's study of "hydraulic societies" examines irrigation-based civilizations to understand power in precapitalist locations. Wittfogel's book led Worster to two other Frankfurt School thinkers, Max Horkheimer and Theodor Adorno, who wrote *Dialectics of Enlightenment* in 1944.[22] Worster uses their critique of instrumental reason to explain the relationship between humans and nature exemplified in western dams. Horkheimer and Adorno accept most of Max Weber's critique of rationality in *Economy and Society*. Weber distinguishes between "formal" and "substantive" rationality.[23] He defines formal rationality as a technique or means of relying on calculability that indiscriminately facilitates. It is the equivalent of instrumental rationality. Substantive rationality, in contrast, is action guided by goals that fit into a belief system. Weber sees formal rationality's indifference to values as a peculiar feature of Western culture; maximizing formal rationality proves morally and politically problematic for him. He notes that people with less power try to limit formal rationality because its results tend to favor the powerful. There is a tension between groups interested in benefiting from efficiency, which is a type of formal rationality, and those interested in the substantive regulation of social life. Weber believes that formal rationality helps bureaucracies increase control, and it also increases irrational results and invites technocracy. This book argues that simplifying solutions to overfishing were formally or instrumentally rational, whereas the solutions that preserved complexity embraced substantive rationality.

Weber argues that instrumental rationality must appeal culturally to gain popularity, and in the oyster case this involved the frontier narratives described below. Proponents of simplifying solutions equated the public good with maximizing production and argued that the way to do this was to expand privatization through oyster farms stocked by hatcheries. They saw the tonging fishery's gear, property, and practices as anachronisms, whereas they described planting, especially industrial-scale planting, and private property as progressive. Literature from colonial studies, particularly Michael Adas's *Machines as the Measure of Men*, argues that colonial officials viewed technology as developing in a linear fashion, with industrial technology as self-evidently superior.[24] Oyster modernists viewed private-property rights the same way. They cast this in an American cultural narrative by continually referencing the Jeffersonian ideal of the yeomen farmer, obviously more progressive than dwellers of the wilderness frontier.[25] Aquaculture created an aquatic frontier, and it is no surprise that colonial themes appear. Modernists argued that private property and industrial technology were further along a linear pathway of civilizational progress. Like their colonial counterparts, they thought this was a universal human law, self-evident to all enlightened observers.

MARINE CARTOGRAPHY

Oyster management agencies spent unexpectedly extensive time making maps. Geographers and others have long read maps as valuable historical evidence. One important book for this study is Raymond Craib's *Cartographic Mexico*. Craib looks at how government cartographers in nineteenth-century Mexico tried to pin down what he calls "fugitive landscapes." Craib documents "the contested, dialectical, and social (not just technical) process by which explorers, surveyors, and cartographers attempted to define, codify, and naturalize space in cooperation and struggle with the people they encountered in the field."[26] Part of the reason they struggled was that they needed to draw lines showing property rights in "places created and recreated through prisms of memory, practical wisdom, use, and collective decisions rather than the lens of instrumentation."[27] This contrast played out in the oyster fishery too. The fixed lines and instrumentation of cartographers, on the one hand, and the inheritance of common-property rights among oystermen, on the other, drove some of the most interesting dynamics in oyster mapping. Craib also notes that Mexican cartographers felt "the tragedy was that of underuse and inefficiency deriving from a presumed lack of self-interest and industry on the part of the Indians."[28] Replace "Indians" with "tongers," and this becomes a perfect description of modernist cartographers of the oyster fishery. They wanted to create maps that showed wasted bay space as a spur to reform. Matthew Edney's study of mapping in British India makes a similar case in a colonial context. Colonial maps show a "British conception of what India should be."[29] Maps not only helped extend Britain's empire, they also functioned as "a significant component of the 'structures of feeling' which legitimated, justified, and defined that imperialism."[30] Modernist maps had a unique power to depict what was there while simultaneously showing what could be there under the right governance. In doing so they elided what was there from the tongers' perspective. Wasted space is only wasted from the view of the colonizing power.

Modernist and populist cartographers drew two kinds of tonger property maps to meet their differing policy goals. Modernist cartographers resembled Craib's state actors in Mexico: they sought to eliminate the wasted bay space that should be filled with productive oyster farms. Their maps depicted a vast extent of empty space. But their maps also needed to seem objective to confer legitimacy. Oyster cartographers developed some of the most detailed maps and painstaking methods; they were pioneers of marine cartography. They did this to justify dispossession of oyster management. If these maps were the only ones made, then the story would be a familiar one of state actors using cartography to help wealthier people and to expand state control. However, other maps fitting the populist model preserved tradition, portraying the existing property rights of tongers and documenting political compromises. The two gospels of efficiency each had its own form of map.

Studies from Progressive Era North American cartography look at the same process of depicting political interests.[31] These studies show the influence of maps on resource allocation, usually to the benefit of upper classes. These studies come out of a tradition in geography interested in the way capitalism redefines space. Henri Lefebvre and David Harvey have been leaders in the field and have stressed capitalism's dependence on the expansion of "abstract space."[32] Space has to be interchangeable and legible so that property can be bought and sold. This took place with oyster-planting-industry lease maps but with outcomes that benefited the larger social-ecological system, along with their support of capitalism.

In addition to creating modernist or populist maps and leasing maps, oyster cartographers also mapped "barren bottoms" and sanitary conditions. Mainly in southern states, maps depicted bottom conditions to show a nascent planting industry where best to start farms. State agencies used sanitary maps to regulate packers and planters by preventing them from harvesting in polluted areas that could transmit typhoid. Packers and planters wanted this form of regulation because it shored up public trust in their product following disease outbreaks. The many types of maps (modernist dispossession maps; populist, tradition-preserving maps; planter cadastral maps; environmental-condition maps; and sanitation maps) illustrate the wide variety of Progressive Era cartography. Progressive Era conservation required making things visible, and cartography played a central role.

These early maps were landmarks in the territorialization of marine space. The territorialization of space is simply assigning new property rights to places. Zoning ordinances and national parks are familiar examples. This has been slower for marine spaces than terrestrial ones, due to less clear ownership, and the difficulty marking property rights in the water.[33] One major milestone was the creation of the Exclusive Economic Zone in 1982, which enabled all countries to exclude foreign resource users within two hundred miles of their coasts. Other examples include an increase in a wide variety of fishing rights, from territorial use rights for fishing (TURFs) in fisheries to individual transferable quotas (ITQs), which both assign the right to fish in a given area and exclude access to outsiders. They all have spatial components: one can only hold an ITQ for a specific location. Another part of territorialization today involves marine spatial planning, which is a form of regional planning applied to marine environments aided by the growth of geographic information systems. Within this context, oysters have been among the easiest marine species to map, certainly one of the most mapped marine species by the end of the Progressive Era. This book looks at the role of cartography in preserving or eroding complex forms of oyster management.

FISHERIES HISTORY

Industrialization often drives overfishing. Jeffrey Bolster's recent study of the North Atlantic finfish fisheries is the definitive work explaining this pattern.[34] Technological change drives ever-increasing catches, and fishermen see the problem coming but fail to stop it. Their inaction occurs because overfishing happens too fast, fishermen benefit from greater catches, and collective action is costly. The last two explanations fit the tragedy of the commons model popularized by Garrett Hardin.[35] In this model, incentives push fishermen to overfish. They gain immediately from overfishing, whereas overfishing's damage is spread out across the whole fishery and felt over the long-term. Numerous studies document this pattern at the regional and global scale.[36]

Fisheries historians have produced nuanced studies that add to and complicate the story of industrial decline. In his book on Alaskan fisheries, David Arnold shows how political and labor history intertwine by analyzing organized labor in canneries.[37] Connie Chiang expands fisheries history by including changing demographic and economic activity, especially tourism, on the shore of Monterrey, California.[38] Brian Payne looks at informal rules and international politics in a cross-border fishery.³⁹ Other fields, such as anthropology, have been diversifying their own studies of industrial fisheries.⁴⁰

Industrialized overfishing occurs more frequently in offshore rather than inshore fisheries. Fishermen see the impact of their actions on inshore stocks. They create territories and enforce conservation rules with greater ease and effectiveness in inshore fisheries, particularly those with less mobile species. James Acheson's work on the history of Maine's lobster fishery provides a classic example of this process.⁴¹ After harvests crashed due to growing industrialism in the 1930s, lobstermen created a conservation system and lobster populations rebounded. Many anthropologists identified similarly successful conservation systems in small-scale fisheries around the world.⁴² These cases illustrate how inshore fishermen have achieved more conservation in industrial fisheries. Payne summarizes the results of this process in his study of an inshore fishery, revealing "a complex system of locally defined codes of conduct" that "sought to limit access to resources so as to corner the market for local communities, and thus naturally limit total extraction."⁴³ The present book examines oystermen's local codes of conduct and how these interacted with the progressive agencies.

Bonnie McCay's and Arthur McEvoy's studies of inshore fisheries parallel Judd and Jacoby's work on conservation in ways that are relevant for this study. In McCay's history of New Jersey fisheries, fishermen preserved older ethics and management forms through the courts. They used civil disobedience and test cases to "try the right."⁴⁴ McEvoy's study of San Francisco Bay fisheries shows the opposite pattern. State managers looked down on the older conservation systems of balkanized immigrant fishing communities and supplanted these "anachronistic" practices.⁴⁵ As with Judd and Jacoby, these studies depict themes of continuance or replacement of inshore fishery conservation. This book presents a case where preindustrial conservation existed, and adds to these studies by examining how simplification affected the encounter between different forms of oyster conservation. McCay's book also offers chapters on the nineteenth-century oyster fishery and its importance for understanding how court cases brought by oystermen shaped the public-trust doctrine. In addition to McCay's text, several other books focus on oyster fisheries. Lawrence Taylor produced the only study of a single oyster town, a Dutch community on Great Bay, Long Island. Taylor provides a detailed explanation of the ways local planters and tongers compromised over marine space.[46] Christine Keiner's study of Maryland oyster politics illustrates how oystermen opposed elite-led reforms.[47] Keiner's book also documents the different views of marine ecology between fishermen and scientists, a central issue in fisheries management today. There are also a few popular books that shed valuable light on the oyster fishery.[48]

Many people promote aquaculture as a solution to industrial overfishing today; this narrative began in the mid- and late nineteenth century. In his book on salmon, Joseph Taylor describes the importance of fish hatcheries as a solution to the problem of dams blocking spawning runs.[49] Jerry Towle documented early fish introductions in California.[50] Both authors explored early U.S. aquaculture as an industrial response to industrial problems. Darin Kinsey's study of Victor Coste, the first modern aquaculture scientist, shows the transatlantic nature of early aquaculture science.[51] This book explores both simplified and complex forms of early oyster aquaculture and considers the reasons why people favored one or the other.

Aquaculture history is a fairly new field, in part because the growth of aquaculture is so recent. As late as 1970, aquaculture only accounted for 6 percent of all seafood production, but by 2016, it accounted for 45 percent.[52] This explosive growth shows no signs of slowing. In contrast, the global yield from wild capture fisheries has stagnated, and many regions have "fished down the food web" by shifting fishing effort to target lower trophic level organisms.[53] Aquaculture now provides an important protein source to developing countries.[54] Growth has been so fast that many people feel we are in a "blue revolution," with fishery impacts on par with the green revolution in agriculture. Changes on such a scale carry mixed results, giving aquaculture a negative reputation as a result. Poor opinions of aquaculture originate from some farms' pollution and waste, including feces, antibiotics, and pesticides. Environmental groups fight genetically modified–farmed fish, arguing that they escape and breed with wild fish. Aquaculturists feed wild fish to their farmed fish; growing farmed fish requires catching a far greater volume of wild fish. Human impacts are equally problematic and include displacement of traditional fishermen and poor labor conditions on farms.[55] At the other end of the spectrum, producers tout the ecological and human benefits beyond increasing global food production. In places where fisheries are declining, aquaculture offers jobs for out-of-work fishermen. Not all fish farms pollute. Some experiment with multitrophic aquaculture, growing multiple species, including ones that feed on the waste produced from fish production. Shellfish and seaweed production bypass the environmental problems associated with fish farms. Barry Costa-Pierce calls these more sustainable approaches "Sustainable Ecological Aquaculture" and their opposite "Industrial Aquaculture."[56]

The dichotomy between sustainable and industrial aquaculture arose first in oyster fishery. Sustainable ecological aquaculture relies on complex social systems, such as the older conservation practices used by tongers. This book details the oyster fishery's main sectors, as well as its actors, canneries, gear, and ships. It also discusses the geography of the fishery and key regional interactions. Overfishing was less of a problem before 1870, but it was important enough to warrant serious conservation measures. The book describes these in detail and then documents the slow crisis of overfishing brought on by industrial growth.

The rest of the book examines solutions to overfishing, the first of which was state law enforcement. Overfishing was most blatant in Chesapeake Bay. Therefore chapter 2 focuses mostly on Virginia and Maryland's "oyster navies," which are an important but overlooked part of U.S. fisheries history. Unlike situations where local people evaded state law enforcement that criminalized traditional use, oyster law enforcement tended to preserve local traditions undermined by industrial overfishing.

Perhaps the most central solution was for state legislatures to found shellfish commissions. Their primary role was to advise state legislatures by collecting information. Chapter 3 describes the ways commissioners promoted both gospels of efficiency. The book analyzes the simplifying solutions of these agencies and the arguments made on their behalf, as well as the alternatives to these solutions that sought to preserve complexity. The book documents the two gospels of efficiency in these agencies and how they dealt with preexisting conservation.

Scientists also debated the two gospels, as they chose between rival oyster science programs. Oyster science originated in Europe, and European engagement with social-ecological complexity foreshadowed what transpired in the United States. The United States Fish Commission (USFC) produced most U.S. oyster science, although some university and state agency scientists offered contributions, as well. Chapter 4 aims to reconstruct their efforts to design oyster hatcheries and analyzes their ideas and institutional context. It explains the forms simplification took in natural science at this time in comparison to the alternatives that sought to preserve complexity.

After exploring scientists' role, chapters 5 and 6 turn to cartography. Chapter 5 begins by assessing the role of maps in the debate over privatization and industrial aquaculture expansion, and it explores why the two gospels of efficiency produced two different types of tonger property maps. Cartographers drew three additional types of maps (planter property maps, environmental condition maps, and sanitation maps), and the variety of oyster maps contributes to our understanding of the range of progressive marine and conservation cartography.

Simplification in fisheries and aquaculture management is a never-ending challenge. Avoiding past mistakes of system simplification is one of the keys to the industry's sustainability. For environmental historians, this book expands on Worster's work to illustrate how we can study instrumental rationality and alternatives to it with a broader array of resources. It also provides a new way of thinking about Progressive Era history by employing a theoretical lens from Scott's influential *Seeing Like a State*.

CHAPTER 1

OYSTER MANAGEMENT BEFORE 1880

LOCAL CONSERVATION AND REGIONAL INTERACTION

The past abundance of oysters is hard to imagine; they were the passenger pigeon of Atlantic estuaries. Nowhere was this truer than Chesapeake Bay. The bay produced an astonishing 17.5 million bushels in 1880. Maryland and Virginia employed almost forty thousand oystermen and cannery workers at a time when the entire country employed about one hundred thirty thousand fishery workers.[1] The combination of extensive shallow water, ample nutrients, abundant microorganisms, and low salinity was perfect for oysters.[2]

Oystermen built an elaborate conservation system prior to the advent of shellfish commissions. This chapter presents an overview of oyster industry history from Massachusetts to Virginia before 1880. The first section of the chapter documents conservation laws and industry practices. The second section discusses evidence found in a particularly useful source, Virginia's legislative petitions. The third examines regional interactions and the slow march of industrialization.

Bonnie McCay's *Oyster Wars and the Public Trust* explains the evolution of nineteenth century oyster politics in New Jersey.[3] Early New Jersey oyster management mirrored forest and fishery conservation in northern New England. In both cases, rural people grew concerned about resource decline and developed solutions to mitigate it. The equity and access goals of rural communities drove conservation, patterning oyster management. Oysters' abundance and proximity to shore made them an important source of money and food for the poorer members of coastal communities. Many coastal towns depended on oysters, and these communities sought to preserve access to their economically important oyster beds. The works of McCay and Judd show that preserving access meant excluding outsiders, and precommission management revolved around maintaining access for locals and excluding outsiders. However, oyster conservation included establishing private rights to planted oysters as well. In some places, private rights to oyster farms clashed with public rights to natural oyster beds, but tongers and planters reached compromises over marine space. Planters' rights expanded alongside tonger conservation.

Local conservation rested on working with complexity. Oystermen understood and adapted to marine ecology. Their conservation practices encoded complex compromises between different towns, classes, and sectors in the industry. Equity, access, and independence formed complicated goals, and specific needs varied between communities due to local social and ecological conditions. This system proved far from foolproof; access could trump sustainability, and tongers completely depleted some locations. However, state agencies still use the system's main practices today because they included sensible ecological provisions and political compromises borne out of long-term knowledge and experimentation. An extensive body of literature documents the successful common-property-based conservation systems of small-scale inshore fishermen.[4] The nineteenth century East Coast oyster fishery became an important success story.

OYSTER LAWS BEFORE 1880

Lime

Oyster laws contained similar provisions across the East Coast states, reflecting a common approach to depletion and conflict. The oldest conservation measures prohibited gathering oysters for lime. Farmers prized oyster shells as a crop fertilizer, but oystermen argued harvesting for this purpose depleted beds (though some states allowed farmers to purchase old shells from packing houses). New York passed its lime law in 1658, Rhode Island in 1734, New Jersey in 1775, Massachusetts in 1796, and Virginia in 1804. All states in this study adopted lime laws, which attests to the very early concern over and awareness of oyster depletion.

Closed Seasons

All states in this study also adopted a summer closed season. Oystermen timed closed seasons to let juvenile oysters develop hard shells prior to harvest. Oysters spawn in the late spring or summer, and closures lasted from April or May until August, September, or October, depending on the location. These laws constituted an important conservation measure. There was also a widespread belief that, due to the timing of reproduction, oysters were unfit for food in months without an *r*, which depressed the summer market. The oldest closed season law was New York's 1715 law, which contained an exemption for Native Americans. New Jersey passed theirs in 1719, Massachusetts in 1834, Virginia in 1836, and Rhode Island in 1864. Many states also prohibited oystering at night, as a measure to aid in monitoring and enforcement, and some banned oystering on Sundays.

Harvest Limits

States set harvest limits in bushels per day. These limits were partly a conservation measure and partly an equity mechanism designed to spread the harvest among more people. Some states set lower limits for the closed season. Most states allowed harvesting for home consumption during the closed season but restricted the amount, usually to about five bushels a day. Five bushels per day obviously exceeded what an oysterman needed for home consumption. However, local farmers often traveled to gather oysters, and they wanted to obtain all they needed in one trip. These rules reflected a widespread norm that it was right to allow local people to use fish and game resources without restriction when they were for home consumption and not for market sale. This right was seen as especially important for the poor, who depended most on these resources.

Cull Laws and Size Limits

Cull laws required oystermen to sort or cull their harvest on the boat. The law compelled them to throw empty shells and undersized oysters overboard, so that they could drift down to where they had been taken up. Oyster larvae float for a short period and then settle on the bottom, and if they alight on soft mud they sink into it and die. They require a hard substrate, such as old oyster shells, for their initial attachment. Culling empty shells maintained these essential attachment sites. Deposited shells provided these attachment sites in places where oystermen knew oysters could reproduce. Many laws achieved conservation as a byproduct of equity and access concerns, but cull laws served purely to conserve oysters. Most states, but not all, adopted cull laws, and they did so later than many other laws. For example, New Jersey passed theirs in 1845 and Rhode Island in 1852. In addition to shell cull laws, some states had size limits. Oystermen had to throw back undersized oysters, a common limit being two and a half inches. Oysters spawn at one year of age, and so size limits ensured smaller oysters remained to breed and replenish the reef. It was also a sound economic practice to leave undersized oysters in place to grow into larger oysters that fetched higher prices.

Gear and Vessel Restrictions

Laws banned or regulated the use of dredges (see figures 1 and 2). The greater capacity of dredges meant they were more likely to

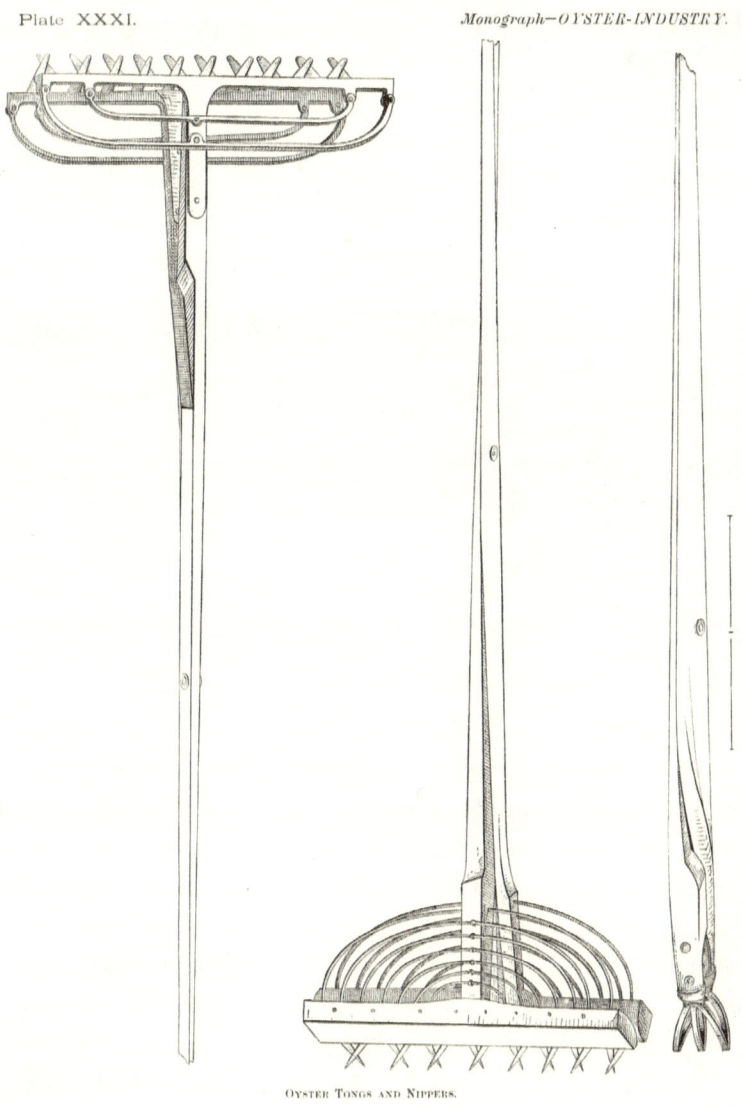

FIGURE 1. Oyster tongs. From Ingersoll, *The History and Present Condition of the Oyster Industry*.

completely deplete oyster beds. In addition, dredges could harvest more oysters faster, leaving fewer oysters behind for other harvesters. Dredges required bigger boats and more workers. Dredging necessitated more capital, helping wealthier people harvest

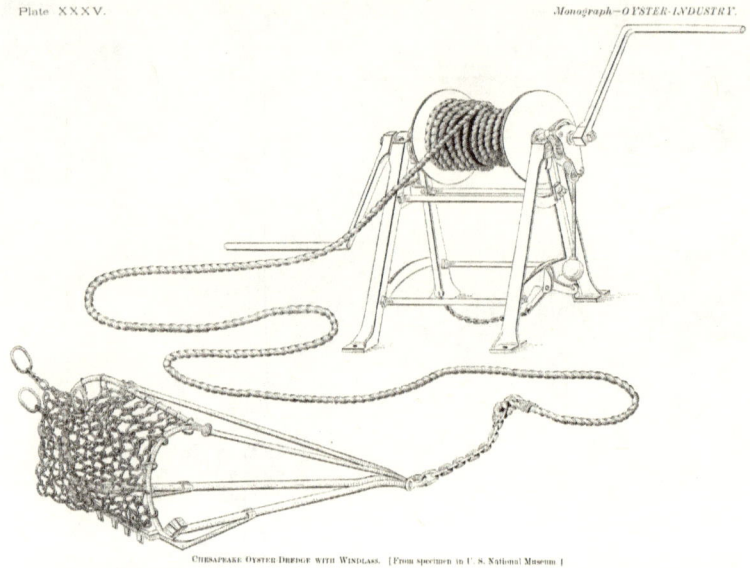

FIGURE 2. Oyster dredge. From Ingersoll, *The History and Present Condition of the Oyster Industry.*

a disproportionate number of oysters. All states banned dredges at one point or another. Sometimes states restricted dredges to deeper waters where tonging was impossible; other times they banned the use of dredges altogether. Some allowed dredges on planting grounds but banned them elsewhere. Vessel restrictions were another way to limit dredging. They fell into two types: laws prohibiting the use of large vessels and laws prohibiting steamships specifically. Both of these aimed to limit dredging. As with many laws, vessel and dredge restrictions combined sustainability, equity, and access concerns.

Residency Requirements

Residency requirements formed another bedrock of nineteenth-century oyster conservation. They restricted outsiders' access to oysters. Residency laws stipulated that a harvester must live in a location for a prescribed period, usually one year, before they could harvest oysters there. These laws often applied to boat owners too. Oystermen crafted residency laws in all states. They differed in how they defined residency. New York, New Jersey, and Rhode Island defined residency at the state level, whereas Virginia and Maryland defined residency by county, and Connecticut and Massachusetts defined it by town.

Once a town or county excluded outsiders, they proceeded to craft provisions within laws that applied only to those specific locations. These laws usually applied to towns, counties, or bodies of water. They were often written in response to petitions from oystermen in these locations. In Connecticut, the state gave towns the right to author their own oyster ordinances in 1766. Massachusetts developed a system of town management in the 1860s and 1870s too. New York's local laws evolved out of the peculiarities of colonial grants on Long Island. Chesapeake Bay's local laws accreted layer after layer of detail. For instance, part of an 1876 Maryland oyster law limited harvesting for family use to five bushels a day in June, July, and August in Dorchester County but exempted harvesting in the Great Bay of the Little Choptank River. This same law reserved a specific bed in the Wye River for Queen Anne and Talbot County residents and also issued a dredge ban for boats within four hundred yards of shore past a certain line in the Wye. Chesapeake Bay legislatures frequently amended these local stipulations. As a whole, residency laws preserved local people's access, and, like most successful common-pool resource systems, they did so by blocking outsiders.[5]

Planting and Leasing

Oystermen moved oysters around. One of the most striking features of the fishery was just how frequently they did this. Oysters are tough: they can survive out of the water for a short period and they are easy to transport alive in containers of salt water. Some of the greatest challenges for nineteenth century conservation revolved around transportation. There were two main reasons oystermen moved oysters. The first involved a practice called "fattening" (or "floating," "drinking," etc.). Oystermen placed their catch in fresher water, usually near the mouth of a creek, where the difference in density and salinity caused the oysters to absorb water, or "fatten," and expel sediment. Many consumers preferred the taste and texture of fattened oysters. Fattening only required a day or two, but oystermen left oysters in these locations for much longer to store them close to markets.

Planting was a very different practice. It grew out of the observation that oysters propagated better in shallower, low salinity water but grew faster in deeper, high salinity water. Oyster predators, such as drills, which have an easy time preying on thin-shelled young oysters, prefer deeper waters. Planters took small oysters from oyster beds and moved them to deeper areas where they would grow more rapidly. They might keep them there for a single winter or up to two years or more. While planters' main motivation was faster growth, they would also move oysters to deeper water for market proximity. Coastal farmers sometimes planted oysters simply to keep them growing adjacent to their farms.

Ernest Ingersoll, a USFC surveyor who produced an invaluable volume on the fishery in 1882, presented persuasive evidence that Native Americans living along the Gulf of Maine planted oysters on a small scale.[6] The first recorded experiment with planted oysters occurred in 1711, when thirty persons placed oysters in Plymouth Harbor in an unsuccessful attempt to form an oyster bed.[7] The next evidence of planting appears in Rhode Island in 1798, when the state granted planters a two-acre lease.[8] In New Jersey planting started in the Shrewsbury and Navesink River area around 1808.[9] From there it seems to have spread north to New York Harbor in the 1810s or 1820s.[10] Leasing plots to oyster planters began on a regular basis in 1822 in Rhode Island and 1836 in Virginia. Planting was less important in Maryland, and it remains difficult to know when it began there.

Planting laws developed in response to the spread of this practice. Laws allowed people, usually state residents, to plant oysters in certain locations and allocated them property rights over those areas. States leased planting grounds and gave riparian owners precedence. Tongers could dispute claims in areas that had naturally occurring oyster beds, however, as these remained closed to planting. This raised vexing questions on the definition of a naturally occurring oyster bed, a subject dealt with extensively in chapter five. The amount of underwater land one could claim varied from one acre to an unlimited quantity, and the duration of leases varied as well. Laws sometimes permitted planters to use otherwise prohibited practices, such as dredging and summer harvesting, on their own property.

VIRGINIA'S LEGISLATIVE PETITIONS

Virginia preserved seventy-eight oyster petitions sent to the state legislature between 1810 and 1855. These petitions provide unique insight into the formation of oyster conservation laws. Petitioners asked the legislature to pass or change laws and also explained oystermen's rationale for petitioning. With one exception, they ask for the same provisions found in oyster laws elsewhere. The value of oyster petitions lies in their extensive discussions of oystermen's motivations in asking for legislative change.

The most common requests in the petitions asked for changes in who could access oyster beds. Oystermen pleaded for the state to ban out-of-state dredge boats and "northern men with large capital [who] fill up our waters."[11] Petitions also asked the state to ban northerners running planting operations in Virginia and sales to northerner-owned packing houses in Maryland. There were several exceptions to this pattern. Chincoteague Island residents claimed they depended on the northern boats to buy their oysters and asked the legislature not to restrict this trade. There were also several petitions asking the legislature to repeal the dredge ban and to allow northern boats access. Petitioners often immediately objected, stating that the prodredging authors were not average oystermen but wealthier persons trying to benefit from increased dredging. These contested petitions illustrate the variation in petitioner views and depict a portion of the conflicts surrounding these laws.

Many petitioners requested laws for their specific locations, usually counties. Often, they asked for laws modeled on ones in other counties. There was an element of competition or conflict driving the spread of place-specific laws. Several petitioners said oystermen who had laws, such as closed seasons, were gaining an unfair advantage by harvesting oysters in other counties. For instance, as stated in a Lancaster County petition, people from areas with local residency requirements were taking oysters from Lancaster County in summer and carrying them back to their protected counties. Petitioners explained that many of them depended on oysters, and that in a few years this practice would destroy their beds. They recommended a county residency requirement for the whole state.[12] A few petitions criticize local laws on the principle that public waters should remain the common property of all Virginians. One discusses a North River law, saying it "operates as a monopoly" that if this were to continue in other places the whole state would be "monopolized," and describes local residency requirements as running contrary to "common property" traditions.[13] The petitions confirm the desire for local laws, but they also illustrate a variety of ways of thinking about the relationship between access and residency.

Access concerns were closely tied to ideas of equity. Petitions often describe the poor's dependence on oysters. One says oysters were the poor's "chief stock of food" and calls illegal dredging "a practice already seriously afflicting the poor and threatening to demoralize the labouring part of the whole community."[14] Another claims, "that with us, oysters are *food for the poor*, whereas when carried away, they are used only as *luxuries for the rich*" (emphasis in the original).[15] The general pattern was to claim that the petitioners were ordinary oystermen requesting laws that would benefit them and protect them from wealthier individuals, sometimes highlighting the importance of these laws for protecting the poor. When petitioners discussed equity concerns, they frequently expressed fear of monopolies. A standard petition states:

> But the proposed law in giving to individuals the right to acquire property in the planting grounds in the public waters will produce

a change in the rights of the people fraught with the most serious consequences to your petitioners, for under the operation of such a law it will not be long before the whole of the public waters and bottoms suitable for planting oysters would be monopolized by a comparatively few while the poor and laboring population will be driven from the rivers.[16]

Their primary fear was that planters or dredgers would continue to earn more and outcompete tongers.

Another common theme was lack of law enforcement. Petitions describe oyster laws as "totally ineffectual" and "so imperfect and defective that they are violated with impunity."[17] Petitions give several reasons for this: "vacilation and continual change" in the laws created confusion.[18] Another explains, "That in consequence of the many changes in these laws they have become so complicated that it has been almost impossible to ascertain what they allow and what they prohibit."[19] Other petitions cite the large number of violators, and the "spirit of taunt and bravado towards the civil authorities" that had grown because of the "uniform success which has attended all attempts to evade these" laws.[20] Another argues that capturers needed better compensation, and yet another suggests that fines were too low. Most focus on the confusion and profusion in the laws and the violators' disregard toward civil authorities.

Petitioners knew oysters could decline. This perception appears frequently in the Virginia petitions. For instance, Gloucester County petitions include "reasons to fear the total loss" of beds, saying nonresidents "will entirely destroy the oyster beds."[21] Ingersoll notes that oystermen knew about local cases of bed exhaustion in all oyster regions.[22] A closely related debate concerned whether dredging inflicted harm on oyster beds. Many people felt dredging helped expand oyster beds by breaking them up and spreading them out. One petition explains this idea:

> Were it true there was the slightest prospect for years or even for centuries of the destruction of these beds under the operation of this trade [dredging] they would forgo the advantages derived from it, for the general good—and without a murmur, but experience has

fully satisfied them that the beds are not only exhaustless, but the oysters have regularly improved during the entire period when they were being removed from the waters of the Rivers.[23]

Here the beneficial effects of dredging are linked to the inexhaustibility of the beds. While this view that dredging spread out beds appears to have been common, others argued that too much dredging could harm beds by not leaving enough oysters to reproduce. Both sides backed up their ideas by citing specific oyster beds. This debate shows how ecological ideas varied, but it also shows widespread fear of resource exhaustion, a fear implied in much oyster law.

One unexpected and unique finding in the petitions is the link between oyster law enforcement and slavery in Virginia. Several petitions from different years and locations ask for bans on northern boats because they were "corrupting" slaves. These petitions claim northerners were making slaves rebellious by giving them alcohol, talking to them about freedom, and encouraging them to pilfer poultry and grain for the ships' crews. They describe slaves as also working too hard oystering, principally at night, which made them too tired to work the following day. The most detailed of these accounts provides a sense of the fear slave owners felt and illustrates their concern for the larger repercussions of this issue (blanks mark illegible words):

> This trade is continued almost exclusively by citizens of other states whose institutions and manners in many ways differ from our own; and they are in general men of that sort who are neither very scrupulous in principle nor very cautious in conduct. Such is the force of public opinion among us ___, that very few of our white citizens engage in supplying their exports, so that they are dependent chiefly on our slaves and free negros. The former labor for them only in the night whereby they are rendered unable to labor for their owners in the day, and in the course of a few years, are laid up with rheumatism and other diseases of a premature old age. In some instances, valuable slaves have been drowned, in pursuing this business too eagerly in the dark and inclement night. Moreover they are paid for the work past in ardent spirits whereby they soon become habitual drunkards. This intemperance is still further ___

by the temptations to theft which the ___ ___ out to them, by either purchasing the stolen goods, or by conning their masters to dispose of them aboard. In this manner they render our slaves practically worthless. But even this is not the worst. Thrown by the nature of this pursuit, into continual contact with other classes—and that too, in the secrecy of night—and interested to win their confidence as far as possible, what can be more natural than to attempt this by injurious comments upon their condition, and affected sympathy in their supposed oppressions?

The petition goes on to describe the emancipation movement's activities and support in their own county. The authors felt the movement was planning violence. They then returned to the northern oyster boats, saying:

> No agent can be more perfectly suited to this work than the oyster traders. Their __, their night operations, their ignorance, their prejudice, their total ___ of all common feeling or common interest with ourselves; their frequent ___ and ___ ___ our slaves and the northern whites . . . Nothing can be easier than for them to incite the most dangerous opinions and distribute them with incendiary writings, without the possibility of detection. With equal ease they can evade detection, and convey intelligence from place to place, whereby the most extensive conduct can be prepared.[24]

This set of petitions shows how conservation incorporated the topic of slavery in Virginia.

Several themes in the petitions conform to the literature on nineteenth-century conservation. Early fishery laws were a reaction to Old World enclosures.[25] The experience of enclosure, coupled with laws restricting fish and game based on hereditary privilege, led U.S. immigrants to desire more egalitarian access to fisheries. The vastness of U.S. resources made this possible. Rhode Island's colonial charter reserved the right for the state's citizens to have "ffull and ffree power and liberty to continue and vse the trade of ffishing vpon the sayd coast, in an of the seas thereunto adjoyninge, or-any armes of the seas, or salt water, rivers and creeks, where they have been accustomed to ffish."[26] Connecticut passed a law regulating weirs in 1716, citing them as a nuisance to migrating fish.

Massachusetts passed a law in 1641, providing free access to fish and fowl from ponds, bays, coves, and rivers for persons near the town where they live, unless prohibited by that town. Conservation laws began at a later point in southern states. Virginia's first fish conservation law passed in 1746 and required chutes for shad around Rappahannock River mills, a requirement that the state soon extended to other rivers. An 1803 Virginia law prohibited dams, weirs, traps, and hedges from obstructing fish passage, saying the Great Falls of the Potomac "afford convenient opportunities to evil-minded persons" and allocating funds to hire a watchman between March and June. This basic pattern extended to other resources, and by the mid-nineteenth century, laws protecting game birds, deer, fish, and terrapins were common in the eastern states. In the same way, oyster laws' restrictions on gear and residency aimed to spread harvests more broadly among local people while excluding outsiders. Closed seasons, lime laws, and cull laws sought to preserve the oyster resources for the future, and petitions confirm the purpose of these laws. Oyster laws match the pattern exhibited in U.S. nineteenth-century local conservation.

REGIONAL PATTERNS AND INTERACTIONS IN THE OYSTER FISHERY BEFORE 1880

Long Island Sound

In Northern Long Island Sound, oystermen depleted several Narragansett Bay and Connecticut beds. In some cases this was rapid. In one case, oystermen discovered a large set on the Potowomut River in 1872 ("set" was the common term for the juvenile oysters that attached over a summer). Soon after, tongers rushed in and harvested all the oysters. This would be the river's last significant set. On many oyster beds, people from far inland would gather along the shoreline to tong oysters for the November 1 season opening. Large crowds would then rush the beds to compete for oysters. Such harvesting methods were common and depict the tension between the desire for access and sustainability. Despite these unsustainable practices, extensive natural beds remained in many areas, the largest being a three-mile-long oyster bed located in Norwalk.[27]

Planting succeeded in Long Island Sound. Planters occupied leases that towns granted. Leasing and planting began in the Providence River in 1822 and was in place in Buzzards Bay by the 1830s. It remains harder to identify when leasing began in Connecticut. Most planters lived in the towns where they worked, except in Buzzards and Narragansett Bays, where Boston merchants leased much of the planting grounds until locals expelled them in the 1840s. Sometimes planters placed oysters on exhausted beds, such as Great Bed near the end of the Providence River, which tongers depleted around 1850. This area later became one of the largest planting grounds. Some planters worked one-acre plots, whereas others owned large planting companies.[28]

New Haven's Packing Industry

New Haven Bay's packing industry is central to the history of the entire East Coast fishery. A tonging fishery developed around the bay's natural beds, and tongers sold catches to one of the first U.S. oyster packing industries in New Haven. Packers sent oysters inland in barrels, which traveled all the way to Albany and then westward over the Erie Canal. New Haven oystermen were some of the first to import southern oysters to their packing houses. Packing companies eventually built branch-houses in major inland cities, such as Chicago and St. Louis.[29] New Haven packers were the first to develop an extensive packing industry, and this enabled them to dominate the U.S. packing trade well into the Progressive Era.

Women and boys "shucked" oysters, removing them from the shell, and then washed them and packed them in wooden casks or metal tins. Early on, packers used casks in cold weather and tins in warm weather. Packing houses stored tins in a cold room, and then packed them together in a wooden container with space for a block of ice in the middle. By Ingersoll's time, packers only used tins and this trade was carried on predominately in the winter. Packing was such an extensive industry that a French scientist sent to survey the

U.S. oyster fishery estimated that in 1863 one hundred fifty persons were employed in two factories making casks and tins for the oyster industry.[30] At its peak in the 1850s, New Haven may have processed over one million bushels annually, but production had dropped to about four hundred and fifty thousand bushels in 1879. Eventually, most of the oysters supplying New Haven's packing industry came from Chesapeake Bay. Referred to as the "southern" or "Virginia trade," this movement of oysters north peaked in the decade before the Civil War.[31] New Haven packers relied heavily on the southern trade during its peak, thereby increasing the pressure on Chesapeake Bay. This natural resource extraction persisted without regard for any conservation practices, as northern packers transported oysters from a resource-rich region to a more industrial one. These activities promoted illegal harvesting and conflict in Chesapeake Bay, even as they took pressure off of Connecticut's natural beds. The southern trade subsidized the New Haven industry and displaced class conflict to the South.

Deepwater Cultivation

After planters claimed the best sites in New Haven Bay, they began moving into deeper water beyond the bay. On the north side of Long Island Sound, much of the ground close to shore was regularly swept by strong currents and tides, which scoured the bottom, presenting a sand or gravel surface, ideal for oyster cultivation. This "deepwater" cultivation was carried out within sight of shore, but in water too deep for tongers. Henry Rowe was the first to cultivate oysters in the sound in 1865, and after his example deepwater planting expanded rapidly. It spread to Narragansett Bay as well. Deepwater planting required much more capital than shallow water planting and tonging, as deepwater tracts needed to be at least fifty acres to be profitable. Planters used buoys within plots to mark where to work. Often planters would also place shells in the water to catch summer spat (floating oyster larvae) and increase their beds. Storms frequently disturbed deepwater beds, buoys were lost, and starfish and drum fish attacked planted oysters. Despite the risk from storms and predators, planters found deepwater planting to be highly profitable.[32]

Deepwater planters generally employed dredges to harvest. Crews culled the harvest, throwing back dead oysters, assorted shells, and other debris. Sailboats used wind power to pull dredges over the beds, after which the crew would haul the oyster-laden dredge on deck and work against the wind. The difficulty of this work is one reason planters turned to steamships in the late 1870s. William Lockwood built the first steamship expressly for dredging. This ship had two dredges that could haul up one hundred fifty to two hundred bushels a day. By 1879 there were seven steamers working on Connecticut's deepwater beds.[33]

Deepwater planting was an attractive model at the start of the Progressive Era. It was immensely productive for the first few decades. However, deepwater planters suffered from the classic problem of monoculture farming: they produced the perfect environment for the explosion of pest populations. Planters fought a running battle with starfish or "five fingers." They dragged a mop-like device behind ships to snare starfish. Planters hauled up and killed vast numbers of starfish, temporarily reducing starfish populations. In the 1910s and 1920s, however, starfish returned in unprecedented numbers and destroyed the deepwater beds. Rowe, the largest planter and the industry's leading organizer, was so distraught by the collapse of the Connecticut planting fishery that he retired to Florida. No one foresaw the end of deepwater planting at the start of the Progressive Era. Many regarded this practice to be the most modern part of the fishery. Connecticut seemed to prove that the solution to oyster conservation lay in expanded planting.

Connecticut also looked like a promising conservation model because it never had an "oyster war." There were frequent disputes over property rights between planters and tongers in the state, but these never reached the proportions found in other regions. One reason for this was Connecticut's limited number of natural beds at the time when planting began. For example, tongers depleted the South Norwalk natural beds in the 1850s, and planting only started after they were gone.³⁴ Just as important was planters' expansion into deeper water areas that tongers never used. Deepwater cultivation would prove difficult to copy, as it took advantage of the way ice sheets had carved the northern coast, deepening bays close to shore. Chesapeake Bay's broad, shallow expanse of flooded river valleys presented opposite conditions. However, the basic idea of dividing bays based on ecological conditions was intuitive and also developed elsewhere. It was a simple spatial division, and it worked best where tongers and planters could divide bays based on clear biophysical differences.

The Mid-Atlantic

Planters adapted to the ecologically varied conditions of the mid-Atlantic region. For instance, in Jamaica Bay, planters had to contend with shallow inlets and shifting sands. Because of the small, shallow channels, they mostly worked from skiffs or flat planting boats. The shallow bay also left oysters vulnerable to ice grinding during low winter tides. Oystermen planted as early as possible and gathered up all oysters at the start of winter. They built special storage houses on the banks of tidal creeks that had ponds dug into them to admit saltwater. Oystermen stored live oysters for winter sale by keeping the temperature up in these storage houses. The channels in the bay also changed frequently, so valuable land could be worthless a year later. The watchmen took advantage of the many islands to build huts next to the oysters.³⁵ Ecological conditions also made Jamaica Bay home to some of the most prized oyster varieties. Consumers recognized oyster "brands" named for places they grew. While these oysters looked alike, local conditions imparted distinct flavors. The most famous were Great South Bay's "Blue Points," and other notable brands included Babylon's "Oak Islands," Raritan Bay's "Sounds," "Keyports," and "Amboys," and Jamaica Bay's "Rockaways."³⁶

Ecological conditions aided spatial division in the mid-Atlantic. In Great South Bay, New York's most productive area, the western end of the bay was better for the rapid growth of adult oysters, whereas the eastern end featured extensive natural beds. Oystermen took advantage of this by moving oysters from the eastern bay to the western planting grounds.[37] Delaware Bay, New Jersey's most productive oystering area, exhibited a similar pattern. Oysters propagated better in the lower salinity upper bay and grew faster in the high salinity lower bay. In 1871 the legislature divided planting grounds from the natural beds along the "southwest line" that split the bay into upper and lower sections.[38] Despite these divisions, there were frequent disputes between planters and tongers over property lines and access.

Towns granted and leased planting property throughout this region. Eugene Blackford, a New York fish commissioner, noted that in New York there was a widespread misconception that a person could claim unoccupied land simply by planting oysters on it. Despite their lack of legal backing, courts upheld these claims, considering them common law. New York planters seldom made maps or kept records of planting bed locations, but they had comparatively few conflicts. They usually managed plots under twenty acres, though some were over one hundred acres in size.[39] In New Jersey, the state legislature granted Shark River residents the right to appoint a committee to make planting grants in 1861.[40] Some New Jersey towns, such as West Creek, set up planting plots without formal legal title.[41]

McCay and Ingersoll provide insight into oystermen's interactions in this region. McCay documents New Jersey tongers' political activism. Tongers gathered in groups and went to the state capitol to argue for protecting traditional access rights. They used mass civil disobedience, usually taking planted oysters, to create test cases in the courts. For instance, Ingersoll reported that planting was common at the Mullica River by the 1830s but had declined greatly due to widespread antiprivatization sentiments.[42] Lawrence Taylor's *Dutchmen on the Bay*, an ethnohistory of the oystering community in Sayville, New York, looks at the complex tonger-planter relationship. Sayville tongers depended on oysters but had other fishery occupations to supplement their income, one of which was working for wages on the planting grounds. There were few truly independent baymen.

Tongers worked closely with their capitalist planter counterparts. The leading planters had started as tongers, and many tongers wanted to follow in their footsteps. There were numerous conflicts over the location of natural beds versus planting areas, and tongers often harvested illegally from planted grounds. Both groups argued over wages too. In Sayville, these two groups shared Dutch immigrant backgrounds, churches, and a sense of identity as baymen. The ethnic isolation and cultural traditions of Sayville oystermen helped mitigate class conflict, as did their sense of shared identity.[43] Delaware's oyster fishery was comparatively small and was mostly owned by Philadelphia merchants.[44]

Chesapeake Bay and the Southern Trade

New Haven packers hammered Chesapeake Bay's oyster beds in the nineteenth century. Northern ships first began harvesting Chesapeake oysters in the first quarter of the nineteenth century, though it is hard to gauge the magnitude of this early harvesting. By 1850 Connecticut packers were taking Chesapeake oysters in large numbers and packing them at New Haven and elsewhere. The southern trade began by supplying oysters for market, mostly packed oysters, but as the Connecticut seed supply diminished, the southern trade soon began supplying northern planting beds as well. Deepwater cultivation began in Connecticut in the 1860s, and these operations depended on seed from Chesapeake Bay. The southern trade peaked in the 1850s.[45] A Virginia government report from 1858 estimated the state sent 8,800,000 bushels north.[46]

The southern trade was lucrative and led to illegal dredging. Maryland and Virginia, like most other states, banned dredging on natural beds, but deterring dredgers was difficult. Articles from the *Baltimore Sun* offer insight into the scope of the problem. An 1851 article reported that Maryland oystermen captured three schooners and one sloop. The state confiscated these Philadelphia boats and sold them as punishment.[47] In 1853 Maryland oystermen caught and sold three more Philadelphia boats.[48] In 1859 Annapolis was "thrown into unusual excitement" when oystermen captured ten schooners after chartering steam vessels to catch them. Nine were from Philadelphia, and one was from Baltimore. When they sold these boats, a quarter of the money went to pay court costs, another quarter went to the informers, and half went to the crew of about twenty who helped catch them. The state dispatched an armed military crew to keep owners from freeing their boats.[49] Heavy fines and even boat forfeitures proved ineffective deterrents for wealthy packers in the 1850s. Sometimes there were legal loopholes. Once dredges were aboard the ship, for example, captains could claim to have legally purchased oysters.[50] Dredge boats also came in groups and often used watch boats to spot law enforcement in time to evade them or pull up dredges. Dredge boat captains made it known they had guns and every intention of defending their ships. Local people had to form large, heavily armed parties to capture them.

The Civil War disrupted the fishery, giving the natural beds several years to rest, and Maryland repealed its dredge ban when the war ended. Lawmakers did this to aid the state's packing industry. They also sought to revive harvests more generally as a measure for supplying work. The new law required all dredge boats to obtain licenses, and boat owners had to be Maryland residents. Increasingly, dredgers had to work beds further from inshore areas, as the state continued to reserve these spaces for tongers.[51] Captures of illegal dredge boats continued after legal dredging began in Maryland. For instance, the *Baltimore Sun* reported that in January 1868 nine mostly Philadelphia-owned boats were caught dredging in county waters.[52] An 1869 article discussed "great consternation" over the capture of six boats at Deal's Island.[53] Such articles were common in the later 1860s and 1870s. Dredge boat crews, who generally came from poorer classes in the cities, were often treated poorly and forced to work in dangerous conditions. Captains, on the other hand, had a share of the profits, which provided them further incentive to break the law.[54]

Dredgers continued to supply the northern industry after the war, but the southern trade waned, in large part because New Haven packers built packing houses in Baltimore to be closer to their source. Caleb Maltby, the first New Haven packer who moved to the city, opened Baltimore's first packing house in 1834 or 1835, shortly after the arrival of the Baltimore and Ohio Railroad. He also shipped oysters in wagons to Pittsburgh. By 1850 many more New Haven packers had opened houses in Baltimore, as had local investors. Baltimore would become the country's largest packing center, and Maltby would become rich as the city's leading packer. Rowe was another leading New Haven packer who became one of Baltimore's largest packers.[55] Maryland and Virginia founded oyster navies that helped oystermen oppose and fight illegal dredgers (see chapter 2). Connecticut's rested seed beds rebounded, as well, which reduced northern sales. The arrival of New Haven packers meant that even as the southern trade declined, illegal dredging continued undiminished.[56]

The town of Crisfield grew into Maryland's secondary packing center. John Crisfield was the president of the Eastern Shore railroad, which he made sure connected to Somer's Cove (the town's original name). Prior to the railroad's arrival, Crisfield bought up much land around the town, which was located near many major oyster beds and was an ideal location for an oyster packing industry. To expand the town and provide wharves on the water, oyster shells were used to fill marshes, leading people to joke that Crisfield was built on oysters. The railroad arrived in 1867, upon which Crisfield's packing industry mushroomed from nonexistent in 1866 to shipping several million bushels a year in the 1870s. By the 1870s, Crisfield possessed over six hundred ships and shipped over a million bushels of oysters annually.[57] This rapid growth, combined with Maryland's law enforcement problems, led to a general culture of lawlessness (see chapter 2).[58]

Oystermen seldom worked in packing houses. Packing oysters was seasonal work, and many of the shuckers went to work on farms or packed fruit during other seasons. In Maryland, about three-fourths of these workers were African American. About one fourth were women, most were Irish and German immigrants or the daughters of immigrants. Few native-born women would take these jobs in a workplace where workers mingled indiscriminately across gender and race lines. Shuckers, who were positioned at tables opening the oysters with knives, received little money for their work, and their repeated motions led to the development of a unique set of health problems.

Other States

Most coastal states developed small oyster fisheries, some of which would grow to rival the eastern states in the twentieth century. North Carolina and Louisiana produced substantial amounts in 1880, whereas other southern states tended to have unmarketable "raccoon" oysters (which were named after the raccoon's small, thin paws).[59] Louisiana and Florida's planting industries grew in the latter part of the Progressive Era. On the Pacific coast, San Francisco Bay had the largest West Coast oyster fishery during the Progressive Era. It was primarily based on planting East Coast oysters.[60]

CONCLUSION: COMPLEXITY IN TRADITIONAL OYSTER CONSERVATION

Oystermen's traditional conservation system did not always work, but it was a significant achievement nonetheless. It succeeded in providing equity, access, and independence, as well as environmental sustainability in many cases. The traditional system worked with complexity in three related ways: it tried to sustain environmental complexity, it contained complex practices, and it encoded complex political compromises. Traditional tonger conservation depended on the natural oyster reefs it aimed to protect. Tongers used their extensive long-term local knowledge to design sensible conservation measures. These measures varied to meet local conditions and were far more complex than later modernist alternatives (see chapter 3). Finally, traditional conservation contained highly complex goals that grew out of conflict. Tongers and planters compromised over space, and towns competed with each other and copied conservation measures. The Virginia petitions provide the most detailed view of early and mid-nineteenth-century oystermen's motivations and goals, which are highly varied and contradictory. Oystermen based their conservation system on compromises between these competing imperatives.

Much of this early management was similar to what Richard Judd found in northern New England, although adapted to a different environment and species. Oystermen's management practices were sensible adaptations to local bay ecology, and much like rural people in northern New England, oystermen perceived large-scale environmental decline. They also clashed with one another over access. Although their conservation measures did not always work, they represent sensible, knowledgeable responses. Modern oyster conservation still uses many of these practices. Oystermen restricted harvesting when oysters were young and vulnerable. They restricted gear and vessels to prevent damage to the beds and to spread the harvest among more people. They prohibited the wasteful practice of gathering oysters for lime and promoted regrowth by culling small oysters and old shells. Brian Payne has shown how early fishery conservation was often a byproduct of the desire for local control, which limited catches.[61] This was true for oyster conservation practices, except for cull laws and size limits, which were across-the-board sustainability measures that in no way excluded outsiders.

There were also several important differences between Judd's cases and that of oysters. First, the oyster fishery was less isolated. Due to poor and eroded soils and short growing seasons, northern New England farmers participated less in the huge grain-export trade with Europe than did the southern and mid-Atlantic states.[62] In the case of oysters, not only was there large regional movement of resources, but wealthy capitalists in one region exploited the resources of another. Railroads, and later steam ships, tied the fishery to distant markets. Continual market pressure was immense, and to many in the new government agencies, older communal forms of conservation gradually seemed less tenable as the fishery struggled to cope with expanding demand.

CHAPTER 2

OYSTER LAW ENFORCEMENT

SURVEILLANCE AND CONSERVATION

Modern conservation requires violence. The new progressive agencies depended on law enforcement officers to force compliance. Karl Jacoby's *Crimes against Nature* is the most extensive treatment of fish and game poaching in the Progressive Era.[1] Jacoby documents a pattern by which rural people broke laws because they saw them as outside impositions that conflicted with their traditional norms and practices. Although Jacoby's cases unfold in parks, his work raises questions about how state conservation law enforcement developed outside parks. Chesapeake Bay oystermen welcomed increased policing to combat the depredations of illegal dredgers and wealthy capitalists. New Jersey and New York planters hired armed guards, later supplanted by state policing without substantially changing the local political economy. Law enforcement corruption was a major problem in Chesapeake Bay. Corruption and depredation by wealthy packers complicate Jacoby's description of rural resistance to conservation law enforcement. Whereas the state criminalized traditional resource use in Jacoby's cases, it enforced preexisting moral economies and political compromises in the oyster fishery. Jacoby's cases also feature exclusion of local people, whereas the

Chesapeake Bay law enforcement officers evicted wealthy outsiders. State policing benefitted most oystermen.

CHESAPEAKE BAY OYSTER NAVIES

Virginia

Before the Progressive Era, Virginia's oyster petitions constantly complained about illegal and nonlocal dredging. Oystermen faced several challenges apprehending illegal dredge boats, many of which sailed from northern ports. Petitioners asked for greater enforcement of existing laws or for the implementation of stricter laws with higher penalties. They cited the dependence on oysters in tidewater communities, for poor populations in particular.

After the Civil War disrupted the southern trade and rested oyster beds, the fishery revived quickly. In 1868 Chesapeake Bay state legislatures established law enforcement agencies popularly known as "oyster navies." Virginia's major enforcement problem was illegal dredging by Maryland boats. Despite laws prohibiting Marylanders from working in Virginia waters, many tongers made short trips across the border. Baltimore and Crisfield dredge boats posed a larger problem. Dredge boats from northern states fished illegally too. Virginia dredgers sometimes worked natural beds or worked in counties where they did not reside. However, the post–Civil War tidewater press mainly contains articles detailing the problem of illegal dredgers from other states.

Reports of the Virginia navy's activities began to appear in the tidewater press following 1868. The *Princess Anne Herald* described the navy, consisting of the schooners *Tangier* and *Pocomoke*, attacking and firing upon five Maryland boats near the state line. They chased the Marylanders to the shore, whereupon the dredgers found reinforcements and returned fire.[2] In 1870 the *Baltimore Sun* reported more gunfire and the navy's arrest of fourteen Marylanders. Maryland's governor interceded, and Virginia authorities eventually released these men and their boats.[3] These disputes led the chief oyster inspector of Virginia and the commander of Maryland's State Oyster Police Force to create a boundary line, which both governors approved as a temporary measure in October of 1870. The governors then appointed a boundary commission in November to settle the matter permanently and thereby ease law enforcement and encourage compliance.

This line led to fewer Maryland boats in Virginia waters and fewer articles on the navy appeared until 1874 with the onset of "the Riggin affair." On September 11, 1874, a Virginia oyster inspector fatally shot a Maryland man, John Riggin, and arrested his four companions for illegally dredging in Virginia waters. The circumstances of Riggin's death incensed Marylanders. His four companions claimed the oyster inspector was guilty of "firing upon Riggin and leaving him wounded and bleeding, drifting at the mercy of the wind and the waves."[4] Virginia prosecuted and convicted the oyster inspector. Maryland's governor asked his Virginia counterpart to pardon the arrested men, but a court convicted them. Following the conviction, the two governors began corresponding through mail, and local newspapers reprinted their letters. Maryland's governor stated that the boundary line was too favorable for Virginia, while Virginia's governor replied that Virginia would protect its rights. Virginia's attorney general published letters saying that the Maryland oyster navy was larger and protected their side of the line better than "the private canoe of Captain Curtis," a reference to the Virginia navy.[5] These cases illustrate the difficulty of maintaining state boundary lines over the water. Part of the problem was that the Potomac River was held in common by both states, whereas Virginia and Maryland theoretically split Pocomoke Sound (where Riggin died). Most of the sound, including a valuable oystering area, belonged to Virginia. Maryland's attorney general eventually came to Virginia and secured the release of the four men, while backing down on the matter of the proper boundary. He stated that Maryland had a "privilege" to fish in Virginia's part of Pocomoke Sound due to established practice, but that they did not have a legal "right" to do so.[6] Virginia oystermen claimed this as a victory.

Articles on illegal dredging in Virginia lessened after this dispute, possibly due to decreased harvests. Overharvesting after the Civil War led to declines in the fishery in the middle to late 1870's. Excellent sets in 1881 and 1882 revived the fishery once again. As news of these sets spread, boats flooded in. Virginia's governor took action to protect the beds, forming a militia to supplement the navy in late 1882. However, this force only made a few arrests, and tongers considered it a disappointment. The governor formed a second militia in late February 1883, comprised of three boats, fifty men, and three light artillery pieces. This second effort still netted no arrests. The governor believed someone had tipped off the dredgers, allowing them to escape. He stated that the militia targeted Maryland boats, although the *Baltimore Sun* reported on many dredge boats from Long Island Sound.[7] In March 1883 the *Baltimore Sun* described another capture, by the regular oyster navy, with eight additional boats driven off by gunfire. The newspaper estimated that at around sixty illegal dredge boats regularly worked Virginia waters.[8]

The state transferred the oyster navy to the Board of Fisheries in 1897. In their reports, the board regularly asked for more money, explaining that the navy was too small and slow for its task. The legislature obliged, and by 1905 the board was spending $20,000 annually on its oyster patrol.[9] Increased funding allowed the patrol to protect the seaside for the first time, and to make an unusually high number of arrests in 1905. They also made their funding go further by borrowing boats and guns. At this point gasoline boats began appearing in the fishery and these boats were faster than any of the four patrol boats. In 1906 the legislature granted an additional $20,000 for a new gasoline-powered patrol boat. Even with the new boats, the navy commander stated that, "Great vigilance and activity are now required to inspect each individual oyster boat."[10] The board reported that dredgers attempted to sabotage the smaller police boats during this time as well. Despite continued resistance from dredgers, the oyster navy expanded its law enforcement capacity and large-scale illegal dredging ceased by 1920.

Maryland

Maryland's oyster navy began with one boat in 1868: the *Leila*, a dilapidated Civil War tug. The navy repaired the *Leila* in 1869 and added twelve sloops to their fleet. Hunter Davidson commanded the navy at its inception. Many of his correspondences survive, as does his 1870 report to the auditor of public accounts. These provide a unique source for understanding the early oyster navies. Davidson reported boarding about three hundred boats in 1868 (half tongers, half dredgers). In 1870 he made eighty-eight arrests, with only fifteen acquittals.[11] He attributed an increase in the number of licenses taken out in 1870 to the increased number of fines levied the previous year.[12] He initiated and led the effort to survey the Maryland-Virginia line after the Riggin Affair, and in his letters he described this as working fairly well.[13] However, Davidson worried that the current oyster law was not working, and he predicted the "early destruction" of the oyster beds as a result.[14] Davidson wanted to map and buoy the natural beds but had neither time nor money. He stated that a major problem with enforcement was that dredgers willingly paid fines associated with their illegal harvesting activities because fines proved too low to act as a deterrent. Many dredgers licensed their boats under proxy owners to evade local residency requirements. Davidson claimed he lacked sufficient ships to fully enforce the law. Maryland justices of the peace prosecuted illegal harvesting unevenly because they were poorly informed about the complex oyster laws. More localized problems arose as well. For example, Somerset County prohibited out-of-county dredgers. When Somerset tongers exhausted their own county's beds, they took out licenses in other counties, leading to armed conflict. Davidson spent much time directly speaking with oystermen and tried to explain the law to them. The overall picture he painted was one where "the trade has run far ahead of legislation."[15]

Davidson also described class conflict. Dredging and tonging were "two great interests, . . . which have always been, and are likely to continue, at war."[16] He characterized this as "the rich versus the poor," stating that, "the worst of it is, that the former [dredgers] rarely lose an opportunity of impressing this fact upon the minds of the latter [tongers], by a too frequent transfer of Oysters from rich inshore beds—reserved by law for tongmen—to the holds of their own vessels."[17] The ubiquity of illegal dredging over the previous fifty years created a group of sailors who thought they were "masters of the Oyster situation." Davidson said that they "keep much secret" to maintain their control.[18] His views matched the moral economy of Maryland tongers. While he did fine them for failing to take out licenses, he also fought illegal dredging.

The Maryland oyster navy archive also documents corruption. It contains a collection of articles circulated in Chesapeake Bay newspapers written by "Licensed Tongmen." Licensed Tongmen accused Davidson of failing to do his job and taking bribes. Davidson responded under the pseudonym "Onwards." He discovered that Licensed Tongmen was a man named Griffith, and after this point, the two exchanged private letters, each accusing the other. Davidson also received a letter from a man named Smith who told him Griffith was trying to become commander of the oyster navy. Smith said Griffith withdrew when he heard Davidson was applying for the job, and he said Griffith wanted the job to solicit bribes from dredgers. Several prominent people wrote letters to tidewater newspapers supporting Davidson. One sheriff wrote that Licensed Tongmen made up statements attributed to Davidson and fabricated evidence. The Maryland archive preserved letters from oystermen and state legislators stating that Davidson always acted in the public interest. This episode highlights the possibility of officers abusing oyster navy posts for personal gain, and it also sheds light on the contests for control of these new agencies.[19]

Davidson resigned in 1872 when oyster navy appointments became part of the Democratic Party's patronage system.[20] His replacement, William Timmons, faced charges of criminal negligence.[21] The case stemmed from the arrest of over thirty boats for illegal dredging in April 1873.[22] At the May trial, Timmons said he lacked the authority to serve any of the warrants given to him, and so the cases were dismissed.[23] A grand jury convened and called for Timmons's removal. The grand jury also pursued a criminal collusion charge, but could not find evidence that Timmons took bribes. Timmons testified that while he did enforce the law, his personal belief was that dredging increased the size of oyster beds and that an "open bay" would benefit everyone. He also said that he had never needed to use guns. This was far-fetched, given previous and future enforcement practices. The Maryland archive contains letters, articles, and petitions complaining that Timmons would simply sail by illegal dredgers.[24] Despite these controversies, the Board of the Chesapeake kept Timmons.

The problem of political patronage continued. An 1889 pamphlet titled "Maryland Oyster and His Political Enemies," characterized "the 'spoils system'" as "the 'star fish' of our Chesapeake."[25] A popular history of the navy referred to appointments as "blatantly partisan." It cited an oyster navy commander explaining in the Maryland legislature how "the captains of these vessels should be good Republicans. Provisions might be made for putting some of the independents in as mates. It is not the right thing to buy democrats into the party."[26] Another urged appointing a captain "who had contributed largely to the success of the republican ticket last year."[27]

Newspaper articles shed light on conflicts involving the navy. The *St. Michael's Comet* said the new navy under Davidson seemed responsible and it "excited much interest." It also described a gunfight between seven tonging canoes and one schooner illegally dredging in shallows off Tilghman's Island in the Choptank.[28] The next year (1869) the Chester River was full of out-of-state dredgers due to a legislative mistake. The law said dredging must be in Chesapeake Bay and not in county waters, which included all the rivers and smaller bays. It failed to specify where county waters ended and the main bay began. Dredgers construed this to mean rivers as well, based on the idea that rivers dividing counties lay in state waters and did not fall under either county's jurisdiction.[29] The *Baltimore*

Sun reported dredgers busily destroying the Miles and Choptank river beds due to the same interpretation of law, which the state attorney general initially upheld.[30] Dredgers rushed into areas they did not work before, and overharvesting began to drive down prices. Davidson and the Board of the Chesapeake persuaded the attorney general to modify his interpretation.[31]

Conflicts intensified in the 1870s. A common example comes from an 1874 *Baltimore Sun* article describing illegal dredging in the Miles River. Tongers went to work one morning and found dredgers on the beds. The dredgers fired on them and they left. The tongers then armed themselves with reinforcements and returned to the site. They captured one boat and its crew, shooting its Baltimore captain in the process.[32] Governor Whyte's 1874 annual address to the legislature stated that the oyster navy was underfunded.[33] By 1876 the *Baltimore Sun* reported dredgers growing more numerous in the Eastern Bay, moving in groups of ten to twenty vessels and working mostly at night. The navy arrested seven or eight ships in the two weeks preceding this article.[34] A battle in early 1878 in Anne Arundel County waters killed two men, which led to a closed-door senate hearing the next month.[35] Dredgers also conspired to assassinate Hunter Davidson in 1871. They boarded his vessel at night and snuck into his cabin, at which point he awoke and narrowly escaped.[36] The 1870s were a time of prolonged lawlessness and armed conflict between tongers and dredgers.

An article from the *Baltimore Sun* described methods of illegal dredging. Seventy-five to one hundred ships worked in the Choptank River and "of course violations of the law are going on." Ships were dredging illegally at the mouth of the Little Choptank. Dredgers worked in groups, and the closest ship dropped its peak sail when it saw a patrol approaching.[37] Another account described illegal dredgers working at night to avoid detection. They used lamps on the mast of a sentry boat to signal the navy's arrival.[38] Chesapeake Bay's geography aided dredgers. Its oyster beds lay mostly in the bay's many narrow "rivers," and these rivers had only one entrance, making it easier to watch for approaching navy ships.

Articles expressing fear of exhaustion and complaining about declining oyster beds started appearing the 1880s. A *Baltimore Sun* editorial from an Oxford writer described the alarm growing among tongers who were worried the beds would be gone in a few years.[39] Articles described the growth of tonger-dredger conflicts and presented tongers as wanting the state to enforce the law.[40] The navy began enforcing the law more stringently after Timmons's departure. The next commander after Timmons, James Waddell, used a telegraph system by which his ships reported their locations once per week to the central headquarters, allowing him to direct and track them.[41] The main oyster navy sloop caught twenty-one boats in 1882, with twenty convictions.

Maryland's oyster harvests peaked in the 1880s, a particularly violent time period. Competition between tongers and dredgers intensified, and enforcement efforts increased. For instance, the Cannon family of Dorchester County led a fight against the oyster navy in 1884. One of their dredge boats fired a warning shot at a navy ship and then openly dredged in closed areas. They then fired on and repulsed the navy schooner. Around one hundred dredge boats began illegally dredging in the Honga River and Fishing Bay. Two local delegations went to Annapolis to ask for help. In the ensuing conflict, a dredge boat ran the navy schooner aground. Two of her crew deserted and the rest threatened to refuse duty. The ship's captain resigned, saying he felt useless. The navy had to dispatch their two steamers to the area with howitzers and cannon.[42] In another instance, dredgers waved white flags at five navy ships to lure them closer before attacking. They drove off four and captured the fifth ship. The dredgers then threatened to kill the crew, who promptly quit. Governor Jackson described the conflict as "a rebellion and nothing less."[43]

The Chester River dredging was the most blatant rebellion. A dredge captain named Gus Rice helped organize illegal dredgers in the Chester. The navy began making arrests in 1881. After this it became more difficult to catch dredgers, and they began to intimidate the navy. Navy officers feared being shot or having their ships rammed and sunk in the cold winter water. Tongers eventually took matters into their own hands. In 1885 they built fortifications along the riverbanks and fired at dredgers. This had little effect. In 1888 the oyster navy finally captured one dredge boat. Local tongers then set two cannons to guard over the river, but dredgers captured the cannons. Dredgers controlled the water at this point, until Rice's flotilla fired on a passenger steamer they mistook for an oyster police boat. This sparked an outcry among Marylanders and the legislature ordered Thomas Howard, captain of the oyster navy, to end piracy in the Chester. Howard sent two sloops to battle the dredgers. Dredgers fired on and sank the first, although the crew managed to escape. They captured the second, stripped it, and left it to drift, making its crew turn the windlasses on their dredge boats for several days. Finally, Howard brought the *McLane* to the scene, the oyster navy's only steamer. Its iron sides and twelve-inch artillery gun made it a formidable vessel. When Howard confronted the dredgers at night on December 10, he and two crewmembers first got in a rowboat and secretly boarded two dredge boats and arrested the crew. They then returned to the *McLane* and attacked the main dredge fleet. Rice set up a blockade of twelve ships, which the *McLane* rammed, sinking two boats. The crews of the two sunken boats were locked below deck and drowned. Although Rice got away, this attack ended his control over the Chester, and conflict began to wane.[44]

As illegal dredging lessened, navy costs began to exceed tax revenue in the 1890s, and the navy had to dock a boat in 1894. They ran out of money completely in 1895 and docked all but two steamers. A 1900 inspection revealed the boats' deterioration; their bedding was "filthy," guns rusty, sails and rigging "only a year old and so neglected as to be very much impaired."[45] The navy often had to borrow money from banks to continue operating. Despite underfunding, the navy slowly improved law enforcement.

Maryland oyster law enforcement history highlights competing ideas about access to resources. Wealthy packers and Chester River dredgers wanted open access, whereas tongers wanted illegal dredging stopped and wanted to preserve local access by excluding outsiders. The rights of marine fishermen clashed in some places, but oyster navies supported the norms of the more numerous tongers.

DEBATES OVER "PRIVILEGE OR PROTECTION" IN NEW JERSEY

In New Jersey, competing ideas about access and exclusion flowed over into fish and game law enforcement. Articles in a Barnegat Bay newspaper, the *New Jersey Courier*, provide evidence of this. One article titled "Are Ocean County Folks All Pirates and Criminals?" reports that "fish and game laws are broken more than all other laws put together" because the "bread and butter of the man and his family are involved." The article goes on to say that fish and game laws were making it harder to earn a living each year. After this, it explains that rural people felt they did not need licenses to hunt for home consumption. The state should only require these for market hunting. The article calls market hunters "pothunters" and considers the term one of "the most contemptuous and opprobrious expressions."[46] This article appeared as part of an exchange with New Jersey's fish and game commissioner. The commissioner agreed that past laws were often "absurd and contradictory." He further stated that until recently a political patronage system controlled appointments to his commission.[47] Articles sometimes refer to the beneficial role of game wardens, as was the case in an article describing them collecting over twenty-six illegal gill nets that monopolized the catch of several fish species.[48] However, a later article complains that fish and game laws still favored city hunters. Wealthy hunting clubs, which the article calls "a nuisance," monopolized the best shooting points. The author points to a new law banning hunting on ice. By walking on ice, baymen accessed these prime hunting locations.[49] These articles show that Barnegat Bay residents rejected law enforcement that favored elites and took away traditional rights, but that they favored approaches to law enforcement that fit their traditional rights by limiting monopolization.

A debate in the *New Jersey Courier* tied these issue to oysters. One side claimed that customary rights gave them the "privilege" to gather oysters and fish anyway they chose. Their opponents claimed that such practices depleted resources and that local people needed "protection" from these depredations. A long article from April 3, 1873, provides a good example and referrs to an earlier (missing) article that had aroused agitation. People were asking why the law did not better protect their oyster resources. The writer says, when this agitation began the "privileged few" said "Let us alone! You must not take from us our rights. . . . But they don't have the right to take and utterly destroy that which belongs to the citizens of the whole county and state." He then discusses summer fishing, saying about forty people "eke out . . . a precarious subsistence" catching the biggest fish and leaving the rest to die. He also explains that seiners were defending their "privilege" to fish with seines, even as this practice put over one hundred men who fished the bay with rods and lines out of work. "These are the *monopolists* of the bay; these are the men who prate of *privileges*" (italics in the original). The writer distinguishes these from two or three large mesh seiners catching sea bass, sheepshead, and rockfish out of Lacy, Union, and Stafford, who did not harm the overall fishery. His aim was to distinguish between "rights and privileges." He argues that in instances where protection replaced privilege, fishermen and oystermen had grown rich. He cites West Creek as a model.[50] Another article titled "Our Shore," describes the decline of waterfowl, fish, and oysters in the region, stating: "we claim these waters to be public domain, owned by the people of the whole state, with equal rights to all, and that in equity no man or set of men have a just right to take and destroy what belongs to the whole people." This article also points to West Creek's example.[51] Another article lists similar declines, also blaming them on privilege, and recommends a state commission to pass and enforce laws.[52]

When oysters entered this debate, and they frequently did, writers claim that oystermen from other counties were taking away too many oysters. Delaware Bay's wealthy planters were singled out for this. One writer compares them to drum fish, an oyster predator. He says, "we have more formidable enemies who come upon us from adjacent counties, and who, having no interest in common with us and caring only for their own advancement, take and carry away oysters and shells promiscuously.... Whilst this continues our business suffers and our people kept poor."[53] One article states that out of five hundred fishermen and oystermen in Barnegat Bay, ninety percent were honest and the other ten percent continued to destroy breeding stock. The writer explains that these people claimed the bay was free and needed no laws. Pointing to these problems, one writer agrees, "These are the fruits of *privilege*."[54] These articles indicate that not everyone supported greater law enforcement. They describe a minority of local tongers and nonlocal planters who favored less restriction, and a majority of baymen favoring better resource protection. These articles depict the ways that wealthy planters, and some local fishermen, argued open access fit prevailing norms.

PROTECTING PLANTER PROPERTY IN NORTHERN STATES

New Jersey and New York provide another example of how state law enforcement continued local people's practices. Newspaper articles from West Creek, New Jersey, describe the town's protective association. Planters claimed to be fighting the "Philadelphia Ring," a reference to wealthier Philadelphia packers who financed illegal dredging. The articles urge that every coastal town needs to "wake up and organize."[55] They go on to say that if "coastal people pull together a law would be passed, but West Creek is indifferent, as they have a custom which is enforced as well as a law would be." This system, they describe as quick, efficient, and cheap. Only occasionally was a "surgeon required to extract out the heavy little consequence."[56] A nearby association in Bridgeport formed by wealthier oystermen in 1868 also opposed Philadelphia merchants. They paid for an oyster patrol and lobbied the state legislature.[57]

In New York, shellfish commission reports mention several protective associations. For example, at Prince's Bay, the Richmond County Oyster Protective Association policed outsiders and themselves. At a large public meeting with the state commissioner they said they did not see the need for state protection.[58] Another example comes from Jamaica Bay. Planters founded the Brooklyn Oyster Protective Association between1882 and 1884, and it included forty to fifty people by 1896. There was no state enforcement when it started, but by 1896 a local police chief had taken them under his wing and sent out a police boat to help.[59] These New York associations protected large and small planters depending on the location. The associations may have worked to exclude tongers; it is important not to romanticize these as reflecting a unified moral economy protecting everyone's interests. State law enforcement eventually replaced these associations.

Newspapers and other sources seldom mention law enforcement problems in Connecticut or Rhode Island. Deepwater cultivation and the southern trade reduced pressure on natural oyster beds. Large thefts from multiple western Connecticut planting beds in 1889 led planters to charter watch boats "at great expense, for their mutual protection."[60] They seized four New York boats near Stamford. Planters requested additional help and in response the Connecticut Shellfish Commission founded a five-person oyster police force in 1895 that included an inspector of the natural beds, who was also a law enforcement officer. Commission reports never mention the activities of this force, which likely indicates little conflict.

LICENSING OYSTERMEN, REGISTERING VESSELS

The oyster and fish commissions performed two activities closely related to policing: licensing oystermen and registering vessels. These made the residency of oystermen visible to law enforcement agents. Oystermen wanted better law enforcement, but they often protested or evaded license requirements, as these were the primary ways states collected taxes on the fishery. Tongers tested the constitutionality of a new Virginia license tax; while they agreed with the need for licensing they felt that the process was too time consuming. The tax was based on the amount they caught, and so they had to report weekly catches to local oyster inspectors.[61] New Jersey oystermen refused to take out licenses when the state stopped shelling, as the state shell commission formerly used license fees for this purpose.[62] Vessel registration followed a similar pattern. Commissions required all oystermen to register their vessels, and registration required proof of residency for the boat owner, captain, or both. Occasionally crews had to obtain licenses based on residency as well. The law then required vessels to display their registration numbers by painting them on their sails or prows to make them visible to law enforcement. Again, this practice helped the state enforce older residency laws.

In some states there was a vigorous debate about how much to tax oystermen and what to do with this money. The Virginia case in the early 1890s is a well-documented example that shows the general contours of these debates. A Roanoke newspaper presents the argument in favor of increased taxation. It says, "The oysters . . . if systematically utilized, will produce a revenue so startling in its magnitude as to cause wonder that they were not sooner controlled, and will eventually quite concern about the baneful State debt."[63] Governor Philip McKinney expressed similar optimistic appraisals, saying oysters could produce one million dollars annually in tax revenue. Oysters featured prominently in the governor's annual addresses to the legislature, alongside the state debt.[64] Virginia's first fish commissioner made similar arguments. He thought the state produced nine to twenty million bushels of oysters annually, worth nearly $10 million. He compared them to wheat, which amounted to about six million bushels annually that sold for $6–10 million. Virginia's seven hundred and fifty thousand wheat acres garnered $56,000 in taxes, whereas oysters remained basically untaxed.[65] On the other side of this debate, tidewater residents said the state created its debt to open the south and west of the state to development. The state should not siphon off oystermen's hard-earned income to benefit other regions.[66] Another common antitax theme was that nontidewater residents knew little about oysters and had unrealistic ideas. One newspaper article argues that McKinney was "again talking oysters," which were his "hobby," and about which he knew nothing. It goes on to say he was trying to interest inland people in oysters but was ignoring the tidewater "on the principle of the blind leading the blind."[67] Another editorial complains that "mountain people" had their property and mines guarded without a special tax, which shows that the legislature responded to them and not to tidewater people.[68] This debate highlights the contests over the revenue that new state agencies could capture.

A few primary sources describe tax collection and licensing. One of these is a report from the chief inspector of oysters of Virginia. An 1867 law created an oyster tax and three inspectors to collect it. The chief's first act was to establish record books. Oystermen immediately petitioned him to change the law, but he felt that they did this to make the law easier to evade. The state issued an order approving their petition, requiring him to change all of his books. He had started collecting revenue in 1869, and by 1870, there were 411 vessels licensed and approximately 800 without licenses. Oystermen felt the military opposed the new law and would not enforce it, leading them to defy tax collectors. The chief inspector told this to a general, who sent twenty armed troops to Tangier Sound, which led to higher rates of tax collection. In Tangier and Pocomoke, "there is a very general complaint" that Virginia citizens and nonresidents harvested and planted oysters illegally. The ships might have licenses and local crews, but they worked for nonresidents. Oyster inspectors seized several ships under this charge but could not prosecute them for lack of evidence. The chief went on to say, "a great deal of bad feeling has always existed between dredgers and the tongsmen."[69]

Maryland has one letterbook surviving from the Board of Public Works that details activities of the oyster navy in 1910 to 1911 and contains press copies of letters sent by the navy's commander, Thomas Howard. Many of these letters deal with licensing.[70] He sent one letter to all his deputies telling them to "keep up a rigid overhauling of the tongers until all have their licenses."[71] Several letters address the deputies' conduct and lax enforcement. In one, Howard notes that he received complaints from Deal's Island that small oysters were being taken illegally. He asked his deputy why he had not stopped this and demanded he do it.[72] Another says he was "credibly informed" that almost all of St. Michael's oystermen were working without licenses, and he was surprised his deputy had allowed for this. He told the deputy to make arrests.[73] Two deputies had failed to send monthly reports. One letter berates a deputy for not collecting tax from a company, which oystermen were talking about "up and down the shore."[74] Another forceful letter requests that a packer take out his license. Howard wrote a formal letter addressed to tongers asking them to obey cull laws, which he suggests would increase prices.[75] Licensing helped ensure continued traditional practices of access and exclusion, but tying this to taxation created ambivalence and distrust between oysterman and law enforcement.

CONCLUSION: OYSTER LAW ENFORCEMENT AND MORAL ECONOMIES

Hunter Davidson stands out in this story as a man who risked his life for tonger rights. One letter from an oysterman asks, "where is Capt Davidson who had charge last year? He is worth all together the present force and ten times more."[76] The history of violence in Chesapeake Bay was strikingly different than Jacoby's cases where local people resisted state-sponsored conservation. Such law breaking was more common in places where the state excluded local people from resources or restricted their traditional practices. Law enforcement agents in the oyster fishery excluded nonlocal, wealthier, or more industrial users. All of Jacoby's case studies involve the creation of new conservation spaces. His "hidden history of American conservation" is actually the American version of a large, international backlash against park-based conservation,[77] a connection Jacoby recognizes.[78] Arthur McEvoy documents the same pattern of government conservation leading to local exclusion in California fisheries.[79] Clearly Jacoby's model can fit fishery and other nonpark resources as well. Chesapeake Bay resembles a class of environmental problems where local people have trouble excluding others, generally outsiders with more wealth and power from an environmental commons or sink. Early pollution reform fits this pattern.[80] In these cases, local people were unable to exclude outsiders from a resource or limit the use of environmental sinks, but the state eventually acquired the power to do so.

This chapter and chapter 1 show that the oyster fisheries had a complex, varied moral economy. The planter-tonger division meant two ways of thinking about property rights existed side by side, one communal and the other more Lockean-liberal. There was also a great deal of disagreement, as in Barnegat Bay's privilege versus protection debate. The moral economy of oystermen could contain divergent views on property and management for a single resource, and these could lead to violent clashes within rural communities. The Chester River shows divisions between oyster communities at their most extreme. Eventually, state law enforcement and surveillance gradually reduced the worst of the illegal dredging, thus protecting tongers and preserving local rights.

CHAPTER 3

SHELLFISH COMMISSIONS

Maryland's first shellfish commissioners faced a daunting task when they stepped aboard a boat in 1882. The state legislature had charged them with assessing the oyster industry and making policy recommendations. Lawlessness and conflict prevailed, and a gold-rush mentality drove overfishing. Few if any of Maryland's fourteen thousand oystermen knew all of the convoluted oyster law. To the north, Rhode Island's lone commissioner fared no better when he took the job. Rhode Island's aquaculture industry spawned a chaotic new property system, and farmers marked boundaries poorly, when they marked them at all. The commissioner commanded scant resources to survey marine farms. He did not even have an office. The first shellfish commissioners surely felt enormous pressure. Crafting policy advice to propel change with limited resources must have seemed almost impossible; yet the need for reform was obvious and urgent. The question was how to have the most impact in nascent agencies with little power.

The need for control led to oversimplification. James Scott's *Seeing Like a State* explores some of the reasons state agents seek to simplify social-ecological systems. One of these is the way simplification seems to afford control over nature and people. Desire to save the fishery, coupled with scarce means to do so, fed the appeal of modernist policy advice, which centered on privatization to expand planting. Modernist commissioners argued passionately that only expanded planting could deliver the industry from ruin. Aquaculture must replace tonging. These commissions cast as antiquated the older conservation systems, with their complex provisions, numerous compromises, and diverse practices. Oyster modernists sought to simplify all this by replacing it with a sea of privately owned oyster farms. Individual ownership would render the past system obsolete.

Not all commissioners saw the problem this way. Populist commissioners argued that the older system had great merit and must be the basis for any reform. They did want to streamline and enforce laws, but their advice centered on amending the old system through state interventions that could shore up traditional management. Populists and modernists pursued Hays's gospel of efficiency in different ways. Populists saw overfishing as wasting a key resource. Modernists saw the lack of oyster farms as wasting marine space. Both wanted a more efficient, orderly industry, and both argued for expanding the state's role. Modernists differed in that they wanted to simplify conservation practices and the moral ideas that underlay them. They sought to replace what E. P. Thompson calls the "moral economy" with maximized production.[1] Populists, on the other hand, wanted to preserve the oystering way of life and culture.

The first commissioners formed part of the Progressive Era's new interventionists. Like many Americans, they believed in grabbing the reins of rapid modernization. Directing change required understanding what was happening, so one of their most pressing tasks was to gather information. Commissioners chose a path summarized by Robert Weibe: "For lack of anything that made better sense of their world, people everywhere weighed, counted, and measured it."[2] The first commissioners sailed off to weigh oysters and count fishermen. The primary function of these new public servants was compiling overviews of the fishery. The endless descriptions and lists that make up the bulk of their commission reports may be seen as evidence of a struggle to make sense of a changing world.

Commissioners poured most of their effort into painting a badly needed picture.

Commissioners then used these descriptions to advise state legislatures on reform. This chapter depicts the way modernist and populist policy advice differed. The first section provides a brief overview of the varied structure of the first commissions. The second and longest section examines the commissioners' advice. It divides advice thematically, comparing modernist and populist versions of each theme. The third section looks at the commissions' institutional alliance, and the fourth describes the USFC approach to gathering data.

COMMISSION STRUCTURE

No two states managed oysters the same way. Only three states (RI, CT, NJ) had permanent shellfish commissions. Rhode Island's was by far the earliest, founded in 1842. Its task was to grant and record aquaculture leases. There are no reports from this early agency. It apparently operated haphazardly, and the state founded a new, more active shellfish commission in 1864 that did begin issuing reports. Connecticut founded their shellfish commission in 1881 and New Jersey in 1883. All three states provided extensive information to their legislatures. Rhode Island and Connecticut also spent much of their time surveying aquaculture property boundaries in their early years.

Four states (MA, NY, MD, NJ) had temporary shellfish commissions. These launched special investigations so legislators could better understand the fishery. They created a picture of the industry and advised legislatures. Massachusetts had one such commission that presented reports in 1905 and 1906. David Belding was the investigator and his reports were classic statements of modernist oyster advising. New York carried out investigative surveys from 1884 to 1887 with the assistance of steamers on loan for short periods from the USFC. These surveys were led by Eugene Blackford, who would later serve as New York's fish commissioner. He sampled bed conditions with a dredge, sent out questionnaires, and held numerous public meetings. Blackford wrote reform laws, and the legislature adopted many of these. Blackford aimed to harmonize and clarify rather than to totally replace or improve existing town laws. His reports present a stark contrast with Belding, as Blackford was one of the most populist commissioners.

Maryland founded a temporary commission in 1882 and a permanent one beginning in 1906. The oyster industry dominated Maryland politics during the first commission. Its commissioners were William Brooks, James Waddell, and Henry Legg. Brooks was a professor at Johns Hopkins and the nation's leading oyster scientist. Waddell was a state representative favoring the expansion of planting and later served as the head of Maryland's oyster navy. Legg was a former representative from a tidewater district who opposed planting and who was instrumental in passing an earlier oyster law.[3] Brooks and Waddell fell on the modernist side of the spectrum, whereas Legg was a populist. They disagreed so fundamentally that Legg wrote a separate "minority report."

New Jersey sent out a temporary commission too, but it also had three other types of commissions. There was a permanent shellfish commission, a set of small district commissions with changing boundaries, a state shell commission that placed empty shells on natural beds to encourage oyster settlement, and a temporary oyster commission tasked with conducting investigations. All four commissions existed concurrently at one point. Missing reports are the norm for these organizations: almost all district and shell commission records are lost. Occasionally nonfishery agencies produced descriptive or statistical surveys, such as one done by the Bureau of Statistics of Labor and Industries of the State of New Jersey in 1883.[4] New Jersey exemplifies the varied institutional arrangements between these states.

Most of these states founded permanent fish commissions slightly before their shellfish commissions: Massachusetts in 1866, Rhode Island in 1870, Connecticut in 1866, New York in 1868, New Jersey in 1870, Maryland in 1874, Virginia in 1875, and Delaware in

1911. Virginia and Delaware were the only states in this region that never had any type of shellfish commission during this period, but Virginia's fish commission frequently discussed oysters.

The USFC concentrated on science, although it did compile statistics and industry overviews meant to guide policy. It published several reports on oysters.[5] Its scientists occasionally expressed opinions in these reports, saying for example that Connecticut's deepwater planting "deserves to be classed among the most remarkable events connected with our coast fisheries."[6] Another major exception to the focus on science was a USFC Maryland advisory survey in 1893 that remains the most detailed statement of the populist position at the time.

COMMISSIONERS' POLICY ADVICE

Agreement on Overharvesting

To understand oyster modernists, one must recapture their sense of being on the edge of a cliff. Both modernist and populist commissioners agreed that oysters were declining in some areas—especially Massachusetts, Maryland, and Virginia where commissioners predicted declines would worsen. In Massachusetts, Belding predicted complete exhaustion of the oyster beds, stating that at present "all hopes for the morrow are sacrificed for the clamorous demands of the present."[7] Rhode Island's first commissioner to write reports, John P. Knowles, complained in 1864 of the "shockingly wasteful and ruinous" practices of the fishery.[8]

There were two notable cases where commissioners disagreed on oyster population declines. In New York, the fish and game commissioners felt that Blackford's first report showed Long Island overharvesting. They claimed oyster beds were approaching "ruin" due to "havoc."[9] However, Blackford never came close to predicting "ruin." A letter from the head of the USFC to Blackford complained that commissioners had misrepresented his views.[10] This case illustrates how some commissioners wanted Blackford's report to present evidence of decline.

The other disagreement came from Maryland's crucial 1884 report. Brooks and Waddell claimed that oysters were declining, but Legg disagreed. Legg's "minority report" stated that oysters were in fact increasing, and he asserted that oysters' natural fecundity made decline virtually impossible. He supplied figures documenting increased landings at Baltimore and Crisfield packing houses. Additionally, he drew a distinction between annual and permanent depletion. Harvesting depleted oyster bars each year, but then they recovered. Legg suggested that Brooks and Waddell mistook temporary decline for a permanent condition. He described large depleted bars, and indeed whole regions of the bay, that he had seen recover after a short rest.[11] Following his notion of temporary decline, he felt that oyster beds needed rest and protection. Despite supporting this protection following harvest, he believed the state did not need a "large and cumbersome navy," nor "high-salaried commanders and crew."[12] Maryland's oyster navy was mainly a sinecure at this time and did little to protect oysters, so Legg's opinion made sense, although that he would later run for oyster navy commander.

Legg's statements on decline are puzzling. When Legg sent out circulars to gather information for the 1884 report, his first question was, "What causes in your county have so reduced the supply of oysters?" The *Baltimore Sun* reported tongers' main answer was illegal dredging and overworking beds.[13] The *Baltimore Sun* also wrote that tongers demanded the state take immediate action. Legg was a candidate to represent Queen Anne County at this time, and he told the paper that oystermen would only find friends in his Democratic party.[14] Perhaps he was adopting positions that were politically expedient by rejecting Brooks and Waddell's recommendations. He certainly cast himself as the tongers' ally.

The 1884 Maryland report sheds light on how the threat of imminent collapse shaped modernist recommendations. Brooks warned about impending collapse in the report, and he was correct that Maryland's harvest levels were unsustainable. It is important to see the reasoning behind Brooks's fears. Oystermen had depleted many smaller oyster beds, and there was a great deal of overharvesting, especially by dredge boats. Oysters were still by far the most important fishery in the state. The importance of the oyster fishery, combined with local declines and overharvesting, led many commissioners to call for rapid and drastic action as the only remedy. It is hard to overstate the gravity of the problem they faced, particularly in Chesapeake Bay. They saw rampant destruction and regular violence. Their dire predictions were more than leverage for intervention. They were sound, sober assessments by experienced observers trying to advance the public good.

Views on Existing Oyster Laws

When it came to existing laws, commissioners agreed that profusion led to confusion. Populist and modernist commissioners alike saw that confusion in existing laws was one of the fishery's main problems, and early reports frequently comment on their defects. Brooks and Waddell saw "over-dredging and unwholesome laws" as major causes of oyster decline.[15] They noted that local laws contained "the greatest confusion and conflict in the statutes." Brooks "procured a coast survey chart and tried to trace on it the requirements of the different local laws, but found the legal boundaries overlapped in labyrinthine confusion."[16] Belding said that the existing shellfish laws in Massachusetts were "the first evil which demands attention."[17] Knowles described Rhode Island laws as "incongruous, inconsistent, and, I will add, suicidal."[18] Knowles thought the laws had contradictory provisions attempting to reconcile different interests. Maryland's second fish commission report explains that "much previous legislation has been ineffective, as based on evidence defective and misleading in character, the result of misstatement and convictions found by conflicting advice given by interested persons and by those guided by too imperfect observations."[19] In Virginia, the commissioners stated that the laws were "partial, imperfect, confused, and inoperative."[20] The state had built up laws, layer by layer, by responding to petitions. The result was "voluminous and complicated."[21] Virginia laws had "confused, and sometimes unintelligible provisions . . . contradictory statements . . . so many exception and qualifications, and special and local statutes" as to make enforcement and public understanding difficult.[22] Oystermen overwhelmed Virginia commissioners with requests for information on laws.

Commissioners agreed laws needed to be more efficient, but modernists and populists had divergent ideas about how to do this. Modernist commissioners sought radical changes. They called for laws to expand aquaculture by privatizing marine space and restricting or eliminating common property. Populist commissioners, on the other hand, recommended streamlining laws while preserving traditional conservation measures. Streamlining laws was a complex recommendation. How could one streamline laws without losing their essential provisions?

Populist commissioners argued for this in a variety of ways. In New York, Blackford felt laws needed greater clarity to promote the settling of disputes. In particular, he wanted to clarify the limits of town versus state jurisdiction.[23] The New Jersey state commission's main conclusion after first touring the state in 1884 was that the lack of comprehensive mapping limited planting of oyster beds. Lack of maps led to constant litigation and disputes between planters and tongers. The main recommendation of populists was to designate and map boundaries, although they considered this solution to be cost prohibitive.[24] Virginia's fish commission recommended harmonization of Virginia and Maryland's closed season dates, and Blackford made specific recommendations about harmonizing closed season dates as well.[25] Of course, streamlined laws needed better enforcement. The first time Virginia's fish commission mentioned oysters (1876–1877) was in reference to the need for a larger navy. They feared that Maryland's navy would drive "that lawless class" (illegal dredgers) into Virginia waters.[26]

The most common feature of populist streamlining advice was commissioners' reliance on the input of oystermen. Commissioners claimed that the industry supported more streamlined laws and wanted a "just, favorable and final solution of a much vexed question,"[27] but they often expressed uncertainty about how best to do this, preferring to defer to local people. In Connecticut, the commissioners wrote that town-managed oyster beds were "so numerous, and so different in character and environment from the deep-water beds and from each other, that uniform laws of regulation might work more harm than good; and each town is the proper judge of what is best for its own oyster-beds."[28] New Jersey's state oyster commission advocated for keeping district commissions for the same reason, saying, "we regard it as absolutely essential to the welfare of the industry that agents of the state . . . must be upon the grounds to give proper attention to the industry."[29] Blackford also cautioned against standardizing all management measures because of variation in environmental conditions.[30] This openness to local management illustrates that the populist commissioners valued allowing oystermen more say in management, as opposed to centralizing state management, and that they were more comfortable with locally specific statutes, as opposed to ones written solely by state experts.

Because they valued local knowledge, populist commissioners frequently solicited the opinions of oystermen. Connecticut's early shellfish commissioners felt they needed the power to hold hearings and gather testimony to "establish order where disorder and confusion now exist."[31] The commissioners acknowledged that there were numerous opinions on the measures needed to protect natural beds, which made it hard for them to know the best choices. They did recommend stirring up oysters, to clean them just prior to spawning, and then closing the season with the onset of reproductive processes. But since the best ways or times to do this were still uncertain, they hesitated to recommend changes in the law. Maryland newspapers frequently commented on Legg's questioning. He asked for information on access, summer planting, conditions of the natural beds, defects in the law, possible remedies, outsider law violation, and harvesting levels.[32] Legg wrote an article for the *Easton Ledger* on the opinions of St. Michael's oystermen, claiming they asked for bans on scrapes (small dredges) and harvesting for home consumption during the closed season.[33] Asking oystermen's opinions about streamlining laws was essential to the populist approach.

In contrast, modernist commissioners questioned the most fundamental provisions of the laws.

Modernist Views on Common Property

Modernists saw privatization as a panacea. They singled out common property as the chief defect of the laws. A lone root cause led to a single solution: privatization. Belding's description of common property typifies this view. He opened his first report by saying, "The first difficulty confronting this proposed system [privatization] is the too frequently accepted fallacy that all lands between the tide marks now are and should be held in common by the inhabitants of the shore communities, to the exclusion of citizens from other sections of the State." Belding blamed oyster decline on "the disastrous effect of this policy." His next step was to describe the link between private property and progress. Modernist commissioners always expressed this in lawlike terms, and they described these supposed social laws as obvious to any unprejudiced, objective person. Belding's report describes common property this way: "This fallacious assumption is contrary to the fundamental principles of all economic doctrines. It may be safely assumed that the individual ownership of property ... is a necessary condition of progress, and has in fact at length become the foundation of all society."[34]

Privatization was seen as the only practical system for halting decline. Private leases would allow natural laws to function smoothly, as "in all business individual initiative and effort furnish the keynote of success."[35] Expanded planting and privatization was the obvious best solution for the fishery's problems. Belding proposed that the state lease most inshore areas to individuals in the form of small lots. Further from shore, he recommended that the state lease plots of unlimited size to both individuals and companies. Belding did assert that every township should maintain public property.

Modernist commissioners recommended varied forms of privatization. Brooks and Waddell felt leases should come with perpetual title. Perpetual lease proposals were an unusual and extreme recommendation compared to other states. Even more controversial was their stance on natural beds. Since almost all areas of Chesapeake Bay contained a few oysters, oystermen could and did claim almost the whole bay as a natural bed. Therefore, Brooks and Waddell felt that the whole Bay should be "thrown open to private cultivators."[36] If public sentiment opposed this, which it did, then they wanted surveys to delineate "legally regarded natural beds" as soon as possible.[37] They noted that it would be extremely difficult to map natural beds, especially now that dredging had spread them out. In particular, they pointed out the difficulty Connecticut faced in mapping its smaller beds.

Brooks and Waddell were aware of their critics. Legg's report states that natural beds must be "held, as a great commons . . . and not sold to a few capitalists, thereby making the rich richer and the poor poorer."[38] Tongers shared this view. Brooks and Waddell did identify monopolies as a problem. Belding also acknowledged this problem with privatization, advised that leases be nontransferable to prevent speculation and monopoly, and stated that there would have to be provisions for the poor to acquire leases.[39] Brooks and Waddell suggested the state could handle this problem by granting anyone their own farm, and by retaining a law limiting planting leases to five acres.

Charles Stevenson's USFC-sponsored 1893 report strongly opposes opening Maryland's natural beds to planting.[40] He begins by explaining the uniqueness of Maryland's oyster fishery, "by far the principle means of support" in the eleven tidewater counties. He calls Maryland the one state that had "persistently refused to encourage an extensive development of private oyster fisheries, devoting instead all its energies toward conserving and protecting the free fishery on the public domain."[41] Instead of highlighting this as the central problem in Maryland's fishery, Stevenson suggests this should be a source of pride in the region and serve as the continued basis for management. His defense typifies populist commissioners' responses to arguments blaming common property.

Connecticut commissioners in the late 1880s argued against expanding leasing too, but for different reasons. They said that many planters had overextended their holdings and shelled more ground than they could protect from starfish. They blamed this practice for increased starfish abundance, stating, "the oystermen must give up their notions of large crops growing without care or labor. They must confine themselves to areas which they can manage and protect."[42] Much of the cultivated areas were "left without attention," catalyzing starfish growth.[43]

Modernist planners favored privatization in part because it was a single solution to a complex problem. McEvoy describes the same pattern in the management of Progressive Era California fisheries. He notes that privatization "was government's way of collecting a wide range of interrelated problems under a single relatively manipulable legal abstraction."[44] Privatization was the linchpin of modernist reforms because it promised to do so much with so little.

Property Incentives

Modernist commissioners continually referred to the different incentives created by common and private property. They believed private property created an incentive to improve resources, as one could capture the benefits from doing so. Lack of title, on the other hand, held back possible improvements, as someone else might sweep up the rewards. As Belding explained, "thoughtful fishermen," who would otherwise control the fishery, knowingly contributed to overharvest and did so because they saw others harvesting without restraint. Logically, they decided to harvest what they could before the fishery was exhausted.[45] This description mirrors Hardin's "tragedy of the commons."[46] The tragedy of the commons appealed to modernist planners because it gave a lawlike explanation for overharvesting and showed a clear link between private property and progress. Populist commissioners agreed that collective action problems could lead to overfishing, but they developed this theme in more nuanced ways. The Connecticut commissioners provide a good example. In their early reports, they describe public beds that were "free to all" as "quickly despoiled by reckless fishing."[47] They cite depletion of natural beds in Europe, Chesapeake Bay,

New Jersey, and New York as examples of this process. Despite the possibility of depletion, populist commissioners defended tongers' character and intelligence and widen the responsibility for conservation to include the larger oystering community. At the time, planters blamed tongers for starfish infestations because tongers were not actively killing the starfish they encountered while harvesting. Planters felt that tongers' negligence allowed starfish populations to build up around the natural beds and attack the planted oysters. The commissioners agreed, explaining, "the avarice of today blinds them [the tongers] to the prospects of tomorrow." Though acknowledging the tongers' limited foresight, the report turns from critique to the larger context:

> The Commissioners would not want to give the impression that all men who work upon the natural beds are open to these charges . . . The Commissioners have found them, with few exceptions, honest, industrious and well disposed. No one can be reasonably blamed for omitting to do that which is the joint duty of all—for failing to cooperate when cooperation is impossible. If public beds, therefore, are to be kept clear of stars, it must be done in some other way than by the voluntary efforts of oystermen.[48]

Here, populist commissioners use the difficulty of collective action to defend the character of tongers and locate the responsibility for conservation with the larger community.

The New Jersey state shellfish commission applied this reasoning to the state's cull law. They began by articulating how the law had helped arrest the decline of seed oysters. However, "the greed of the tonger, prompting him to take everything, so that he may lose nothing," soon reversed these gains.[49] The cull law was hard to enforce and oystermen evaded it by asserting that they had not yet thrown the shells back but that they intended to do so. The commission recommended revising the law so that tongers could only catch a certain amount before culling. They claimed this would meet with "universal approval" from oystermen. They felt tongers only disobeyed the law because they were sure everyone else was doing the same, due to its easy evasion. The commission also disliked the law allowing anyone to harvest two bushels without a license, describing it as "simply a legalized nuisance . . . [and] an excuse for shirking the law altogether."[50] Their cull-law discussion depicted oystermen following the logic of incentives in a way that harmed the fishery, but it also explained how the legislature could employ a traditional management measure to address these issues. The commissioners analyzed collective action problems in a populist way that maintained tradition, even as their analysis accused tongers of "greed." Many commissioners expressed similar ambivalence on this complex topic.

Commissioners in other states often analyzed cull-law problems in the same way. Stevenson repeatedly said the cull law was the most useful conservation tool Maryland had, but unlike the closed season, no one obeyed it. Tongers disobeyed because they could get twenty cents a bushel for undersized oysters, which were previously legal. Enforcing the cull law was challenging. Joseph Seth, commander of the Maryland oyster navy, explained the problematic nature of the cull law in Stevenson's report. The navy searched vessels and enforced the law by dumping one barrel out of fifty on deck, making oystermen cull it immediately. They could not sell anything below the legal limit. However, small oysters did not have to be thrown back if they were already off the bed where they were caught. Oystermen gave away these unsellable oysters free to the packers. Because of this, Seth said, "I find all classes to agree with me in saying that the cull law should be vigorously enforced, and all as unanimous in both violating it and trying to screen violators from arrest by the fishery force."[51] The state amended the law the following year. Stevenson and Seth explained the problem as a collective action dilemma created by the discrepancy between individual and group incentives. As with the Connecticut commissioners, they proposed using traditional conservation mechanisms to address this issue.

Stevenson and other populist commissioners sometimes applied collective action analysis to overharvesting on natural beds as well. Stevenson claimed Maryland was divided between two "great interests," tongers and dredgers, who "wage war unitedly on the planters."[52] He rejected arguments that blamed the tongers' character and instead cited a collective action problem as the primary issue:

> The great trouble with the present methods and regulations is not with the close seasons or with the implements employed, but, as in other States, the oystermen take no individual interest in the preservation and development of the reefs on which they work, their sole object being to obtain at the moment all the oysters possible, without reference to the future supply. Individual interests clash with the public good. While it is the public or general interest of all that each oysterman should refrain from taking the small and poor oysters, taking few during bad markets, and give attention to removing enemies and leaving the reefs in the best condition for further reproduction and growth, it is his individual but temporary interest to take all he can get, big and little, fat and poor, in good markets and in bad markets, and with the least possible expenditure of time. As with other men, the individual gain of to-day outweighs the public good of tomorrow.[53]

Ideally, tongers would prepare beds and be careful to protect the small oysters, but these measures were unlikely in a large "public domain."[54] Populists and modernists agreed that short-term individual incentives promoted overharvesting. Modernists cited this dynamic to argue for privatization, whereas populists used it to argue for building on traditions in ways that could help tongers overcome inherent incentive problems.

Historical Narratives and Comparisons

Aquaculture created an aquatic frontier, and on frontiers dispossession requires justification. To provide this, modernist commissioners situated the oyster problem within larger historical narratives. As with colonial justifications for dispossessing native people, modernist commissioners equated enclosure with improvement.[55] Commissioners posited an inexorable progression from common to private property, expressed as a self-evident social law. They saw this shift as an engine of and prerequisite for improvement. For proof, commissioners cited numerous and diverse examples. Commissioners used surveys to make the fishery visible. In turn, they framed survey data to illustrate supposed social laws by reporting on how enclosure correlated with improved conditions. They claimed to be laying bare the fundamental operative principles of the fishery and advised legislatures to base their laws on these. They hoped to substitute objective laws for political arguments.

This advice simplified ethics. It narrowed the goal to maximizing a single variable: productivity. This was the ethical basis of the Taylorist side of Progressive Era reforms.[56] As with privatization, it appealed because it promised to identify a social law that showed one optimal arrangement. Such laws seemed powerful since they revealed the causes of problems at their root. Single causes inspired belief that changing one linchpin, property rights, was the key to unlocking progress. This thinking led to greater optimism and an appetite for radical change.

Why did modernist commissioners advocate these simplified solutions? The calm characterizing Connecticut's planting industry, when compared to the chaos of Maryland's oyster commons, presented a vivid contrast. More important though was the sense of crisis and potential mixed together. Commissioners saw themselves, quite reasonably, at a turning point, believing they faced the prospect of steep future declines. If they could only make people see the fundamental principles of enlightened management, they could be on the cusp of a much more prosperous era. If they could inspire decisive action, they could snatch victory from the jaws of defeat.

The New Jersey commission's advice on leasing barren natural beds illustrates the way they saw progress as objectively rational. The commissioners expressed incredulity toward the current policy prohibiting leasing in these areas, saying it "can hardly be conceived" and it "seems beyond comprehension" that people could not cultivate barren former beds. They acknowledge that doing so "would cause such a howl of wrath. . . . Yet it is really difficult to see why any can with good reason object."[57] They cite the obviousness of their argument, saying "it would really seem that such a measure in oyster farming should require no argument to prove its desirability, on the principle universally accepted the world over."[58] This perspective treated traditional norms and practices as backward, as anyone who could see "universally accepted" principles would agree to privatize barren beds. New Jersey commissioners thought opposition to planting on defunct natural beds came from tonger resistance to the prosperity of others. Their 1901 report also mentions as examples Virginia, Maryland, and Connecticut, claiming all leased "nonproductive bottom," which is misleading. At this point, Connecticut was leasing areas, but only after examination and public hearings, while Virginia and Maryland did not lease nonproductive areas designated as natural beds. The commissioners visited Connecticut a year before, and this may have influenced their report.

Belding again provided an articulate version of this perspective. He couched the need for privatization in a history of Massachusetts resource and property law. He said the early Massachusetts great pond ordinance was just at the time, but only because of the state's small population in the 1600s. In the 1900s "this communistic system is distinctly unsound, and is in direct opposition to the principles of social and economic development."[59] Belding also made a comparison to farming, an almost obligatory technique for modernist commissions. He argued that common-property oyster beds were the equivalent of leaving farmland unplowed so that people could pick blackberries in common. The practitioners of traditional oystering were "mentally unbalanced."[60] Belding used farming metaphors to temper criticism of other shellfish commons, saying they were like wild meadows. Oyster beds, however, were like gardens and had to be tended. This was why oysters needed places under private ownership, though other shellfish could be kept in common.[61]

Populist commissioners rarely discussed progress in a lawlike fashion. Blackford provides an interesting example of the populist view on the inevitability and desirability of expanded planting. He held up Connecticut as a model that New York should emulate, claiming, "all the leading oyster experts of the country strongly recommend the system."[62] But he also wanted to carefully maintain natural beds as seed nurseries.[63] When he discussed the decline of natural beds, he said, "It can readily be seen from this that the oyster industry is rapidly passing from the hands of the fisherman to those of the planter and oyster culturist."[64] He then explained how this was both "good and bad." It was good because planted beds produced more oysters, but it was bad because planters did not compensate tongers for their losses and diminished seed supply.

Frontier analogies were another staple of modernist narratives. Knowles provided a classic example of how commissioners described the history of frontier settlement in a lawlike fashion that linked private property to progress:

> A sale of the wild lands of the Federal Government to emigrants, that the wilderness may blossom as the rose, with the arts, institutions and structures of New England civilization, no statesman ever yet opposed, on the grounds that the trappers, hunters and squatters, accustomed to scour those lands for game and plunder, might complain of infraction of their natural rights, and expulsion from the "free and common" hunting grounds, where, perchance, their fathers and grand fathers vegetated in poverty and semi-barbarism,—and, worse than all, trained up their offspring, only to fill their fathers' places.[65]

Modernist commissioners invoked popular frontier imagery, linking tongers to poor, primitive hunters and thieves, in order to enhance the persuasive power of their arguments.

Characterizing Oystermen

Colonizers justify frontier dispossession by claiming it will improve the dispossessed.[66] Curtailing common property would force tongers into more productive work. More strikingly, modernists claimed that more productive occupations, especially working on planting farms, would improve the character of former tongers. Modernists depicted tongers as backward and planters as progressive, which was closely tied to their frontier analogies and linear view of progress. Their advice also contained an aesthetic or technological bias. Michael Adas explains how Europeans in colonial settings often judged other cultures based on a technological hierarchy that placed Western industrial technology at the top.[67] This was the way modernist commissioners wrote about the difference between planting and tonging. Connecticut's planting fishery—with its steamships, dredges, and packing houses—presented a stark contrast to the tonger with his rake-like tongs and small boat.

Knowles tied this view of tongers to common-property traditions, saying that the "pestiferous notion that oysters, in their native element, cannot become individual property, and that therefore, to take them wherever found is not *stealing* in morals, though it be in law, would find propagandists and advocates no where but among 'long-shore-men of bad reputation for honesty, and landsmen of no reputation worth having" (italics in original).[68] Belding described tongers as "incapable of working together for the best interests of the towns or of the public." He also discussed ethnic and class issues, saying the shore was "combed by . . . irresponsible aliens and by exemplars of the 'submerged tenth.'"[69] He identified two classes of fishermen. The first was a "permanent resident, usually native born, bound to a definite locality by ties of home and kin and long association,—a most useful type of citizen." Whereas the second was "a more rapidly increasing class,—foreign born, unnaturalized, nomadic, a humble soldier of fortune, a hanger-on in the outskirts of urban civilization, eking out an existence by selling or eating the shellfish from the public grounds. Too ignorant to appreciate the importance of sanitary precaution, the alien clammer haunts the proscribed territory polluted by sewage, and does much to keep the dangerous typhoid germ in active circulation in the community." Belding felt that this class typically engaged in "petty buccaneering." He suggested that private property would force "these irresponsible wandering aliens to acquire definite locations," thereby improving their character. Belding also discussed "an unprogressive element . . . who prefer to reap where they have not sown; who rely upon what they term their 'public right.'"[70] It is unclear if this last comment referred to immigrants or merely tongers in general.

New Jersey commissioners expressed similar, although less extreme, views. According to the commissioners, current practices on the natural beds "entail poverty, ignorance and their attendant train of evils upon those who are content to eke out a scanty subsistence in working them."⁷¹ On the other hand, "in those sections of the State visited by the Commission, where oyster planting is most extensively engaged in, the people, as a rule, were found to be in a busy and prosperous condition; and on every hand evidence of enterprise, thrift and good citizenship were to be observed."⁷² These quotes illustrate the commission's bias toward planting and depict how this tied into the way commissioners characterized oystermen.

McDonald Lee, Virginia's fish commissioner from 1906–1912, claimed that, "many parts of the oyster country are afflicted with a worthless class, who go north as waiters or hostlers in summer." A permanent residency requirement would keep out "this vagrant class."⁷³ The other benefit of this proposal was that "it means the farmer can find more help," as it would keep oystermen in Virginia in the summer. Lee said that tongers felt everyone had rights to oysters, and "they glory in their smartness if they can take them without being apprehended."⁷⁴ Where tonging decreased, this "weeded out" some of the lawbreakers, leaving "a better class" behind to continue tonging.⁷⁵

Lee applied the modernist reasoning to African American tongers in a predictable fashion. He said that "some of the colored and a large majority of the whites" were good citizens.⁷⁶ About half Virginia tongers were African Americans, according to Lee, so the implication was that most African Americans were part of the "lawless class." Lee said whites complained that blacks were hard to find as cull-boys (a helper who culls oysters while the other person tongs) because they started tonging so young. White oystermen often had to take their children out of school to fulfill this duty. Lee advised raising license fees as a way to keep blacks out of the industry, but he recognized that not all whites would agree to this. He felt a measure of this sort would not only benefit whites looking for cheap labor, but might be the salvation of black oystermen." The "improvident negro" spent what he made as fast as he could, and this proposal would force him to work more hours and make more money as an employee. At present, "the average negro tonger . . . is the personification of independence," giving him more time to spend money.[77] Lee felt that curtailing public property would help undermine the livelihood of the black oysterman, keeping him in check. Lee's statements add racial prejudice into the larger theme of forcing tongers to become efficient wage laborers for their own good.

Stevenson again presented the most articulate populist alternative. He defended the morals of Maryland tongers, saying:

> There are few workmen in America more independent than these. At almost anytime during the season a tongmen can in a good working day catch from four to twelve bushels of oysters, for which there is always a demand almost at his door. Then having sufficient to supply his temporary needs he usually takes things easy. While some are indolent and work only when compelled by necessity, yet as a class they compare favorably in industry and morals with any other body of men similarly situated.[78]

Here he challenges the common stereotype that tongers were lazy and compliments their independence. When discussing current laws, he aligns the conduct of tongers with reasonable traditional management practices, saying, "the fishery in Maryland is not, as frequently supposed, a haphazard undertaking conducted by a class of men depending for success on violations of the State laws, but is on a firm, orderly basis, any sudden, revolutionary change in which would work great hardship and distress to the thousands of citizens depending on it for a livelihood."[79]

The differences between Stevenson and Lee reprises the split between American perceptions of farmers as Jeffersonian bastions of democracy on the one hand and backward rubes on the other.[80] Dichotomization came easily to observers of the oyster fishery because its two technology and property systems were so different. The presence of two strikingly different modes of oystering fueled thinking about linear frontier progress. It was reassuring to think tongers possessed low morals, as it was less troubling to evict persons who stood in the way of progress and who were partly to blame for their fate. Indeed, eviction would benefit tongers' character. Dispossession was a moral duty.

Role of Science

But how could the state expand planting? Science offered salvation. Modernist commissioners believed scientists would develop hatcheries that would aid privatization and expand planting by ending dependence on public beds. Brooks was the country's leading oyster scientist and a vocal proponent of hatcheries. He and Waddell write that "the supply of oysters must be artificially increased, for the natural fertility of the oysters is not great enough to withstand even the present drain upon them, and the demand for oysters will certainly increase from year to year."[81] Increasing demand would swamp any legal remedies.[82] Brooks makes the same argument in his book, *The Oyster*, which was a popular treatment of the oyster problem in the late nineteenth century. In it, he writes that the principal cause of decline was that "THE DEMAND HAS OUTGROWN THE NATURAL SUPPLY" (capitalized in the original).[83] Brooks and Waddell urge that their investigation justifies "the worst foreboding," that the oyster beds were in "imminent danger of complete destruction" due to increasing demand.[84]

There was a great deal of truth to this, of course. What makes it a modernist theme is the way that Brooks links science and property. At the time, Brooks felt that science could increase productivity by identifying how to properly grow oysters in hatcheries. Brooks and Waddell explain that cultivators had to place hatchery-grown oysters on private leases, not public beds. They claim that, "the only obstacle [to scientific production methods] . . . is the existence of the sentiment that since the oyster grounds belong to the whole people, they are not the proper field for labor and industry."[85] They express certainty that hatcheries would require private property, as no one would be inclined to invest in common property improvements. They suggest that most fisheries operated as commons because people could not improve them, but that soon this would no longer hold true for oysters. They go on to compare oysters to farming potatoes, equating privatization with the "progress of civilization."[86] They continue this motif throughout their 1884 report: "Civilized races have long recognized the fact that the true remedy is not to decrease demand, but to increase the supply of food.... We live in a highly civilized age, and if we fail to grasp its spirit we shall go to the wall before the oyster cultivators of the Northern States, just as surely as the Indians have been exterminated by the whites."[87] This presents an additional twist on the theme of social laws. When demand inevitably increases, science will come to the rescue, but only planters with private rights will utilize these scientific findings. Brooks's view grew out of the Lockean notion of mixing labor with property found in modernist historical narratives.

Marshall McDonald, like Brooks, was both a commissioner and a prominent scientist. He served as Virginia's fish commissioner from 1878–1888 and head of the USFC from 1888–1995. Although a modernist in most ways, he was less optimistic about oyster hatchery science than Brooks. He felt that fisheries suffered from "wanton spoliation."[88] Shad were almost entirely gone from Virginia by 1878, which McDonald blamed on dams and improper harvesting methods and technology. For him, the solutions included fishways around dams, artificial propagation in hatcheries, and introducing new fish species. At first he felt that oysters needed similar remedies. McDonald quickly implemented most of his proposed solutions. He designed the "McDonald fishway" in the late 1870s, and it became a leading design. Shad numbers began to rebound due to hatchery operations and fishways. In addition to experimenting with shad, McDonald introduced species such as carp that spread successfully. In 1888 he became head of the USFC and worked to expand their hatchery operations. These solutions proved harder to apply to oysters, requiring extensive research. He spent his first five years as Virginia fish commissioner studying oysters before outlining a plan. Despite the success associated with his fish hatcheries, McDonald came to feel that artificial oyster cultivation would fail and that Virginia could only halt decline through "rational legislation."[89] He was "satisfied the starting point is in converting the oyster domain to private property."[90] Not all modernists were sure science could save them.

Connecticut and New York commissioners posited a more populist role for science. They wanted planters to share best practices, a relationship modeled on farmers' institutes. In their discussion of starfish, commissions admitted that it was difficult to know how to proceed with management and even suggested prohibiting shooting coot (a bay duck that ate starfish). In one report they listed twenty different conflicting quotes they had heard regarding the best ways to combat starfish populations. Eventually, they recommend bounties. Following this recommendation, tens of thousands of barrels of starfish were destroyed annually in the 1880s. Later, when Connecticut planters had overextended into areas where planting failed, the commission recommended extending a buyout program to town-designated areas in state waters. They were unsure why these areas failed and said that oystermen offered conflicting theories. What they felt was needed was a thorough comparison of the best areas with areas unable to support oysters. This would take many years and vast amounts of time and money. Until they reached an understanding, they suggested that oystermen must continue to "grope in the dark" through "perplexing and costly experiments."[91] Blackford also repeatedly stressed that planters could profit by sharing information about advanced methods. In his first report he states:

> Unfortunately at present there are localities where the persons who are engaged in this kind of work have no conception that there are any methods which can advantageously take the place of those which have been established since the "long, long ago" by old customs. Such ideas can only be rendered obsolete by showing these persons that there is something better.[92]

In his next report, he blames "the lack of scientific culture on the planted beds" as a cause of low harvests.[93]

Commissions in New Jersey, Virginia, and Maryland routinely reprinted scientific findings in their reports. Maryland's 1880 fish commission report suggests that artificial cultivation might work as a solution, but "it remains a matter of conjecture" and "it will require extended experiments before we can feel assured that the protection afforded in this manner will be sufficient."[94] In contrast, the first

Virginia report recommends opening a fish hatchery.[95] Spencer Baird, the first head of the USFC, offered personnel assistance, and the commissioners decided to build four hatcheries. They were "perfectly satisfied . . . that enough is known about fish culture to ensure its success."[96] This report was also the first to feature a scientist: J. R. Page of the University of Virginia. Page reprinted a long report by Victor Coste, Europe's leading aquaculturist and a specialist in oysters. Page believed that overharvesting would soon deplete Chesapeake Bay and that the fishery would have to adopt French planting methods to continue to exist. Page went on to describe why these methods were the only realistic solution. He wrote that fishermen were too greedy and politicians simply pandered to what the fishermen wanted. What Chesapeake Bay needed, he said, were scientists who saw the laws of nature that should guide legislation.

Hatcheries helped modernist commissioners argue for a single solution to the oyster problem. If the law of increasing demand stressed oyster beds, then the solution was for scientists to create hatcheries, which modernists felt was the only way to raise production. Of course, only planters would use hatchery-raised oysters. As with farm science, in the case of oyster hatcheries it was easier to explain how science would meet the needs of larger producers. The modernists solution was based on revealing fundamental laws. It also contained an ethical narrowing: the older conservation system's complex goals of equity and access gave way to the measurable aim of maximizing production. Hatcheries supplying expanded planting fits Scott's model of simplification. Hatcheries would replace natural beds and enable private property to replace complex common rights.

Optimism

Faith in science bred optimism. It was also easier to be optimistic in the absence of evidence to the contrary. The Massachusetts reports exhibit a number of optimistic statements that also appear in the reports of other states. Belding believed planting could develop "untold wealth" through the "reclamation of large portions of the waste shore areas."[97] This optimistic theme is common in many legislative advisory reports. Belding was presumably familiar with oyster population constraints, but this failed to temper his enthusiasm. The modernist commissioners were initially optimistic about artificial cultivation in particular. T. B. Ferguson, a Maryland fish commissioner, stated that it had "prospects so bright" that he lamented delays in related experiments.[98] Brooks and Waddell were of course optimistic about the ability of science to improve productivity. They stated that the fishery would eventually be worth hundreds of millions annually, at a time when Maryland harvests were only worth around two million a year.[99]

Populist commissioners tended to be more cautious. Stevenson thought that others were greatly exaggerating the potential of planting, harming planters in the process. He suggested that exaggerating potential wealth increased the tonger desire to maximize planting areas. Connecticut was highly productive, but he estimated deep-water planters averaged twenty-five bushels an acre, not the inflated four hundred bushels that some thought possible. He went on to say that no state had ever completely removed natural beds on purpose, and he saw these coexisting with planted beds. The latter could take pressure off natural beds and provide a market for seed oysters. In his mind, tongers could be the ones to start planting: "The cultivating systems here outlined are by no means antagonistic to their interests; on the contrary, they more than any others are to reap the benefits. These men are familiar with the bay; they are familiar with the character of the grounds and with the methods of handling oysters; they are already fitted out with boats and implements for engaging in the business."[100] Populist advisors often said that planting and tonging could be mutually beneficial. They were also more realistic about potential planting yields.

INSTITUTIONAL ALLIANCE OF THE COMMISSIONS

Another way to promote oyster modernism was through national organizations and alliances. Shellfish commissioners founded the

National Association of Shellfish Commissioners (NASC) in 1909, and a group of large planters and packers founded the Oyster Growers and Dealers Association (OGDA) in 1908. They cooperated closely and initially promoted a modernist platform. Literature on the "organizational synthesis" explains how government agencies and professional groups formed alliances for mutual gain.[101] In the literature on agricultural history, Charles Rosenberg describes these public-private partnerships as "entrepreneurial." More entrepreneurial scientists gained more support.[102] Oyster commissioners often lacked the power to make legislatures heed their advice, and therefore they needed and sought political allies in the private sector. David Hamilton calls these partnerships "associative state-building," which denotes the way government officials tried to expand their authority and influence through these networks.[103] This was another reason agricultural science tended to benefit larger producers: big producers could move legislatures to support science. Commissioners hoped a national alliance with large planters would convince legislatures to speed up privatization.

Charles Bacon founded the NASC and was its first president. His view represents common sentiments at the NASC annual meetings. Bacon was head of the New Jersey Bureau of Shellfisheries at the time. He founded the NASC to "exchange griefs and lay plans to win success."[104] Despite serving as a commissioner for seven years, Bacon felt he had failed to convince the legislature "that the oyster is not a joke." He said, "I have been, with the other Commissioners of my own state, so cast down by the failure of our Legislature to legislate for its general good, that I have felt totally discouraged and ready to quit the service."[105] The NASC was a venue where commissioners debated problems and solutions, and their chief aim was to improve legislation. At their first meeting, which drew sixty-four commission members, Frank Wood, New York's Superintendent of Marine Fisheries, expressed the purpose of the new organization in the opening speech. He said, "we hope by our Association here, by mingling with each other, exchanging views, to get at better methods, to get at unified laws."[106]

At the second convention in Mobile in 1910, Bacon outlined the setbacks the new association faced in its legislative advising:

> In several of our states there have been seeming setbacks in the efforts of some of our Commissioners to push forward with legislation that was meant for the betterment and advancement of the Industry. . . . The point of strongest resistance to these efforts has been the influence which ought to be most strongly arrayed for the movements, the men engaged in the industry themselves. But it is so difficult to convince some of these hard-headed and honest sons of the deep that we are striving with all sincerity for their good.[107]

The conference papers covered three topics: science, sanitation, and planting. Numerous scientists presented at NASC meetings, and most of their talks related to planting. The association's mission statement stressed the science-planting link too. It outlined that the purpose of the association was "to promote the cultivation of edible and bait mollusks; to gather and disseminate information on the methods adopted in various places."[108]

Bacon headed New Jersey's special temporary advisory commission in 1902. The New Jersey Commission for the Investigation of the Oyster Conditions toured the state and made recommendations to the legislature. Its report no longer exists, but the *New Jersey Courier* presented a series of articles on the commission's recommendations.[109] The commission's main recommendation was to eliminate the state's shell commission because shelling was based on "a crude conception of the state's duty in such matters and a still cruder knowledge of the law governing the propagation of oysters."[110] The commission felt that shelling offered no real benefits. Bacon and his colleagues also argued for the sale or lease of all bottoms, including natural beds. Although they recognized that such a proposal would arouse violent opposition, they went on to characterize any opponents as "unqualified and ignorant." They also attacked the 1902 act creating the Ocean County District Commission. The shell commission responded by justifying its existence. Its commissioners claimed that the majority of planters were "greedy and covetous . . . grabbing up everything in sight." They possessed "an antipathy to anything in legislation that will restrict their greed."[111] Prior to the shell commission, it was common for planters to induce tongers to catch seed out of season. Planters disliked the shell commission for its enforcement of public bed lines. Bacon was clearly heavily pro-planting as well as open to radical change in the fishery, and he may have thought that his best chance for influence was through a political alliance with large planters.

Rowe founded the OGDA in 1908 to address declining sales following typhoid scares. It was an association of the largest planters and packers. The OGDA president and select members gave speeches at NASC meetings. Numerous planters attended the NASC meeting each year, demonstrating the close tie between the two professional groups. Both initially had New York headquarters.

FEDERAL INFORMATION GATHERING

The USFC focused mostly on science but also created one enormously detailed overview of the industry. The USFC made its first effort to create an overall picture of U.S. fisheries in conjunction with the 1880 census. They hired five field assistants to carry out extensive surveys, assigning them to the fisheries of the Atlantic, Pacific, Gulf of Mexico, Great Lakes, and to oyster fisheries. Baird justified giving oysters their own survey, saying, "Certain branches of trade which are in the hands of a distinct class of men are well worthy of special investigation. Chief among these is the oyster trade, which absorbs more capital than all other branches of fisheries, and which has never been thoroughly studied."[112] He hired Ingersoll for this task. Ingersoll's study is still regarded as a benchmark by shellfish scientists.[113]

Baird's instructions to Ingersoll survive and show the importance of local knowledge. Baird instructed the five field assistants to visit every settlement and write the fullest possible description of the field. Prior to the survey, Baird sent out circulars to all fishing towns. Baird used these to compile a directory of all post offices within three miles of the coast and hundreds of names of persons willing to talk to the surveyors ("fishery-capitalists, manufacturers, skippers, fishermen, collectors of customs, post-masters, and lighthouse keepers"). Baird's methodology included a long, detailed list of approximately sixty questions. It explains that old newspapers "cannot be too strongly recommended" and the value of the oldest inhabitants' information "cannot be overestimated." Following the 1880 reports, Baird said the USFC had twenty to thirty thousand pages of manuscripts, and that these went a long way toward creating the first accurate picture of the nation's fisheries, a process which relied heavily on local knowledge.[114]

Ingersoll's report follows Baird's instructions for the most part. He spent twenty-two months gathering information from knowledgeable oystermen, packers, and merchants. In smaller towns, he relied more on small planters and tongers, whereas in the areas with extensive planting, he relied more on larger planters. He always visited the town personally and clearly talked to many people, except in Maryland. Here he switched to reprinting information verbatim from one informant, a proplanting oysterman, and did not report on every town. Ingersoll's statistics were based on what oystermen told him, so their accuracy is only approximate. Despite these limitations, his report provides an impressive and comprehensive picture of the oyster fishery.

Early government reports often utilized local knowledge to generate a picture of oyster fisheries, and scholars have begun to look more closely at early scientists' utilization of local knowledge.[115] Erastus Bigelow could not have written his landmark *Fishes of the Gulf of Maine* without his extensive relationships and conversations with fishermen.[116] Charles Townsend based his whale biogeography studies on whaler's knowledge and logbooks.[117] Bigelow is still in print and scientists continue to use the "Townsend charts" today to determine baseline whale populations.[118] USFC scientists also went overseas to study the oyster industries of other countries with the goal of searching for practices that could improve the U.S. fishery. Bashford Dean traveled to Europe in 1890 and to Japan in 1901. His reports resulted in few changes, partly due to the variation between foreign and domestic prices; U.S. oyster prices were too low to support the labor-intensive French and Japanese practices. Despite this, Dean felt that U.S. fishermen had much to learn from other countries.[119] Dean's reports were part of a larger effort to collect agricultural knowledge from around the world. F. H. King's *Farmers of Forty Centuries* is the most well-known example.[120] King was Chief of the Division of Soil Management of the U.S. Department of Agriculture, and he traveled to Japan, Korea, and China with the intention of understanding the "permanent agriculture" practices of peasants Both King's and Dean's studies are remarkable for their humbleness at the high point of U.S. imperial expansion.

COMPLEXITY AND THE TWO GOSPELS OF EFFICIENCY

Hays's description of Progressive Era conservation explains that its broadest significance lay in transforming "a decentralized, non-technical, loosely organized society, where waste and inefficiency ran rampant."[121] Oyster commissioners sought to impose order, end waste, and improve efficiency, but they argued for two distinct solutions. Stevenson, Blackford, and other populist commissioners recommended preserving local norms and practices. Stevenson tried to show the reasonable nature of tongers' methods, which he considered practical adaptations; he felt that any future improvement needed to build on these traditions. Blackford gave the same advice in a fishery with greater planting. He never cited social laws as justification for his advice but relied on empirical observations instead. Both he and Stevenson valued science and believed that science could spread new and useful ideas for all oystermen, but they valued oystermen's knowledge as well. Populist commissioners appear to have dedicated more time to meeting with and talking to oystermen about their experiences than their modernist counterparts. Perhaps their contact with oysterman increased their respect for them. Respect and contact were likely reinforcing.

At the other extreme were modernist commissioners like Belding, Knowles, and Brooks. These men were optimists who saw great potential wealth in the fishery. They viewed older traditions as wasteful and backward, and for them the future lay in planting. They cited social laws of historical progress to explain this belief. Relying on teleological ideas about technology and property, they compared oyster production to farming and frontiers. In short, they wanted to radically restructure the industry, and privatization was the linchpin.

This modernist narrative had its roots in colonialism and enclosure. Richard Drayton identifies a narrative common in colonial thinking: that progress required the enclosure of common property.[122] He documents how this began in England and continental Europe, with the slow spread of the enclosure movement. Other scholars, such as E. P. Thompson and Raymond Williams, explored this phenomenon within England,[123] and Drayton illustrates how colonial officials exported it around the world.[124] Adas adds a technological dimension: he examines how Europeans saw technological superiority as a mark of their own civilization, dividing people on a ladder of progress based on tools.[125] These two colonial phenomena come together in the oyster fishery. Modernists saw tongs as inferior technology, and they perceived common property as equally antiquated. As in colonial settings, they used this vision of progress to justify dispossession.

These narrative themes were the cultural background for oyster commissioners' advice, but there was also a professional imperative. McEvoy notes that privatization was an attractive solution because it seemed to offer a flexible way to solve multiple problems at once.[126] In the case of the oyster fishery, privatization also fit with commissioners' ideas of progress, and it dovetailed with their preconceptions about technological advancement. In addition, privatization was compelling because the limited resources and limited ability to sway legislators toward bold action. Interventions needed to produce results beyond the initial act, and privatization was the lone candidate.

The Taylorist side of progressivism relied on promulgating efficient principles for social order. Several factors led to this in the oyster fishery. Commissioners' social laws claimed to explain all the problems of fisheries, and they promised a powerful solution. This solution focused on the single variable of property, and although it would be difficult to implement in the short run, they thought this would make the fishery eventually almost self-governing. Imagined social laws gave commissioners hope that they could do more with less. The other reason efficiency principles were appealing to oyster commissioners was a shift in scale. Producing the first comprehensive knowledge of large, complex systems invited simplification and abstraction. Langston's description of the first federal foresters in the Blue Mountains illustrates this.[127] Oyster commissioners had to produce the first knowledge about a complex and diverse fishery. They had few resources for this and felt pressure to produce useful results, a situation which encouraged oversimplification. Simple abstract depictions of problems led to narrow ideological solutions. Narrow solutions have simple goals, such as maximizing productivity, and rely more on single-variable solutions. This is what unites oyster commissioners' call for privatization with foresters' attempts to promote orderly succession. One simplified a social system, the other a natural one, but the causes had much in common. The challenge of complexity and scale encouraged Progressive Era natural resource managers to adopt the Taylorist approach. But this was far from universal; some took another, more populist route. This division in the oyster fishery produced two competing gospels of efficiency.

CHAPTER 4

NATURAL SCIENCE

U.S. oyster scientists chased a contradiction. Their first research program focused on "artificial cultivation," which was their term for breeding and growing oysters in hatcheries. Most oyster scientists held modernist views and wanted hatcheries to maximize production. Ironically, many also fought against narrow definitions that limited the USFC's application of science to production. USFC oyster researchers put all their energy into perfecting oyster hatchery science, even as they resisted pressure to make the USFC focus more on fish hatcheries. Why did oyster scientists adopt a hatchery-focused research program in the first place, and how did they understand their role more broadly?

David Hull advises looking at "intellectual lineages" as a method for studying the history of science and advises identifying concepts at the centers of these lineages.[1] Hull's ideas explain why scientists choose between rival concepts, making his work especially appropriate for understanding the evolution of oyster science. The intellectual lineage of U.S. oyster science stretches back to Europe in the 1850s and the work of Jean Victor Coste, the pioneer of European aquaculture science. Coste focused on using hatchery science to maximize production. Karl Möbius, another prominent European scientist, provided an alternative, arguing that hatcheries could never boost wild oyster populations. U.S. scientists ignored Möbius's advice and advanced Coste's ideas as their solution to the problem of oyster decline. This chapter presents an explanation for why they chose to pursue Coste's modernist lineage instead of its more cautious alternative.

This chapter begins with a detailed narrative of experimentation conducted by oyster scientists in the nineteenth century. It then follows Andrew Abbott's "system of professions" model and examines how oyster scientists described the problem and their solution for it.[2] Abbott argues that professions justify their role by explaining how their expertise makes them uniquely suited to solve specific problems. Through this process, professions lay claim to problems and solutions. Scientists defined the problem facing the oyster fishery similarly to modernist commissioners; however their solutions promoted applied science rather than legislation. This section of the chapter spends considerable space exploring the solution of maximizing production and reasons scientists advocated for it. The next section looks at correspondence between scientists to examine how they saw their larger professional role. Unexpectedly, many prioritized pure over applied science. Another unexpected finding from these letters was their concern over political patronage appointments that might serve personal gain rather than the public good. The chapter suggests why this problem may have intersected with the debate about pure versus applied science. The conclusion surveys the terrain covered and argues that the choice of Coste over Möbius seemed less contradictory then than now.

TWO EUROPEAN AQUACULTURISTS

American scientists often cited French scientific findings as a rationale for action. French oystermen had long fattened oysters with similar techniques to those oystermen applied in the United States, but in the 1850s French scientists sought to move beyond this approach for the first time. In 1853, a chance encounter drew Coste's attention to oyster culture. The French government had sent Coste on an expedition to study the potential for fish culture in the Mediterranean. On this trip he stopped at Lake Fusaro in Italy and saw people collecting oyster spat for planting. Although there were old Roman records of oyster farming, Coste believed that Lake Fusaro was the only place still practicing oyster planting in Europe. Coste's trip convinced him that similar collection methods would work for oysters on the French coasts. Scientists intervened in France because of declining oyster beds and the growing success of French fish culture.[3] France became the world's leader in fish culture, and Coste led this field.[4]

Coste and others often referred to Lake Fusaro as the cradle of oyster culture, investing it with almost mythic status. Coste published pictures of the lake depicting the point of view of an explorer crossing a ridge and seeing a revelation below, which contrasted with the technical pictures he usually included. Coste described the small lake as preserving an uninterrupted tradition of oyster culture founded by Roman cultivators two millennia in the past, furthering the lake's symbolism as a cultural refuge.[5]

In 1853 the French government asked M. de Bon to restock oysters in the Rance River and Saint-Malo by means of oysters gathered at Cancale. This experiment was successful and proved to de Bon that transplanted oysters would still spawn. His success allowed him to establish an experimental park at Saint-Servan in 1854. In 1855 "he announced to the minister that the question of artificial reproduction was for him definitely settled in the affirmative," the first of many overly optimistic projections from both sides of the Atlantic. Coste visited de Bon at Saint-Servan in 1857, and this confirmed his earlier theories about the possibility of using spat collectors in aquaculture. He convinced de Bon to experiment in this direction too, and in 1858 de Bon asked the Ministry of the Marine for permission to begin spat-collecting experiments at Cancale. The next year his experiments at Cancale were copied on a much larger scale by private culturists, and de Bon reported that "the experiment was crowned a complete success." Coste also began studying oyster aquaculture. He published a report in February 1858 that attracted much attention. In it, he predicted that the whole French coast could be made to produce abundant oysters, and he asked the government to finance experiments demonstrating the feasibility of his dream.[6]

The Ministry of the Marine provided generous support to Coste. He took three million oysters from Cancale and Tréguier. He deposited them in April of 1858, employing two small government steamers to tow a flotilla carrying the oysters. He used shells as collectors in the same places and anchored and suspended long bundles of sticks to act as spat collectors. At the end of the spawning season spat covered the collectors. Following this success, Coste published another report in December 1858 showing his results and asking for support to duplicate these efforts across the entire French coast. This report again received much attention and publicity. In July 1859, the Ministry of the Marine gave Coste a steamer to direct his experiments and coordinate with oyster culturists working under the French government. He took half a million oysters from Cancale and distributed these at Saint-Brieuc with the intention of enriching its bottom. He purchased two million more oysters from England and took these to Bordeaux where they were shipped by rail to the Mediterranean and distributed at Thau and Toulon. He restocked Brest and used English oysters to stock an oyster reservation at l'Anse de la Forest close to Concarneau that was meant to supply nearby beds. The following year, in 1860, Coste established two model "parks," or oyster farms, at Arcachon to serve as breeding beds for the basin and as a source for trials of different collectors.

Coste's initial success led interested parties to solicit numerous concessions from the Ministry of the Marine, especially along the Brittany and Normandy coasts, the coast along the Loire River to the Gironde Estuary, and also at Arcachon. Oyster farmers, some of whom invested large sums of money in these enterprises, rapidly established farms and began experimenting with spat collectors. Many of these places experienced large harvests in the early

1860s. The most successful were at Saint-Brieuc, the Island of Re, and Arcachon; they also had decent success at Brest, Toulon, La Rochelle, and Marennes.

These first French oyster farms were unlike anything in America. The French made extensive use of spat collectors, and after early experimentation, the most popular collectors were those made of ceramic tiles coated with a weak mortar. The mortar flaked off easily, making it easier to detach young oysters. Farmers suspended ceramic tiles to intercept oyster larvae by giving them a clean, solid surface for attachment. Larval oysters drifted in from nearby beds. After the spawning season, farmers removed spat from tiles and placed them in ponds or "claires" that they dug into shallow coastlands. High tides inundated the ponds, bringing in food twice a day, and when tides receded, the banks of the ponds retained the water. Oysters matured in these ponds. Oystermen started this system in the late 1850s, after de Bon and Coste's experiments, and expanded it to include numerous local variations on this basic method. The French system was more labor-intensive and depended on higher oyster prices than the U.S. counterpart.[7]

After a few years of success, most of these experiments failed. Storms scattered the oysters and collectors at Saint-Brieuc. Fishermen took many of the oysters planted at Brest, and their natural beds declined at the same time. There were rapid, unexplained declines at Île de Re, Île d'Oléron, La Rochelle, Cancale, and along the Rance River, and oystermen abandoned all these areas. Only at Arcachon was there any sustained success. Arcachon's government parks were still operating in 1865, but even there the natural beds declined, and the fishery became moribund due to an inability to collect spat. Some of this decline was probably due to poor site selection in the first rush to expand cultivation, an understandable phenomenon given that no one had ever attempted it before. However, Coste became severely depressed when his early success turned to failure. He grew despondent and retired, dying shortly thereafter. His colleagues attributed his death to the collapse of his oyster schemes.

Scientific reports described these failures as "the ruin of all hopes based upon oyster culture."[8]

Not everyone thought oyster culture would spread as rapidly or easily as Coste predicted. The Ministry of the Marine thought restocking would take longer, and they were less discouraged by the first wave of failures. They passed regulations in 1853 mandating a closed season determined by local inspectors, reserving natural beds as common property, and prohibiting the sale of undersized oysters, all with the aim of protecting natural beds. De Bon noted that the new oyster parks were mostly dependent on the natural beds for their spat, so their protection probably facilitated the revival of France's oyster cultivation. This revival began at Arcachon, where the initial experiments had succeeded longest. Private farmers, rather than government scientists, led this expansion. They learned from these early setbacks and improved their methods, and by 1875, oyster farms were spreading to many locations; Arcachon and the Gulf of Morbihan emerged as the two leading centers.[9] Oyster aquaculture use of spat collectors and ponds is widespread in France today.

France was the model so many U.S. scientists cited as the way forward for U.S. oyster cultivation. It was an odd choice given that French cultivation was more labor-intensive, requiring oystermen to maintain ponds and spat collectors, and depended on higher prices. Also, the French Ministry of the Marine was a colonial agency more interventionist than any U.S. agency with authority over oysters. It funded a large-scale experiment based on the work of two scientists alone in the 1850s. Coste's experiments also failed in the short run, although cultivators revived the oyster parks Coste inspired by 1878. To many scientists, the revival of oyster parks in France vindicated Coste's vision and the idea that science could spur the expansion of aquaculture.

American scientists could have chosen to follow Möbius, rather than Coste. Möbius was one of Europe's leading authorities on the oyster, and he ultimately disagreed with Coste's vision on scientific grounds. He began his career agreeing with Coste, and his early writings contained optimistic statements about the possibility of oyster culture. When describing his own 1869 experiment at Norderney, where he built ponds in the sea flats, he discussed prospects for expanding oyster beds, saying, "All that is necessary, then, in order to increase the size of these beds is to render the sea-bottom between them habitable for oysters."[10] Like Coste, his experiment ended in failure when starfish, crabs, and storms destroyed his oysters. The other event that influenced his thinking was the opening of a canal between the North Sea and the Baltic. The North Sea fauna did poorly in Baltic waters, and this led Möbius to question the idea of unlimited oyster expansion.[11]

He soon developed the concept of a "bioconone," a word he coined for an interconnected and interdependent assemblage of species and their aboitic environment. Möbius came to feel the tight linkages between species and between organisms and their environment forced each species into what ecologists now call a niche. He thought it was unlikely that a species could expand its range or population without deleteriously altering these relationships. He reasoned that oyster farms had limited potential for expansion. Trying to increase oyster populations would upset the balance between organisms and produce unintended consequences, including insufficient feed, increasing predation, and declining ecological conditions. He wrote that undisturbed oyster beds were probably near their population limits already, and although this meant that it should be possible to restore depleted areas, Coste's optimistic project would never last.[12]

The USFC translated and printed Möbius's writing on the concept of an oyster bioconone, and they also printed his work on oyster reproductive biology, as he was Europe's leading authority on the subject in the 1880s. However, U.S. scientists never cited his bioconone ideas, whereas they frequently cited his biological studies. In contrast, U.S. scientists not only translated and reprinted Coste's papers, they consistently lauded him as the father of oyster culture and as the model American scientists should emulate. The important distinction between Coste and Möbius was their disagreement about a bay's ability to sustain greatly increasing oyster populations.

Möbius believed that natural oyster reefs were about as large as they could be, given ecological constraints, whereas Coste believed that coastal bays could sustain much larger oyster populations. Both cited anecdotal examples to back up their claims; neither had definitive proof. Lacking irrefutable evidence, U.S. scientists used other means to choose between these two mutually exclusive intellectual lineages.

THE RACE TO SOLVE ARTIFICIAL CULTIVATION, 1878-1885

One reason U.S. scientists followed Coste and not Möbius was their perception that solving the riddle of oyster reproductive biology would revolutionize the fishery. They felt that a single scientific answer could change history. A female oyster produces millions of eggs, of which only a tiny fraction survives. U.S. scientists thought they could keep a much larger portion alive under laboratory conditions, which would give them vast quantities of young oysters they could use to restock depleted bays. All they had to do was learn how to fertilize and rear oysters. As scientists sought to surmount this obstacle, a breakthrough always appeared tantalizingly close. Scientists continually stated that they were about to reach their goal; success looked near enough to touch.

In the mid-1870s, U.S. scientists did not know whether oysters were hermaphroditic or had separate sexes. European scientists had found that the European oyster was hermaphroditic, and in 1879 William Brooks discovered that America's Eastern Oyster had separate sexes.[13] After determining this, Brooks and others turned to the issue of artificial fertilization, which Brooks saw as the first step toward successful large-scale hatchery propagation. Brooks was also the first to successfully rear oyster larvae in a laboratory. He observed these larvae for twelve days, at which point they died due to fouling of the water. Keeping the larvae's water free from injurious organisms proved to be a key stumbling block to successfully rearing oysters in laboratories. The seawater they needed always contained tiny organisms that preyed upon oyster larvae, and scientists could not filter the water to remove these pests without also filtering out the oyster larvae.

Brooks's experiment illustrated that oyster larvae were not simply borne randomly by the current as previous research had stated. They could rise or drop depending on the water's salinity. This mobility helped keep the larvae near the location where they originated. Freshwater from streams tends to stay on top of the bays because it is lighter, and thus higher salinities are found near the bottom. These streams often push surface water out to sea. Oyster larvae drop when they encounter low salinities and rise when they encounter higher salinities. Incoming tides have a higher salinity and push oysters inland. This behavior helps them avoid being swept out to sea. Brooks's first experiments proved highly successful. He quickly determined that oysters had separate sexes and controlled their drift as larvae. Most significantly, Brooks demonstrated scientists could fertilize oysters and keep them alive in a laboratory. These achievements were an enormous step forward for the science of oyster cultivation.

Brooks's success inaugurated a period of intense scientific work aimed at rearing oysters in laboratories and hatcheries. In 1878 H. J. Rice, a fellow in natural history at Johns Hopkins, was working for the United States Coastal and Geological Survey (USCGS) at Tangier and Pocomoke sounds. Rice tried to fertilize oysters in a laboratory setting, but he procured his oysters from shoalwater. These oysters, he later learned, spawn early and were no longer useful by the time he collected them. Needless to say, his experiments failed.[14] In 1879 Brooks moved his work to Crisfield to obtain better breeding oysters and bay water. Rice joined him there.[15] Brooks began devoting more of his time to artificially cultivating oysters in 1880. Francis Winslow, an oyster scientist and cartographer who worked for the USCGS and USFC, also began experimenting with oyster cultivation at this time. Winslow was in Europe experimenting with fertilizing Portuguese oysters.[16]

In March of 1882 Winslow joined Brooks, who had moved his work to Beaufort, North Carolina. Winslow's letters detail the challenges they faced. In them he attributes his previous failures to insufficient oxygen levels, excessive fouling, and lack of adequate food sources.[17] One of Winslow and Brooks's key problems was obtaining suitable seawater for aquaria. They decided that oxygen, carbonate of lime, and perhaps currents of air or freshwater needed to be added to the jars. They also noted the importance of food supply for young oysters and regarded the selection of oysters as another key factor affecting success. Oysters had to be breeding but could not have excess dead sperm, as this polluted the water. The scientists had to undertake microscopic investigation before selecting oysters, and sometimes they had to use inferior oysters. Many oysters that appeared ready to spawn had eggs that never developed. This might have been due to oysters not producing eggs all at once, and Winslow recommended studying the histology of ovaries in detail to settle this matter. Brooks and Winslow also found they could take out small amounts of the generative organs, but they needed to take care not to include parts of other organs. Male organs had to have the sperm washed out immediately, as exposure killed them. Then eggs had to be brought into contact with sperm immediately after washing. Winslow recommended using a small number of oysters so that they could attend to detail. Organ fragments had to be thrown away after they settled. Additionally, temperature was critical. When they transferred oysters to water with slightly higher temperature, the generative matter deteriorated. High temperatures hastened the segmentation of fertilized eggs, and low temperatures slowed it. Rapid temperature changes destroyed eggs. The scientists found that sixty-five to seventy-five degrees was the optimal temperature under which to conduct this process. In his letters, Winslow also describes density, currents, aeration, lime, and food. He says nothing could be done about infusoria (microorganisms that feed on oyster larvae). It was difficult at this point to say which factors mattered most. Winslow recommended proceeding slowly and scientifically.[18] His comments illustrate the importance of controlling variables, and his correspondence presents a useful description of which variables mattered and why.

Once he began working with Brooks, Winslow sent periodic reports to Baird at the USFC. The first of these discusses how they met with failure, the reason for which was "not clear." Brooks and Winslow had tested the effects of current and aeration, and found that these variables did not affect spawning. They did discover however, that adding large amounts of lime sped up oyster growth. They also discovered the problem of infusoria and found that the presence of dead eggs and embryos fed these microorganisms and increased their abundance. They stated that "their ravages . . . [were] greater than expected." Also, weather had been poorly suited to raising oysters. But their lack of success was due to "something unexplained." Despite this, Winslow wrote that "Neither Brooks nor myself despair of eventual success."[19]

Subsequent letters from 1882 show that they barely passed the stage Brooks reached in 1879. They were able to fertilize oysters and did manage to speed up larval growth, but they never successfully raised young that reached the attachment stage. Unaided, it took oysters from six to thirty-six hours "to complete the segmentation of the egg," but Winslow and Brooks brought this figure down to between six to ten hours. It formerly took six to eight days to reach the "advanced stage," and now one to two days sufficed. They succeeded in speeding development by adding lime, guarding against infusoria, equalizing temperatures, creating the best specific gravity, and supplying ample food to oyster larvae. They reduced infusoria by boiling shells used for lime and by taking great care to remove swimming embryos from the mass of eggs. The best way they found to feed oysters was to insert small amounts of mud from oyster bottoms, but it was hard to avoid smothering the young with this practice. They believed that lack of food was "the probable cause of our failure to meet with complete success."[20]

Since they could not keep the larval oysters alive long enough for them to attach to collectors, Winslow proposed depositing the unattached young oysters in the water. He proposed going to private grounds in Connecticut to try out this approach. He asked for a letter of introduction to Addison Verrill, a scientist and pupil of Brooks's at

Yale.[21] Winslow then proceeded to New Haven with a batch of these very young oysters. By August, he had deposited them on Rowe's Connecticut planting grounds.[22] A letter from Rowe describes these oysters as developing well, though he found it hard to believe that he could distinguish them from naturally occurring oysters.[23]

A second team of scientists had better luck in 1882. In 1881, the USFC and the State of Maryland began what would become the most important artificial propagation experiments during this period. Maryland leased land at St. Jerome Creek near the mouth of the Potomac River beginning in 1880, and the USFC took over the lease the following year.[24] The USFC wanted a site where they could experiment with the French pond culture system.[25] T. B. Ferguson had visited France in 1878 to study pond culture, and he was the first manager of the St. Jerome Creek station. John Ryder served as the chief scientist there, and Marshall McDonald joined him in 1882.[26] McDonald was the assistant commissioner of the USFC at the time and an engineer who designed hatcheries and fishways. McDonald's first major advance was designing an apparatus, a circuit of jars with filters, for keeping water clean in oyster aquaria. Then on July 22, 1882, McDonald and Ryder recorded the first instance of artificially reared oysters attaching to the sides of their aquarium. These oysters surprisingly attached only two hours after fertilization. These lived for four days until high water temperature killed them. Ryder and McDonald then arranged for well water to run around the jars to lower the water temperature, but for unknown reasons they failed to duplicate their success that year. Ryder gained valuable information on shell development from this experiment. At this point he thought the shell development was the key to understanding how spat attached.[27]

Ryder also thought scientists needed to learn more about the preferred food sources of oyster larvae. Opinions differed greatly.[28] He had done a little work on microscopic organisms in Chesapeake Bay but believed that scientists needed to increase their knowledge on this subject. His work suggested that oyster food sources were highly variable, and he thought that variations in food, driven by variations in environmental conditions, might account for the variability in oyster bed conditions. He said, "All of this [is] little touched, and today's students just want to compile lists of new species, so we will likely not know for a while."[29]

Rice achieved the attachment stage in 1882 as well. Blackford provided him with oysters and other material support in a building at New York's Fulton Street fish market. Rice was able to use a new apparatus he had developed after his initial experiments with Brooks. Rice's apparatus used two siphons to circulate freshwater into and remove old water out of the system. He considered circulation to be key to keeping oyster larvae alive. However, he was unable to keep circulation at a steady rate. He then tried using cloth strips as water conduits. These drew water in or out using capillary action, and Rice found he could regulate these much better than siphons by adjusting the size of the cloth strip. The apparatus conveyed new water into the system, which lessened fouling and infusoria. The cloth apparatus enabled Rice to keep larvae alive for longer than anyone had previously: fifteen days.[30] On July 27, only five days after Ryder and McDonald achieved the same feat, Rice saw one of his oysters attach itself to its container. The oyster was two days old at the time. Rice rushed downstairs to tell Blackford, who rushed up to try to dislodge it. According to their reports, both were jubilant.[31] Although they would later learn of Ryder and McDonald's accomplishment, at the time they thought they were the first to reach this important milestone. Just as with Ryder and McDonald, however, Rice was unable to repeat his success that year.

The two brief attachments in 1882 raised high hopes for 1883, and scientists did indeed achieve substantial advancements. Rice and Blackford continued working in New York City, and Rice again witnessed one of his oysters attach. This time it lived for fourteen days, which set a new record. Rice learned how oysters attached from this experiment.[32] Winslow and Brooks had less success. Winslow delayed in writing to Baird, hoping that this year he and Brooks would succeed. Instead he states: "we have had bad luck and bad luck since the middle of June," and communicates that they were "unable to secure attachment of the spat. Our first experiments were full of promise."[33] Toward the end of the summer they did find attached oysters fastened to the glass of their collectors and troughs, which marked the most progress so far. However, they had the "greatest trouble, an unaccountable one," fertilizing eggs,[34] despite their ease of doing so the previous year. Later, Winslow explains that this had been a poor year for setting locally and again mentions the difficulty of renewing the water without losing the oysters.[35] Next, Brooks invented a set of inclined troughs that trapped oysters and let water flow, like gold pans. The apparatus proved successful in keeping oysters in, but for some reason their oysters failed to grow. At the end of the summer, Winslow proposed going back to Long Island Sound, presumably to check on the prior year's experiment.[36] He also asked for information on Ryder's work.[37] Ryder was now working alone at St. Jerome Creek, where he constructed ponds based on the French pond model. Cloth barriers allowed the flow of water and food in while keeping larger oyster predators out. He introduced fertilized eggs, and these not only attached to collectors but also lived and grew. This was the first time artificially fertilized eggs had been successfully grown into mature oysters in the United States.[38] Following this success, Ryder wrote a *Forest and Stream* article entitled: "The Oyster Problem Solved."[39]

Ryder took the lead in U.S. artificial cultivation experiments in 1884. Winslow and Brooks grew discouraged by their lack of success in 1883 and stopped experimenting.[40] In New York, Rice died, putting an end to his experiments. Ryder built a more extensive pond system at St. Jerome Creek, where William Ravenel joined him. Once again, they were able to make artificially fertilized spat attach to collectors in these ponds. Oysters grew best in ponds with ample circulation. Ryder and Ravenel continued experimenting with pond culture in 1885. In their forty-square-foot pond, Ryder placed one hundred bushels of oysters, and in a four-hundred-foot canal, he placed twelve hundred bushels of shells and four hundred collectors. He estimated these oysters produced one hundred billion fry, and "this vast multitude of oysters will be wafted back and forth through the shells 360 times during the season, thus insuring the fixation of the largest possible percentage of embryos."[41] By this time, he had constructed twenty spat-collecting apparatuses in the ponds.

Ryder's 1885 reports and articles claim that his findings would revolutionize the industry. He writes, "the hope that I might solve, or help to solve, the oyster-problem practically, has served to constantly encourage me for the five years that I have been working with that object in view."[42] In an article entitled "The Oyster Problem Actually Solved" he states, "the future of the oyster industry in the South is henceforth ensured."[43] He admits to the failure of his previous work and the work of others, but he asserts that he now knows why they failed and knows how to succeed.[44] By the end of 1885 Ryder was not only satisfied that pond culture could work in the United States, he believed his research solved all major technical hurdles to artificial cultivation. Convinced his work was finished, Ryder left Maryland and moved on to other things. He worked on oyster greening and anatomy, but he never experimented with artificial cultivation again.

Ferguson and Ravenel tried to keep cultivation experiments going at St. Jerome Creek, but sediment and slime ruined their 1886 season.[45] Whether this was due to Ryder's absence, as he continually stressed the importance of circulation, or bad luck is unknown. Since pond culture was difficult, Ferguson decided to cultivate on a larger scale outside of the ponds. He placed spat collectors in the main pond's connecting canal. The canal was two hundred feet long, and zigzagged to increase the area. The crew of the research ship, the USFC *Fish Hawk*, came to dig a bigger pond and sink a new well, but the ground was too hard so the pipe found no water.[46]

Lack of any positive results in 1886 led the USFC to curtail experiments at St. Jerome Creek in 1887, and the area was placed under the supervision of a watchman. During this interval an anonymous researcher conducted smaller experiments with the finding that naturally fertilized oysters grew better in ponds than artificially fertilized ones. But neither naturally nor artificially fertilized oysters grew well enough to make pond culture commercially viable.

The USFC commissioned a report that recommended keeping the station open since the ponds were already built. Despite the report's findings, the USFC closed the station in 1889.[47]

The closing at St. Jerome Creek ended the first period of U.S. oyster science. After Brooks's initial experiments, there was a rush of intense work, from 1878 to 1885, on artificial fertilization and attachment. One is struck by the sense of expectation conveyed in these sources; to the oyster scientists of this period, success was always within their grasp. They would reach a certain stage, only to be unable to repeat the results, usually for unknown reasons. By 1886 scientists realized that the challenge of artificial cultivation was too formidable (though Ryder believed he solved it), and they largely ceased pursuing it.

OYSTER SCIENCE AFTER 1885

References to artificial cultivation experiments appeared sporadically after St. Jerome Creek closed. The New York legislature asked Blackford to repeat Fulton Street market experiments, and he went to Cold Springs Harbor to attempt this in 1892. He dug a canal to connect the station's two ponds to the ocean so that he could propagate oysters and saltwater fish. He began by placing into one of the ponds mussel shells and then oyster embryos, on which spat settled from nearby spawning oyster beds. He had trouble getting new water to circulate into the system. The water temperature in the ponds was constantly shifting and killing all the young oysters. Water from a nearby marsh also leaked in through a pipe and covered his oysters in slime. His report and work seem much less rigorous than the work of earlier scientists. He was trying to prove pond culture could work, but there were more technically proficient ways to do this, and his work offered no conclusions.[48]

Two other scientists took up artificial cultivation experiments in the 1890s: H. F. Moore, who worked for the USFC, and Julius Nelson, a Rutgers University biologist. In 1898 Moore experimented with ponds in Lynnhaven, Virginia, without any success. He resumed experimenting in Louisiana between 1905 and 1909, planting seed oysters and using spat collectors. None of these experiments led to useable techniques.[49]

Nelson, who was appointed as a biologist at Rutgers University after earning his PhD under Brooks in 1888, represents the second generation of oyster scientists. He was less optimistic about hatcheries than the former generation. As a result he worked less on artificial cultivation and more extensively on natural history. A fire in 1903 destroyed most of his papers, making it difficult to document his oyster work. Remaining records show that he worked on egg fertilization in 1901, embryo development in 1902, and getting embryos to live into the shell stage in 1903.[50] Later, he built experimental ponds.[51] Nelson worked on artificial cultivation throughout his career, but he continually stressed how long it would take to achieve success and how important small steps were to this process.[52]

HOW SCIENTISTS DEFINED THE OYSTER PROBLEM AND ITS SOLUTION

The Problem: Inevitable Decline

Andrew Abbott argues that professions are organized in a system within which they vie for jurisdiction.[53] By "jurisdiction," Abbott means that different professional groups claim they are best suited to take action in a certain area. A profession competes for jurisdiction by defining problems its members seek to address and then articulates the specialized solutions that they are better positioned to supply than their competitors. Scientists defined the problem of the oyster fishery and offered solutions. This section describes statements by scientists about the fishery's problems and examines the solutions they proposed.

Almost all oyster scientists agreed that oysters were declining or had declined in the past. McDonald's first sentence in his 1880 report reads: "The facts that there has been a great decrease in the annual product and in the value of our fisheries is too patent to require demonstration."[54] Similarly, Brooks opens a speech printed in the

Baltimore Sun saying, "There has not been anywhere exhibited in the United States a more reckless squandering of natural wealth" and asserts that this was common knowledge. He was emphatic that oysters had only five to ten years left.[55] Many other scientists predicted eminent exhaustion of Chesapeake Bay oysters. The only instance where a scientist disagreed with these warnings was Joseph Collins, a USFC scientist, who claims in a *Fishing Gazette* article that Chesapeake Bay oysters were inexhaustible.[56]

One possible explanation for oyster decline was changing environmental conditions, which several scientists described as a common opinion among tongers. Scientists repeatedly rejected this perspective. Sometimes they listed the various environmental causes that were supposed to have contributed to declines and then refuted these in turn. More often, they lumped the assumed causes together and claimed that they were false without providing explicit refutation. Instead of natural causes, they laid the blame on overfishing. However, they discussed overfishing as a symptom of a more important underlying cause.

Scientists tended to portray this underlying cause in the same terms as the modernist commissioners. The larger narrative that emerges from these statements is one that explains oyster decline as a part of a historical process. Fishermen managed oysters as a commons at first, which scientists equated with open access conditions. Alternately, they pictured common property as an archaic form of management. Either way, oyster commons were described as inappropriate for the modern world. Technological and population changes rendered them obsolete. McDonald suggested that this social progression reflected the history of fisheries everywhere in the world.[57] These historical explanations assigned a lawlike quality to the development of fisheries and resource management in general. Private property emerged as the cornerstone of progress because of the incentives it created. This narrative rests on the assumption that people never invest energy into improving a natural resource unless they can claim the full benefits of their labor. Private property is considered the necessary precondition for resource improvement.

Oysters declined because, without improvement, harvesting could not keep pace with increasing demand.

Tradition blocked progress. Because people grew accustomed to particular practices, like exercising their rights to common property, they were slow to change and failed to reform their behavior. Scientists suggested that tongers were "killing the goose that laid the golden egg" and were "suspicious of any attempt at improvement."[58] Tongers looked at artificial cultivation, which was progressive and modern "doubtfully . . . with disdained curiosity," and they resented all efforts to restrict their "prerogative to capture the very last fish in our waters."[59] This prerogative not only caused overfishing, but also created opposition to cultivation. As Nelson puts it, "This [cultivation] is never done under conditions of a free or public fishery. It is in the interest of conservation that oyster farming be introduced to supplement natural production. The foremost difficulty encountered in this connection is the opposition of those who believe in harvesting what nature produces without contributing to the labor of cultivation."[60]

Scientists also depicted the traditional system as parochial because of its local management. McDonald writes: "The whole industry then [1880] was regarded as a purely local interest, and no view which did not measure down to the narrow personal views of those directly concerned in it, could pass through the doors of that committee and have consideration in the legislature."[61] Scientists sometimes said that traditional management had disposed oystermen to rank highly the preservation of natural beds, making them feel that preserving these would ensure prosperity. However, scientists regularly remarked that this reasoning was erroneous. Preserving natural beds only restricted supply, which raised demand and undermined protective efforts.[62] This narrative historicizes the problems with tradition. It ties local management practices back into the larger picture of resource management's inevitable evolution. Resource management history follows a lawlike progression, which positions the oyster industry at a crossroads. It could continue toward exhaustion or embrace progressive methods with science leading the way.

Scientists did write statements that reveal they were less unified than the basic outline above suggests. For instance, Brooks favored prohibiting dredging on natural beds, and saw their protection as essential for preserving the seed supply.[63] Many scientists agreed. Most did not want to eliminate natural beds, and some like Brooks did not object to tongers maintaining these as commons. McDonald writes, "Spat-producing oyster beds . . . of course should be preserved for all time and under State administration and regulation, since, where they are in sufficient numbers and suitably distributed, they present an inexpensive means of maintaining the oyster supply."[64] According to Brooks, these areas needed a cooperative organization of oyster fishermen devoted to improving the natural beds. If tongers could not form one, he felt that it would be better to privatize oyster beds. Belding and Nelson agreed with the former idea and suggested that oystermen needed cooperative organizations to improve their common beds.[65] Brooks also thought oyster planting did not require much capital and could be profitable for small-scale farmers, although it did "need constant and intelligent attention."[66]

Scientists' descriptions of past management practices vary in their sophistication as well. Belding acknowledged that common property was not the same as open access, and he had detailed firsthand knowledge of Massachusetts town-based oyster management.[67] McDonald states, "The object of public fish-culture is to assure the utmost utilization of the resources of our waters," but in regulating fisheries, lawmakers must be careful not to "embarrass or harass" fishermen with undue regulations.[68] Oddly, few scientists cited illegal dredging as an important cause of decline, despite constant complaints about this from oystermen in Chesapeake Bay newspapers.

Nelson's report on Prince Edward Island's oyster fishery, which was written at the end of his career, is a good example of a more nuanced view that still adheres to the larger modernist narrative. He blamed decline on overfishing and countered many natural-cause theories. No one on the island was practicing conservation because of fishermen's attitudes, and these were based on their lack of familiarity with planting. Nelson stated that on private farms self-interest equaled the public good, whereas the opposite was true on public beds. He approved of Canadian oyster laws, but he felt that they did not do enough to achieve conservation. Measures such as closed seasons and closing depleted beds were insufficient. Furthermore, oystermen were able to legally harvest some planting areas. Nelson noted that oystermen did not want the government to privatize public beds because they were afraid capitalists would monopolize these. He acknowledged this as part of the struggle between capital and labor and suggested that greater control by capitalists was inevitable. Though Nelson expressed sympathy for the difficult transition the tongers had to undergo, the above statements fit the general modernist narrative.[69] Professions need to coherently define problems, and oyster scientists provided a definition that served their interests. If they had argued that illegal dredging was the main problem in Chesapeake Bay, then science would have had little role in the solution. Instead, they argued that outdated common property was to blame.

The Solution: Hatchery Science

What role could natural science play if private property rights were the key to progress? How could studying oyster embryos propel privatization? Part of the answer was that science could lay the basis for an improved oyster fishery by providing information for planters. One day, when oystermen accepted private property, the fishery would progress and productivity would increase. Planters would be eager to receive the latest scientific knowledge. Winslow invokes this rationale: "In view of the rapid deterioration of the oyster beds it appears advisable that all information, regarding the life and habits of the oyster, that can be obtained should be [illegible] speedily and made public for the benefit of the oyster culturists, as that class must in a short while increase and need what we may in a measure be able to supply."[70] Planters would want to increase spat with artificial cultivation. Scientists would experiment with the best ways to manage hatcheries, which they saw as part of their role because no one else would do it. Individual fishermen would not build a hatchery since everyone else would have access to the fish after release. Oysters were different in that they did not move around once planted in the water, at least after the larval stage, and so planters could plausibly defend a claim to them. However, artificial cultivation was complicated, and so the industry would still need scientists to conduct the experiments that would propel it beyond technical obstacles. Ryder argued his pond system would be for use only "upon areas which are positively and absolutely under individual, proprietary control."[71]

Scientists also had to convince tongers to overcome their prejudice toward private property. For twenty years, Brooks had been engaged in "the attempt to teach the people of Maryland the necessity of supplementing the bounty of Nature with the industry of man," and he believed that Chesapeake Bay needed "a whole army of skilled instructors."[72] Nelson agreed with Brooks on the scope of this project, saying that it took years of education to teach oystermen the benefits of planting.[73]

Education depended on demonstration. Tongers would see scientists' success and gravitate toward progress. As McDonald puts it, "retrograde" methods of dealing with oyster conservation were unlikely "now that public attention has been called to it."[74] He ties technological advancement to an evolutionary narrative saying, "as the planting interest expands under the present conditions the disposition will also become more general to contract the public areas to such a point as to reserve only spat-producing oyster beds."[75] At a meeting called by the Richmond Chamber of Commerce to initiate a public education campaign, Winslow observes that oystermen were "suspicious of any attempt at improvement" and "they also suppose to know what is best for them. That they do not makes no difference."[76] He goes on to say no one could force change on oystermen, but once scientists demonstrated the superiority of planting, tongers would readily adopt cultivation. He discusses at length how French scientists played this role at the outset of European oyster culture.

This educational role depended on the same ideas about human nature contained in the scientists' vision of history. That narrative assumed a universal, predictable, and rational human nature. Applying this to education, scientists thought that once oystermen saw the scientific truth, they would inevitably adopt modern practices. This might take time, but it was inevitable. Scientists would change tongers' behavior by making progress visible.

Progress was already visible in certain places. Perhaps the most common model scientists cited to explain why the industry should move toward planting was farming. Scientists compared oysters and migratory fish, pointing out that oysters stayed in place, which positioned oystering closer to farming or raising stock than fishing. They felt migratory fish should remain a commons, whereas oysters should not. Scientists would then compare oysters to various crops; comparisons to potatoes were particularly numerous. McDonald asks what would happen if wheat fields were commons?[77] Brooks compares gathering berries to modern farming on private property and cites the difference in productivity.[78] Scientists linked farming's productivity with private property and its incentives. By 1880, scientists were raising German carp successfully in hatcheries and distributing them to nearly every state and territory. Hatcheries were also growing salmon and shad and restocking them in rivers where they had been depleted.[79] Fish hatchery successes made artificial cultivation seem more likely and encouraged scientists to believe that they could dramatically expand oyster farming.

European science served as another model of progress. Scientists continually praised Coste, which was odd given his failed experiments. Coste attributed his failures to his lack of support, and U.S. scientists must have agreed. Their main theme was that Coste paved the way forward with his pioneering studies. Ryder hoped he could introduce French methods in the United States. Artificial cultivation would allow planters to dispense with tile collectors, as "the older methods are universally cumbrous."[80] Nelson wrote that he expected oystermen to eventually drain New Jersey salt marshes to create oyster ponds, emulating those in France.[81] Winslow in particular described French government science as a great benefit. Not only did Winslow advocate for following Coste's scientific path, he also suggested using science to demonstrate progress in the same way Coste desired.[82]

Scientists also continuously pointed to Connecticut and Rhode Island as successful models. Planting expanded in these states during the 1880s and 1890s, and scientists cited this as evidence for the need to expand it elsewhere. Brooks compared these states to Virginia and Maryland's current "nearsighted" policy in an 1884 speech. He complained that Chesapeake Bay's large and influential body of tongers had always used natural beds and would resist planting as long as any oysters remained on them.[83]

Handy models spawned optimism. At first, scientists expressed great optimism about their ability to transform the industry. Even Möbius, eventually the most oyster pessimistic scientist, was originally sanguine. Ryder argues, "The uncertainty which had hitherto attended oystraculture must disappear in the face of intelligent experiment."[84] Brooks is optimistic too, writing:

> I have been able to carry the oyster much further than anyone has ever done before with the American oyster, and I have met with no difficulty that seems to be insuperable. The subject is one that requires very delicate management, and the difficulties are much greater than I had anticipated, but I feel confident that all that is now needed is proper apparatus, and that *the question demands nothing but a little patience and ingenuity*. (italics in the original)[85]

Brooks believed Chesapeake Bay would be able to raise four hundred million bushels a year (its maximum output had been below twenty million). Winslow remarks that, "neither Brooks nor myself despair of eventual success."[86] Brooks agrees, saying, "I feel though, that I have command of the subject."[87]

Why were scientists initially so optimistic? One reason may have been a self-selection process. Scientists who felt more pessimistic about expansion of planting would have taken their career in a different direction. Limited knowledge may be an important explanation. Lacking evidence to the contrary, why not be optimistic? These oyster scientists did have Coste's failure and Möbius's warnings, but these likely seem more noteworthy in hindsight. At the time, these had to be balanced against subsequent successes in France and Connecticut. Fish hatcheries looked successful at this point too. The ecological side effects of expanded planting, especially starfish invasions, had not yet fully come to light. The same was true for fish hatcheries such as carp. Fish hatcheries and deep water planting tipped the scales for scientists.

Optimism was also inspiring. Brooks provides the most compelling statement linking optimism to the historic role of scientists. He compares Chesapeake Bay to the Nile, saying both were highly fertile, though the former was suitable for one crop only: oysters. Just as the Nile drained immense areas and carried fertile silt, so did Chesapeake Bay. That this silt was underwater made no difference; these important nutrients fed tiny marine plants. Although he had no idea how to quantify their population, he described vast concentrations of these plants and documented the speed of their growth. Oysters were ideal for turning these tiny marine organisms into human food. Brooks submits: "The fitness of the oyster for this work—bringing back to us the mineral wealth which the rivers steal from our hillsides and meadows—is so complete and admirable, so marvelous and instructive, that it cannot be comprehended in its complete significance without a thorough knowledge of the anatomy and embryology of the oyster."[88] The great river valleys formed the cradles of civilization, and Chesapeake Bay was one of these. "Man will some time assert his dominion over the fishes of the sea and will learn to send out flocks and herds of domesticated marine animals to pasture and fatten upon the vegetable life of the ocean."[89] This speech illustrates how Brooks's vision sweeps up geographic analogy, native pride, and grandiose expectations. Destiny awaited the Chesapeake Bay.

Brooks's pupil Nelson was optimistic too, but expressed more reservation than any other scientist. He began his work after the first wave of failed studies, during which time he was at Johns Hopkins. In explaining his hesitance about cultivation, he says, the "one hitch in all this beautiful arrangement" was that the labor and cost made artificial cultivation unprofitable.[90] Another example of his measured thinking comes from a few articles from New Jersey and New York newspapers. These praise his work, saying he was nearing an important breakthrough. Nelson responded to these by cautioning that successful oyster culture was still many years distant. He wished to avoid raising false hopes. One exchange with the *New Jersey Courier* is especially interesting. The paper reports, "His most recent efforts . . . have been crowned with the success he has sought so persistently, and it looks as though the problem of 'seed' is practically solved."[91] The paper's editor was instrumental in procuring funds for Nelson's first coastal laboratory, and the same experiments that this article describes; yet Nelson wanted to keep expectations realistic. He replies the following week, saying he believes he has made "encouraging progress" but has not solved the seed problem. He wanted to avoid overexaggeration that might result in disappointments.[92]

The descriptions above fail to capture the scientists' personalities. Sources provide evidence of this for Ryder and Nelson, whose views represent the most and least optimistic of this group. Understanding how Nelson thought about science requires knowing something about his religious views. There is evidence for these in three speeches collected in his papers, "A Half Century of Darwinism," "Sex and Health," and "Relation of Biology to Theology."[93] In each, he explains the correspondence between religion and science. Citing Henry Drummond's *Natural Laws in the Spiritual World*, Nelson states, "There is profound agreement rather than superficial disagreement between Darwinism and the Gospels," and "Bible students should earnestly seek to study natural sciences."[94] These speeches posit that the laws of nature flow from God, just as the Bible contains laws governing human conduct. Nature's law contains a third testament; natural science teaches one how to live morally.

The consistency and completeness of these arguments in Nelson's public lectures offers convincing evidence that these ideas informed his view of biology as a profession. Nelson probably saw his work with oyster propagation and spat collection as uncovering laws of nature that would yield a morally enhanced industry, not just a more productive one. He would help eliminate waste and increase production, but more importantly it would lessen conflict among different classes of oystermen. Expanded cultivation created a more moral social order, and science would light the way.

In a telling section of "A Half Century of Darwinism," Nelson discusses the need for scientists to lead social reform. He says, "Human health was evolved under the natural conditions of savage and animal ancestry. Now man is subjected to the new environment of civilization and its luxuries, its artificial surroundings and its strains. The question is will he adapt himself or will he become extinct [as ancient civilizations].... Only an expert Darwinian is competent to debate such questions."[95] One can see how this perspective might apply to the oyster industry. Conservation worked well in the past, but under modern pressures oystermen needed to adapt or become extinct. Only an expert scientist could uncover God's laws of nature to lead the way forward. This view elevates the scientist, but it humbles him, as well, as uncovering God's plan requires expert Darwinians with extensive training. Nelson's religious perspective seems to have tempered his optimism in comparison with his contemporaries, although it also suggests the role of scientists as guides.

Ryder, by contrast, was undoubtedly the most optimistic scientist. As with Nelson, his views on evolution take center stage. He searched for a theory of evolution that did not contain natural selection and thought he found one in 1874. He calls it the "dynamics of phylogeny." The subject appealed to his sense of the scope of his ability. He states, "Here is field enough for a Darwin. I almost shrink from the task when I consider its magnitude.... It completes Darwin's work on a far grander scale than Darwin ever dreamed of."[96] Ryder, who published two hundred and seventy-eight papers in his short lifetime, describes a flash of insight that led him to this evolutionary synthesis, saying, "I sat up late last night after the whole thing flashed across my mind in an instant, and did not sleep for two hours after I went to bed because my brain was going like a dynamo.... Wolfe and Schwann mark two eras in the history of hypothesis. I shall mark a third if I live to complete the sketch of the vast hypothesis.... My disappointments vanish into the uttermost inane when I think of what it has been possible for me to achieve."[97] He then drops the subject and does not openly discuss it again, which his biographer found hard to understand. This example highlights Ryder's expansive sense of his mission and ability. Another quotation on his evolutionary theory illustrates the same perspective:

> It is my hope to reduce the doctrine of evolution into a simple realization of Newtonian principles. The three great Newtonian laws of motion are at the bottom of the whole matter. Some day I shall be able to tell a great deal that I have kept to myself in order to test its truth.... I have at least worked out a new theory of inheritance which must ultimately replace those of Weismann and Darwin, or at least furnish the foundation by which the data and phenomena of variation can be co-ordinated with the great universal principle of the conservation of energy.[98]

These quotations make it easier to understand Ryder's involvement in oyster science. There was a short period of intense activity, followed by his revelation that he had solved the problem of the industry completely. Then he abruptly switched to other concerns. His optimism arose naturally from his strong confidence in his own ability.

This section presents five reasons scientists favored artificial cultivation. It was the only solution promising to produce tangible, short-term results. Scientists held modernist views that private property must expand and hatcheries could aid this. They believed their most productive educational role was teaching oystermen the value of planting. Scientists' paucity of knowledge recommended fish hatcheries and Connecticut as models. Lastly, scientists' personalities gravitated toward optimism in their abilities. In light of these characteristics, it seems logical that oyster scientists pursued artificial cultivation.

CONTRADICTORY MODERNISTS

Pure versus Applied Science

The correspondence of scientists paints a more contradictory picture. These letters reveal that many scientists prioritized pure science over hatchery research. They believed pure science would have an economic impact, but they felt it incumbent on them to keep the order straight. As McDonald puts it, "scientific investigation, however remote it may seem to be from immediate economic application, is the only sure foundation upon which to build the practical methods of fish culture. . . . Practical fish culture and scientific inquiry must go hand in hand."[99] Scientists should discover new facts about oyster life to lay the "sure foundation" for conservation. A letter from McDonald to George Goode, the second head of the USFC and another proponent of pure science, says it was important for people "representing the broader side of the Fish Commission work" to stay in touch with "the practical man." He describes scientists as becoming "more and more intolerant of views that are shaped purely by selfish and utilitarian aims." He considered scientific research to be the true and only end of the commission, but fishermen "and average fish culturist" saw this as valueless.[100]

A series of letters from Nelson to the New Jersey Shellfish Commission depict some of the funding difficulties that pressured scientists to produce more immediate results. Nelson writes in 1903 that "our laboratories and other appliances are not much to brag on; it could not be otherwise with only $200 per season for all expenses, food, travel, apparatus, and such matters as pertain to the establishment of such a station." He then asked for $1,000, saying that last summer's experiments were "promising" (he crossed out "successful") and now at a "very critical point in their investigations."[101] Nelson requested funding for a lab boat the following year, saying that it would be helpful if he could move his experiments to places where spat was setting well.[102] Nelson also wrote two strongly worded letters to the legislature in 1905 and 1906 regarding inadequate funding. He complained about having to take the time to write reports for Bacon, who was publishing them in the commission's annual report, saying that he was only furnishing the report because he was legally required to do so. He also complained about the state reducing his budget. Nelson stated that he had decided to dedicate the remainder of his life's work to oyster culture but asserted that the state was not providing adequate support.[103] In 1907 Nelson's tone changed. He had received money for his houseboat laboratory, and his letter was pleasant.[104] However, it took Nelson a few years to buy the boat, and his papers contain several letters to New Jersey senators requesting additional funds.[105]

Eugene Blackford provides a striking example of a populist commissioner arguing for modernist science. His policy advice articulated thoroughly populist aims. His letters to the USFC, in contrast, all adopt a utilitarian perspective. Blackford writes about "the importance of throwing the entire strength of the Fish Commission into the improvement of our fisheries." He stated that the USFC's supporters wanted to see more results than what the commission's scientists had produced so far. "Scientific inquiry and collection of specimens should be made entirely subsidiary to the practical work of the Commission."[106] The need to produce tangible results pushed the USFC toward fish culture. Hugh Smith replaced McDonald in 1913 and established the primacy of applied science at the USFC. Smith received a letter from Gilbert Grosvenor, head of the National Geographic Society, asking him to speak to the society in the winter of 1915–1916. Smith replied that he would be happy to publicize the commission's work. He titled his talk "Farming the Waters." It provides an account of the activities of the federal government in maintaining and improving the supply of useful animals in the interior and coastal waters of the United States.[107] Modernist scientists chased a contradiction: they argued for pure science while prioritizing a single solution, oyster hatchery research.

Scientists versus Spoilsmen

Another unexpected finding in the USFC archive was the sheer number of letters devoted to combatting patronage. In these, scientists express the conviction that only rigorous scientists should advance in the commissions. Interpreting these letters requires caution because they deal with issues of professional jockeying, loyalty, and promotion. It is not always possible to tell if a writer is telling the truth or just trying to align with one side in a conflict. In one case, a writer blatantly describes different accounts of another scientist's motivations to different people.

The letters from scientists express an underlying assumption that science should provide knowledge for the public good. In contrast to this stood the "spoilsman" who used political appointment for personal gain. The recurring fear posed in these letters is that elected officials would appoint people to head the USFC and state commission as favors for political aid. These usurpers would then divert the commissions' resources to line the pockets of political allies via contracts and continued appointments. Science, in this telling, functions as a criterion to identify and weed out corruption. Theodore Porter shows that quantification plays the same role in government agencies more generally.[108] Agencies quantify costs and benefits to attest to the fact that their programs are providing the greatest good for the greatest number compared to competing programs. The idea that one can numerically measure the greatest good for the greatest number is a highly modernist simplification of the public good, but it is likely better than corruption.

USFC scientists relied a great deal on personal opinion and correspondence to gauge corruption. They successfully used personal communication to defend their top posts from corruption. No one could accuse McDonald of using his post for personal gain; he even asked Baird for a modest raise, saying he had "money worries."[109] Keeping the USFC's highest offices free from the "spoils system" helped the credibility of scientists with the fishing industry and legislatures. It presumably helped maintain a sense of shared mission. Disinterestedness may have been a personal cultural value posing as an objective measure, but, when it came to corruption, it functioned as if it really were objective.

A typical letter from McDonald to Brooks illustrates the larger pattern. McDonald writes that "a lame person . . . without much scientific knowledge" was trying to get appointed as commissioner.

McDonald thanked Brooks for voicing his views to the president, who needed to hear from scientists. McDonald goes on to say that Verrill sent him "a very fussee letter" saying scientific men saw McDonald's administration as a failure because he stopped paying Verrill. McDonald claims that Verrill failed to render promised services and "behaves like a spoilt child."[110] The same letter shows McDonald extolling the importance of the commission's scientific work, but indicates that at least some scientists thought he was failing in this regard. These two letters agree that scientific experience was essential for top USFC appointments.

This role for science comes to light most prominently in letters about the professional ambitions of Fred Mather, Eugene Blackford, and T. B. Ferguson. In the 1880s and 1890s Mather was the superintendent of the New York commission's Cold Springs Harbor hatcheries, where he propagated trout and other fish. As described above, he first experimented with artificial cultivation at New York's Fulton Street fish market in the summers of 1882 and 1883. He was asked to duplicate these experiments at Cold Springs Harbor in the summer of 1892.

His studies were haphazard and unsuccessful. Despite this, he also held a position as assistant to the USFC. In a letter to McDonald, he mentions that he has "struggled hard to keep the characters apart." He apparently had ambitions to move up in the USFC, once writing that Baird had promised to promote him, and that he had hoped to eventually win appointment as the next commissioner. Since he was not promoted, he was thinking of leaving fish culture, "As it held little for a man of ambition."[111] The same letter alludes to other offers and indicates that he was trying to leverage promotion. Blackford refers to Mather's professional jockeying in one of his letters, saying, "I don't know what ails the man, except that he has a big head on him."[112] Other scientists sometimes refer to Mather's scientific work in disparaging terms. McDonald answers Mather courteously in all his correspondences, but when writing to others he says Mather was "base," and he wanted to drop the USFC's connection to Cold Springs Harbor. Eventually he stopped answering Mather's letters altogether. A few other scientists, such as Ryder, express similar views about working with Mather.

There seem to have been two reasons why other scientists disliked Mather: his political ambition and lack of scientific training. He had no formal training as a scientist, although he had been involved in fish hatchery work for the USFC since 1872 and was Superintendent of the New York State Fish Commission from 1883 to 1895.[113] He lived for ten years in the western United States, and he had worked as an editor for *American Field* and *Forest and Stream*.[114] Several letters presented a sense of personal antipathy toward Mather, presenting the possibility that other scientists simply disliked his personality. However, his careerism and lack of scientific training appear to have been the heart of the matter.

The New York commission was particularly prone to this sort of problem, or at least more evidence survives supporting this. The governor vetoed funding for two new hatcheries in 1892, saying the state was building them for political reasons. He also stated that political manipulation led to three of the five existing state hatcheries being poorly located.[115] Blackford was also the subject of several letters that evoked the same scientific criteria.

Blackford's case is more complex. Mather distrusted him, writing to McDonald that when he propagated salmon for the USFC at Cold Springs Harbor, Blackford "interfered, and you know the result."[116] He felt Blackford and the state commission was trying to "step in and claim credit for work it ridiculed years ago."[117] Blackford had other enemies too. Seth Green, a prominent USFC scientist, eventually succeeded in evicting Blackford from the New York Fish Commission.[118] He attacked Blackford for conflict of interest over his ownership of a fish wholesale business.[119] Blackford claimed Green disliked him because he supported the Republican candidate who lost the election and suggested that Mather had something to do with his removal. Blackford said the New York commission had become "a political machine."[120] He later characterized the man who replaced him (L. D. Huntington) as "totally lacking in a number of things that go to make a gentleman," and he said he could not cooperate with him on the New York Fish Commission's contribution to the World's Fair.[121] He went on to say a circular from Huntington announcing a fishery congress was "wild and asinine" and made fishermen laugh. Blackford had "no use for him . . . he is a boor and does not know when he gets courteous treatment."[122] Blackford also wrote a letter to McDonald in which he discussed the need to keep the fish commissions clear from strictly political appointments. In this letter, he expressed approval for Goode's appointment to head the USFC on those grounds. He wished Goode would reconsider and stay in charge permanently.[123]

It is not clear how McDonald, the recipient of these letters, felt about Blackford. He claimed to be "highly indignant" at Blackford's firing in 1892, and Blackford wrote him a letter asking for his support in 1885.[124] However, in 1889, Ryder wrote to McDonald to say that Blackford was trying to take McDonald's job. He writes, "I have absolutely no faith in Blackford, but all faith in you. I think it simply outrageous to make the office the prey of spoilsmen."[125] Ryder said he would use the Philadelphia Academy of Science to support him. In a subsequent letter, McDonald thanked Ryder for his support, but replied that he believed Ryder was mistaken about Blackford's ambitions.[126] Ryder had received a letter from Joseph Collins informing him of Blackford's plans. Later Ryder recommended Collins to McDonald as an ally, saying he "can thoroughly depend" on him. Ryder himself wanted to keep out of appointment office, writing that, "university bickerings are enough for me."[127]

Ferguson provides a more straightforward example of corruption. Ferguson was a fish commissioner in Maryland and worked for the USFC as an assistant commissioner. Other scientists often opposed him, claiming he was unscientific and mainly interested in career advancement. Blackford wrote McDonald letters saying that Ferguson wanted to succeed Goode. He writes, "The man we have to fear is Major Ferguson, and needs to be watched. Anything I can do here to thwart him, you may rely upon."[128] When the U.S. Senate was debating buying Battery Island for a hatchery, Blackford wrote that this was Ferguson's way to get a "convenient ducking ground."

He asked to be kept informed about his movements and offered to "open fire on him from several quarters."[129]

An unintentionally humorous example of Ferguson's reputation concerns his aborted attempt to conduct an 1884 oyster survey. The USFC loaned him the *Fish Hawk*, but the captain—Lieutenant Wood, who commanded the *Fish Hawk* for much of this period—refused to work with him. In a letter to the secretary of the navy, Wood writes, "I cannot with self respect, again consent to be placed under the immediate authority of Mr. T. B. Ferguson . . . as past experience has taught me that he uses the Fish Commission and the Naval forces connected with it, on every possible occasion, to further his private ends."[130] He sent a copy to Baird as well. When the secretary of the navy, replied that Wood must follow orders, Wood found ways to disrupt the survey. He ran the ship aground surveying in water he knew was too shallow, put in for coal at unnecessarily distant ports, sent down a diver to survey oysters as a way to slow the process of sampling beds, and generally made every effort to ruin the survey without evading the letter of his orders. Ferguson eventually gave up, saying, "The work so far has been a complete failure and a useless expenditure of time and money."[131]

What stands out in all three cases is the fear of turning commission appointments into political rewards. Scientific production guarded against this. It could prevent men like Mather and Ferguson from qualifying. Identifying good scientists rested partly on personal judgment and communication. It is difficult to ascertain whether this was another factor leading scientists to favor artificial cultivation, as one could be a good pure or applied scientist. What is clear, however, is that scientists fought against a shortsighted materialism. They feared creeping utilitarianism and political patronage, both of which valued immediate gain over the slow quest for scientific truth.

CONCLUSION: ENABLING EFFICIENCY

If oyster scientists opposed shortsighted productivist goals, why then did they direct their energies toward hatcheries? The literature on early fishery science explains scientists' preference for hatcheries in terms of their desire to achieve immediate results.[132] Tim Smith's history of measuring fish stock depletion, for example, argues that American and European fishery science privileged hatcheries because scientists were concerned with fixing immediate management problems.[133] Hull advises looking at "enabling conditions" to better understand why scientist adopt a specific intellectual lineage.[134] Möbius provided an authoritative alternative, but his findings would have led scientists to studies of ecological interactions, which provided few immediate benefits due to ecosystem complexity. Coste's program promised much more impactful short-term results. Increased productivity promised to depoliticize conflict. This solution was politically palatable to legislators funding science. Legislatures preferred fish hatcheries as a solution to the contentious conflicts between fishermen and dam builders, conflicts that pitted artisanal resource users with traditional rights against wealthy industrialists. Scientists were also highly optimistic. They lacked knowledge that was difficult to acquire in the marine environment, therefore they relied on models that seemed to point to Coste's accuracy. The aquaculture expansion in Connecticut and France and the success of carp and other hatchery species were their main models. Scientists saw an educational role for themselves akin to cooperative extension. They wanted to make progress visible by proving the superiority of hatchery-based planting. Finally, hatcheries played the same role as privatization for the commissioners: they were the key to unlocking progress. Scientists imagined a single solution that could revolutionize the fishery.

Privatization and hatcheries exerted gravitational force on each other. They merged into a single, powerful solution. Most scientists viewed improvement in ways similar to the colonial discourse on technology. They imagined a linear technological progress as inevitable and desirable. They viewed tonging and common property as outdated stumbling blocks. Planting fit their cultural predispositions and this narrow view of progress that led them to focus on maximizing production via artificial cultivation. The way science and policy linchpins dovetailed lent credence to both.

These enabling conditions paint too tidy a picture. Scientist held contradictory views. The irony of choosing Coste was that doing so undermined advocacy for the USFC's pure science mission. The best book explaining these contradictions is Joseph Taylor's *Making Salmon*. Taylor's description of Baird captures early USFC thinking: "Fish culture was his bridge; it promised practical results painlessly, and science would improve its methods over time. Hatcheries allowed him to build and maintain political backing and funding for less obviously utilitarian science projects such as investigations of tiny aquatic life or encyclopedic classification of North American fish species."[135] Many of these scientists resisted the mania for applied science based on narrow production-maximizing goals, even as they funneled oyster science to exactly that end. They also fought against political patronage. Scientists did want immediate results, but they held loftier aspirations for their commissions. Pure science and patronage put some of the messiness back into their choice.

Another actor pushed scientist toward hatcheries, the marine environment. Abbott's *System of Professions* suggests why oyster scientist may have had few options. To survive a profession must posit problems and solutions. What solution could early oyster scientists, or any fishery scientist for that matter, offer to overfishing? Hatcheries could increase supply. Broader ecological studies were particularly difficult for marine science, as exploring ocean environments presented a formidable challenge. Jennifer Hubbard suggests that marine scientists only began to appreciate and study ecological complexity after the advent of scuba gear in the 1950s.[136] The change in attitudes from Brooks to Nelson signified a small step in this direction. People choose simplifying practices in situations with acute problems and little knowledge. Sophisticated environmental management requires detailed studies that take decades to develop. Solutions like artificial cultivation, that promised to achieve so much with so little, must have been particularly appealing. The marine environment blocked scientists from learning how to improve the fishery the way agronomists improved fields. Lacking knowledge and options, they did what they could to help.

CHAPTER 5

MAPPING NATURAL BEDS

Mapping shellfish sounds easy. Oysters stay in one place and live close to shore in shallow water. But as with oyster legislation and science discussed in the previous chapters, mapping oysters was a contentious process. The more avidly cartographers pursued it, the more controversy they sparked. Mapping oysters meant mapping property as well. Property rights adhere to real objects, but they are also negotiated social constructs. They apply to real oysters on the bay bottom and are also legal abstractions embodying decades of conflict and compromise. This dual nature of oyster habitats vexed cartographers of the late nineteenth century. Mapping oysters without attention to tongers' perception of property rights invited protests. Cartographers had to simultaneously map real oysters and diversely imagined property rights. States did map oysters extensively by 1920. Modernists and populists worked out different solutions to the dilemma. Modernists drew maps to pave the way for expanded planting, whereas populists mapped to solidify traditional property rights. Progressive cartographers turned the two gospels of efficiency into two types of maps.

This chapter first examines the problem of defining natural oyster beds. It then turns to "straight-line" mapping in northern states, which used simpler mapping techniques to divide bay space along biophysical gradients, separating tonging and planting grounds. It then discusses small-scale commission mapping in New York and New Jersey. All of these projects encoded traditional spatial rights in their maps. In contrast, modernists led Chesapeake Bay's three mapping projects, one of which tongers turned to meet their own ends. The three Chesapeake maps, then, provide a comparison between populist and modernist mapping.

DEFINING NATURAL BEDS

The first question confronting cartographers as they mapped tonger property was, what is a natural bed? Traditionally, the term "natural bed" meant an oyster reef, and it excluded planting grounds. Cartographers needed to map these spaces to reserve them for tongers and open the rest of the bay to planters. However, the definition of "natural" was increasingly at issue because it was the legal term used to define marine property boundaries.

A Maryland case in Dorchester County furnished what became the guiding definition of a natural bed. In July 1881 Judge Charles Goldsborough decided that a natural bed was any place with enough oysters for someone to make a living tonging it. The "Goldsborough Definition" drew on a previous court decision, crystallizing the debate, and resulting in a traditional compromise.[1] Following precedent, Goldsborough distilled this compromise born from conflict, not a new definition. He was the same judge who brought William Timmons before a grand jury and charged him with taking bribes as head of the Maryland oyster navy. Newspaper articles on the Timmons case depict Goldsborough as sympathetic to oystermen. His definition was a reasonable attempt to translate the traditional tonger-planter compromise into an abstract, usable legal framework.

Despite Goldsborough's intentions, there were several difficulties associated with integrating this tradition into an administrative framework. The first concerned places with a few scattered oysters. How should the new commissions define places with so few oysters that no one harvested them? If they classified them as natural beds, this would greatly expand tonger property. Goldsborough's solution was to define natural beds as places where oysters occurred in concentrations sufficient to provide tongers a livelihood. Several surveys tried to quantify the density of oysters required to merit inclusion in this definition. In particular, the Chesapeake Bay surveys of H. F. Moore and Charles Yates went to great lengths to operationalize Goldsborough's definition.

Natural bed boundaries often changed, especially following storms. Cartographers sometimes recommended establishing common property boundaries a certain distance around the current beds to create a buffer that would allow for natural movement. Others recommended resurveying beds periodically and adjusting boundaries accordingly. Oyster prices shifted too. The exact number of oysters required for a tonger's livelihood changed when prices fluctuated.

Cartographers also had to surmount the challenge of well-known but presently exhausted beds. Should these locations have the same public property rights as extant oyster beds? Since no tongers presently harvested them, this would seem to be a moot point. However, tongers frequently objected to surveys that missed these locations, arguing that oysters might return, or that they could be brought back with shelling and seeding measures. Others believed that granting defunct areas to planters would open the door to further encroachment. Some cartographers made a conscious decision to omit these places, others set a cut-off date (e.g., it was considered a natural bed if it had oysters in the last ten years), and still others tried to map these nonexistent beds. Mapping extinct oyster beds presented its own difficulties, as cartographers had to rely on oral testimony.

Dredging created a final problem. Over time, dredging spread out beds, causing their boundaries to change. It broke up oysters that were clustered together. If the smaller oysters or shells were thrown back, they drifted down in a more dispersed pattern. Due to its extensive dredging industry, Chesapeake Bay was an extreme case. Dredging had disrupted and expanded oyster reefs well before the first mapping in 1878. The beds were so dispersed by the time of Moore's James River survey (1909) and Yates's Maryland survey (1906–1912) that vast areas of the bay had oysters where none existed before. In all other states, cartographers classified such extensions as natural beds. This was the only possible solution for cartographers, as any attempt to determine where the beds ended before dredging began would be futile. The solution was politically feasible north of Chesapeake Bay because expansions were not big enough to limit cultivation significantly. One proposed solution to the problem of mapping Chesapeake Bay's oyster dispersion was to classify the entire area where oysters now lived as natural beds. However, such a solution would greatly limit cultivation. The opposite was for tongers to admit defeat and acknowledge that it was too late to map the natural beds. However, opening the entire area to cultivation was politically impossible. Any middle ground required compromise, as there was nothing in the environment that lent itself to neat division.

The social nature of the Goldsborough definition created problems for cartographers whose scientific tools were not designed to map a variable and contentious social construct. It was unrealistic to expect cartographic science to objectively settle a complex political question. And yet, state intervention required oyster management to make decisions on a legal basis, so commissions somehow had to map tonger property. Cartographers adopted one of two solutions: they either created simple straight lines that divided bays with larger buffers for tongers, or they used rigorous methods to precision-map oyster beds. Populists used straight-line mapping to preserve traditional compromises. The modernist alternative was more technically sophisticated, but it simplified traditional conservation's political compromises. This is the paradox of oyster mapping: the most intricately detailed maps simplify the older conservation system.

STRAIGHT-LINE MAPPING IN CONNECTICUT AND RHODE ISLAND

Rhode Island's commission reports did not mention mapping natural beds. Restrictions on planting to areas over four-feet deep obviated the need for detailed maps. Rhode Island's solution to the difficult question on mapping natural beds was to simply divide Narragansett Bay by depth. In Connecticut, cartographers began mapping natural beds in 1881, synchronous with the execution of oyster cadastral surveys (see chapter 6). Their commission reported that they "experienced no little difficulty" in this because "great difference of opinion exists as to what constitutes a natural bed; while testimony as to their size and shape is conflicting and untrustworthy."[2] The commission held extensive public meetings to hear opinions on the locations and the extent of beds. Tongers wanted the commission to construct larger natural bed boundaries, and planters wanted them smaller. Commissioners stated that the grounds adjacent to natural beds were valuable due to seed supply, which heightened tensions over boundary placement.

The commission discussed the difficulty in adjudicating these debates:

> What, according to the intent of the law, is a natural bed? Various definitions have been attempted. In one sense, all oyster beds, whether a result of cultivation or of accident, are natural beds. But it is not in this sense that the term is commonly used and understood. That is true in the general sense, but it does not describe the natural bed which the law designs to recognize and protect. Small isolated patches of natural growth oysters cannot be deemed natural beds within the meaning of the law; but when such patches are found scattered over an extent of ground in sufficient abundance to remunerate the oystermen, a greater or lesser number of years in succession, for the labor of gathering them, there is a natural bed as the law recognizes and protects. This is substantially the idea of those who have labored on the beds for many years. In their testimony before the Commissioners, a natural oyster bed with them was an uncultivated bed where they could find oysters "in paying quantities"—where they could do "a fair day's work"—and this view is substantiated by legal authority.[3]

Connecticut's 1881 law defined natural beds as places that had oysters in the last ten years and were not "designed or planted by man." The commissioners cited the Goldsborough definition, and they used it to interpret the 1881 law. They claimed that although oystermen disagreed about what constituted a natural bed, their general concept fit the Goldsborough definition.

Cartographers faced other problems that led them to the straight-line solution. Connecticut bed boundaries varied from year to year. The general shape and placement of these beds did not change much, but the edges moved a great deal. It was hard to mark irregular edges with buoys. They also encountered problems determining the "south line" of the beds, which is where they became too deep to work. Their definition was, "the most southerly line claimed by any oystermen who work on the natural beds."[4] The commissioners' solution to all these challenges created by tonger rights was to construct straight lines enclosing the natural beds. They drew lines where prominent shore objects made it easier for oystermen and law enforcement officers to find them. These reserved areas were larger and more arbitrary than would be the case otherwise.

Applications to lease many exhausted beds were approved, but oystermen presented numerous conflicting opinions about the location of former beds and the presence or absence of oysters. The commissioners expressed "grave doubts" about finding a workable solution.[5] They sample-dredged many areas and usually confirmed that beds had been barren for a long time. They still had to reject many applications due to conflicting testimony. Commissioners pointed out that barren beds might be leased later and recommended reducing the unproductive period to five years.

The commissioners of Connecticut and Rhode Island finished mapping natural beds in 1885. Together, these covered 5,805 acres. The largest were near the towns of Stratford (3,055 acres) and Fairfield (1,237 acres). Commissioners were proud of their work and viewed it as historically important, saying, "Connecticut is putting into practice the best system of oyster culture in the world. . . . The eyes of the world are upon Connecticut at the present time. . . . Every country which has an oyster fishery is trying to solve the same problem, viz: 'How to protect beds and give oyster culturists right of property in the fruit of their labors.'"[6] This mapping dealt with the basic problem of defining natural beds by creating simple borders that erred on the side of protecting tonger rights. This basic pattern helped avoid large-scale conflict over mapping, and Rhode Island's four-foot measure represented a similar approach. Both attempted to map oystermen's preexisting norms. These older norms were complex and hard to pin down, but they focused on preserving access for local tongers. The way commissioners encoded this complexity was to devise maps with buffer areas and straight-lines to preserve the basic aim of the older system. This was easier to do because planters in these states tended to work in deeper waters.

STRAIGHT-LINE MAPPING IN NEW JERSEY

New Jersey's two largest production areas, Delaware Bay and Barnegat Bay, used straight lines to split natural and planted beds. In 1899 the state oyster commission contracted an engineer to survey natural beds[7] and create the first map of Maurice River Cove, which "proved so extremely interesting to the oystermen."[8] According to their report, the oystermen approved of the map and crowded around to examine it. This survey led the commission to draw the "Southwest Line" separating upper and lower Delaware Bay. Tongers harvested the upper half as a commons, and planters held lease in the lower section. This simple division decreased conflict. All of the natural beds save one were in the upper portion of the bay. Oysters propagated better in the upper bay's lower salinity waters. The lone outlier was a large natural bed in Maurice River Cove, Delaware Bay's biggest estuary. This was in the lower section and adjacent to Port Norris, the bay's largest packing center. More conflict occurred here than elsewhere in the bay. If Delaware Bay had contained more inlets with abundant oysters, it would likely have seen additional conflicts. Instead, tongers sent most of their seed oysters to the planting grounds in the lower Bay. Barnegat Bay's line divided its northern and southern halves too. At one point, district commissioners wanted the line changed to run north-south. The advantage would be that seed supply and planting grounds would be adjacent to one another. This proposal ignored both ecological differences and longstanding tradition in the bay.[9]

The New Jersey District Commission mapped most natural beds, and their few surviving reports shed light on challenges of populist mapping by small-scale agencies.[10] The Ocean County District Commission's 1903 report stated that the commissioners lacked adequate funds to map oyster and clam beds. Faulty equipment forced them to abandon the survey for the year. Clams and oysters were equally valuable in this region. Deciding how to divide these areas was difficult and controversial because of many overlapping claims. Both groups also fought with planters over space. Commissioners admitted to accidentally assigning clam beds to oystermen. Predictably, this created animosity and distrust. The commissioners wrote that many baymen thought the whole survey was being done for the benefit of the oyster industry at the clammers' expense.[11] In 1904, the Ocean County District Commission adjusted clam lines again in Tuckerton and Great Bay. By 1905, their survey work was nearing completion. The commissioners had established baselines that would make future surveys easier to conduct. They also reported that clammers and oystermen were happy with the restaked clam line.[12] These few surviving district commission reports demonstrate the relative weakness of these small agencies.

A letter in a trade publication titled "Thirty Years Reminiscences of a Veteran Oyster Planter" describes conflicts with the commission in Atlantic County.[13] The author states that in 1903 ninety percent of all oystermen and clammers in Atlantic County signed a petition asking for "equal rights" with what the state gave Cumberland County, which brought peace there. This referred to the Delaware Bay line. The legislature refused that year, and refused again in 1904, 1905, and 1907, despite eight hundred signatures on a 1905 petition. In 1908 Ocean County commissioners did set up a line dividing Barnegat Bay. The author says oystermen were pleased with the commissioners, who were "honest men." However, the new commissioners began leasing clamming grounds to oystermen. The article argues that the commissioners wanted to give the bay to rich capitalists. This article provides an excellent illustration of the various struggles parties endured over the control of these small-scale commissions and their mapping efforts. It also describes how local people sought the creation of maps to help settle these disputes. One letter uses the case of a tonger murdered by an oyster farm watchman to explain why Barnegat Bay needed a line like the one constructed in Delaware Bay.[14] Straight-line maps were not panaceas, but they could reduce conflict.

MODERNIST CARTOGRAPHY IN CHESAPEAKE BAY

The Baylor Lines

Three Chesapeake Bay cartographers embarked on modernist mapping projects. They crafted maps to expand planting and reduce tonging. James Baylor was the first modernist oyster cartographer, and he mapped all of Virginia's natural beds from 1892 to 1894. Virginia used these maps into the 1970s. The USCGS furnished Baylor with instruments and projection paper, while the USFC provided the steamer and crew. The survey delineated 201,216.3 acres of natural beds, leaving more than 400,000 acres open for planting. After completing the work, Baylor reported a high demand for the thirty resulting charts; he quickly ran out of the maps and asked the legislature for funds to print more.[15]

State law mandated that a judge in each county appoint someone with long-term experience working the beds to identify bed locations for Baylor. Judges appointed tongers. These men were the final arbiters of bed boundaries under the law. Baylor produced straight-line maps like the ones to the north, which simplified administration and policing efforts. This was partly because he lacked time and money for a more rigorous, detailed survey. The law also forced him to rely on the testimony of judge-appointed tongers, and tongers desired a map that would protect their rights. Baylor's boundaries included many areas void of oysters. Tongers forced Baylor to draw a straight-line, populist map.

This was not the map Baylor wanted. Sources allow us to reconstruct the views of the three Chesapeake cartographers (Baylor, Moore, and Yates). All three favored expanding aquaculture leasing and limiting natural bed tonging. They hoped their surveys would promote this end. The contrast between their desires and what transpired attests to their lack of control over the mapping process. The experiences of Baylor, Moore, and Yates illustrate the role that cartography played to negotiate modernist plans for fishery reform.

Baylor was a hydrographic and geodetic engineer who worked for the USCGS. He was also a Confederate Civil War naval veteran. He mapped the U.S.-Canada boundary line with his Canadian counterparts and resurveyed the Virginia-Tennessee and Pennsylvania-New York boundaries. His coastal work included mapping Mobile and Perdido Bays in 1892, which included surveying oyster populations. He later mapped Louisiana oysters in 1904.[16]

Several pieces of evidence provide insight into Baylor's ideas about the oyster industry. One is a set of pages held in his personal collection of papers on which he wrote notes and calculations. In these pages, he detailed his thoughts on the link between education and productivity. He saw increasing productivity as a pressing issue for southern states. These notes appear to be preparations for a report or article. The calculations show the populations and literacy rates of different countries. According to his data, America produced nearly half the output of Europe, despite Europe's much larger population. Baylor attributed American productivity to "labor saving machinery and intelligence of workmen. . . . The waste of labor in Russia is prodigious. . . . [Russians] live out their lives in drudgery, . . . [and their poverty] is due to the ignorance of the people." He adds that the, "density of population has no necessary effect on the productivity of a country, or even on the rate of wages." He cites France as the country with the highest wages per capita. The pages also refer to Charles Dabney's article "A World Wide Law." Dabney was president of the University Tennessee at the time. Baylor also cites Dabney's speech titled "Education and Production," which compares Massachusetts and Tennessee to advocate for greater spending on education.[17]

Baylor made the links between education, productivity, and oysters explicit in a speech before the Richmond Chamber of Commerce.

He began by saying the South lagged behind the North in industrial education because they could not afford better schools. He argued that machines lessened the cost of production, but workers needed training in mechanical arts before the use of labor saving machinery could spread. He mentioned a farmer whom he advised to use labor-saving machines as they did in the North. The farmer told Baylor that he had tried, but no one in the region could repair them. Baylor then applauded Texas for wisely investing the profits from the sale of their huge public domain into schools. He explained that the South would continue to lag behind economically until it could improve its agriculture. He finally turned to oysters, saying, "No product on earth or water can be more largely increased by human intelligence and labor."[18] Baylor thought Virginia should adopt northern methods. He did not mention planting by name; the implication would have been clear to his audience. The conference where he spoke was called to launch a proplanting education campaign. When combined with the notes cited above, Baylor's writing expresses a narrative that goes as follows: education improves productivity everywhere (this is a social law), the South lags behind the North economically due to a self-perpetuating cycle of poverty and lack of education, oysters are a key place to break this cycle because production increases can happen with relatively little education and time, and education means getting the populace to follow the example of northern states.

This narrative put the need for education into historical context and featured prominently in modernist thinking on oysters. Baylor added a distinctly southern twist, heightening the stakes of modernizing the oyster fishery. Progress for the South required adopting the North's industrial methods. This required enhancing southern education, and the South lacked money for schools. Industrial methods in the oyster fishery (planting and canneries) required relatively little education and promised large revenue. Baylor's desire to break the cycle of southern poverty is understandable, and it helps explain his production-oriented progressivism. Experiencing defeat against the industrial North in the Civil War must have shaped his appreciation for the power of industrial productivity and regional competition.

A planting advocate named William Ellinger had an extensive correspondence with Baylor preserved in Baylor's papers. Their letters shed further light on Baylor's interest in expanding planting. Ellinger described their work together as "founded on a mutual interest," and the letters mostly pertain to Ellinger's efforts to promote planting. He wrote as though Baylor supported him in this, and he often asked Baylor for help or thanked him for his assistance. He was clearly keeping Baylor up to date on his progress, and Baylor was keenly interested. Ellinger used phrases such as "the glory of our generation" to describe the eventual expansion of oyster planting in the South. He was trying to spread acceptance by changing public opinion in his own county first. He said both he and Baylor felt regret that "the oyster question should be the football of politics."[19] Both were also worried about oyster decline and held disparaging views about tonging. Ellinger described tongers in one letter, saying, "Sick? Yes Mr. Baylor such news as you write is contagious. It makes me sick too. I think that a class whose rapacity and wastefulness has nearly destroyed the noblest Bounty nature ever bestowed when [illegible] reaches forth for not only what is left but claim also that which were if left to its rightful owner the Commonwealth might be made a source of profit to the citizens of the State."[20]

Baylor also received letters from B. H. Haman, a Maryland legislator who led the fight for expanded planting. These letters indicate Baylor's support for Haman's bills to allow aquaculture leasing in Maryland. In response to a Baylor letter, Haman said perhaps Baylor could strengthen part of Haman's proposed legislation on planting.[21] Haman asked Baylor's advice on numerous matters, and he asked for help organizing a movement for oyster aquaculture. Baylor was also opposed to monopoly. He fit planting into the yeoman ideal that was so important to Virginian culture. He states in his 1894 report, "the ideal system would be to have the oyster area divided as much as possible into small farms."[22]

Baylor wrote a series of letters to the *Richmond Times* that explicitly argue for the modernist narrative of common property and frontier progress. He laments that "public opinion can override any law," even a good one. He defines a good law as one that follows the progressive maxim that "the greatest good to the greatest number is the humanitarian aim of government."[23] In these letters, he provides a lengthy discussion of the northern oyster industry. Virginia held several natural advantages, according to Baylor. He also acknowledges the state's limited access to markets. He explains the problem with the oyster commons, saying, "These were the common rights of the first settlers. This is the usage in all new communities. As man advances in civilizations the policy is to assign to the individual everything susceptible of ownership. Thus only can human energy and enterprise be encouraged, the material wealth of the country increased, opportunity for full development of mind and body obtained, and what is called civilization made possible." He notes that the current property system maintained poverty, calling it the "height of folly in this progressive age." He stresses that people kept the oyster beds as a commons solely because they had been one in the past. Everything was a commons once and tongers should display "cheerful acquiescence" to the inevitable change.[24] Virginians could never compete with interior states in producing staple crops, but they could compete with anyone in oysters.

Baylor's discussion of natural beds also contains ambiguity. In one letter, he suggests that natural beds should remain state or public property. They should be carefully regulated to maintain spat for planters. He goes on to say that tongers must make money from natural beds "until they are induced to become small oyster planters."[25] Baylor felt that natural beds should be preserved but that this could only be accomplished if planting expanded to reduce harvest pressure.

Baylor combined modernist views about the inevitability of private property with Southern concerns over lack of industry and competitiveness. His sought to make maps that would restrict tonging and open as much area as possible for planting. His maps, however, reserved extensive areas without natural beds for tongers. He felt his work was incomplete and needed extensive revision. Baylor never had the opportunity to remap oysters. Planting advocates had to wait until 1909 for H. F. Moore to begin this process.

Moore's Resurvey

Moore's views are best documented in a paper he read to a fishery congress in Tampa Bay. Moore outlines the problem as follows:

> I can see no hope for the continued productiveness of our natural beds if they are made to bear the brunt of the yearly increasing demand. . . . Those who have studied the problem are a unit in the belief that the solution lies in the general adoption of oyster culture under private ownership and as a result of private enterprise. The Government can do but little. Wise laws rigidly and judiciously enforced can stimulate private ventures and retard reckless waste of public possessions, but our oyster beds can never be repopulated by the methods which have in many cases proven so beneficial in restocking our streams with food and game fish.[26]

Moore recommended cull laws and closed seasons as solutions. He opposed government-funded oyster hatcheries, stating, "The methods of fish culture are not now, and probably never will be, available in propagating the oyster."[27] He believed that fish culture was proper work for the government because fish dispersed only to be caught by the individuals who did not contribute to their cultivation. This removed any incentives for private propagation. On the other hand, he believed that because oysters remained where they were planted, the private sector could undertake propagation.

Moore also discusses the property question:

> The logic of our history would dictate the throwing of the tidelands open for occupation, yet in how many states are the laws, and more especially public opinion, practically if not intentionally prohibitive? A policy far different from that in land above tides is supposed to be justified in dealing with that portion of the State's domain lying beneath the sea. There is a reluctance to part with the tide lands, and it is thought preferable to allow them to lie barren rather than to permit individuals to acquire permanent possession. There can be no doubt the best results are obtained when the oyster grower holds his lands in fee simple.[28]

He also states that "thrifty citizens . . . will hold aloof" without private property rights because they feared tongers would steal their oysters.[29] Moore believed that the government should tax sales and not property to improve planting incentives.

Moore then discusses how incentives could be brought about. He cites Connecticut's success, saying that while it was due in part to market proximity, an important consideration for his southern audience, it was also due to the industry of citizens and "enlightened public opinion." He suggests that "enlightened public opinion" was missing in Virginia:

> Adverse public opinion . . . is one of the greatest difficulties with which he [the planter] has to contend. Theft of property beneath the tide is palliated by some as an act of retributory justice against a common enemy, and a man who will steal oysters would scorn to enter his neighbor's poultry house. This peculiar moral obliquity is rooted in ignorance, and must be combated by education, supplemented by more than occasional salutary castigation from the strong arm of the law.[30]

Moore, like Baylor, saw private property and planting as more productive and viewed both as requirements for progress. Moore and Baylor pointed north for proof.

The USFC provided Moore with funding to remap Virginia's James River from July to September in 1909. Moore's goal was to open areas within the Baylor lines to planting by demonstrating that they lacked natural beds. Because he was funded by the USFC, Moore was not bound to use tonger guides as Baylor had been. To fix the Baylor survey, Moore endeavored to make his work more scientific and objective than Baylor's. Moore used sextants and three-armed protractors. While these were not as accurate as "the best theodolites" used by the USCGS, they proved quite sufficient for his work. He located beds by dragging a chain line with a copper wire. The wire vibrated when pulled over shells, and he recorded these locations. His ship ran transects, and Moore checked its position by sextant readings every two to three minutes. He took a sounding every twenty seconds and sampled the hardness of the bottom. He then recorded the wire measurement for that section as either "barren, scattered, or numerous." If Moore recorded numerous oysters, he dropped a numbered buoy.

A second boat would tong up a sample, taking a standard number of grabs per distance. Moore made measures of the areas grabbed by tongs at various depths, and he used them to adjust the data. Tongs cover less area with depth, which made it appear as if fewer oysters occurred in deeper waters. This method gave an exact record of conditions within a few yards. For the entire survey, the trailing boat made 590 buoy examinations, while the lead ship took 10,440 soundings, used 1,369 instrument reading locations, and chain dragged 226 transect miles, all in the James River.[31]

Following the Goldsborough definition, Moore then converted his data into a map of natural beds by developing an economic measure. He divided the beds by the number of bushels a tonger could take in nine hours. This was a function of density and depth. A tonger could gather more oysters faster in shallow water, so a natural bed needed lesser densities to support a tonger in shallow conditions. Moore and his team observed how fast tongers worked to develop these metrics. In his report he provided an estimate of density needed to make a living given recent prices.[32] Moore avoided discussing in detail what constitutes a livelihood, as he felt this was a judicial matter, but he had to use some standard in classifying productive regions.[33] Due to the division of labor in the survey and by design, no one could know the final results until they compiled all data at the end. Moore states, "The author himself could form but a vague idea of the general results until the charts were completed and the results almost written."[34] Moore designed by far the most detailed oyster map to date.

The results indicated that natural beds were formerly more distinct. Their outlines had become less sharp, and they had often expanded or merged as a result of dredging. Many areas with few oysters listed as "depleted" were in fact new areas where dredging had scattered shells, though some of these were already overworked. The survey found some private beds within the public bed boundary established by the Baylor survey, although it was difficult to locate exactly where some of the boundaries were, due to "the flimsy nature" of markers.[35] Baylor's boundaries were poorly marked in 1909, and several shore reference markers he used were gone by this point.

Out of 26,408.4 acres within the Baylor lines on the James River, Moore classified 3,227 as "dense growth," 2,078 as "scattering," 1,848 as "very scattering," 3,884 as "depleted," and 15,371.4 as "barren." According to Moore's map, only 27 percent of the designated natural beds were productive, and 58 percent were entirely devoid of oysters (see figure 3 for an example). Moore's report stated that he favored opening these barren areas to leasing.[36]

Despite Moore's rigorous methodology, which was a model for later natural bed cartographers, the Virginia legislature never used his survey. It had no impact on management at all. Both Moore and Baylor favored expanded planting and decreased tonging. While

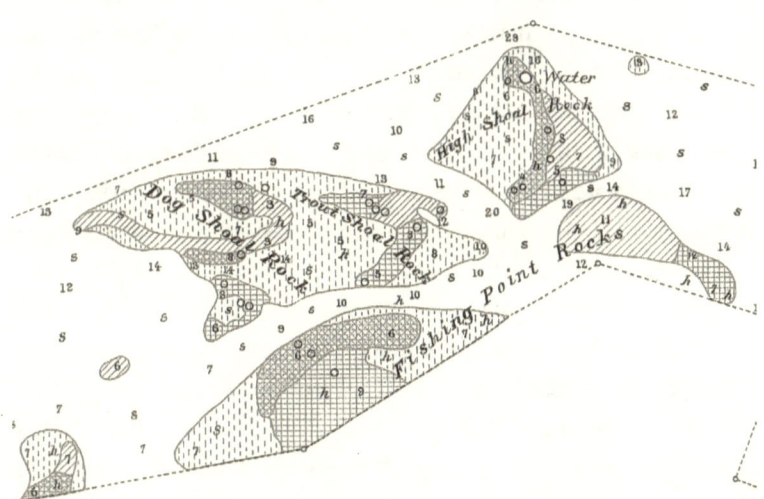

FIGURE 3. Detail from Moore's map of the James River. The dashed outer straight lines are the Baylor Lines. The hatched areas within them are oyster beds, with denser hatching indicating greater oyster density. The map also shows depth in feet and popular names for oyster reefs. This area is roughly two miles long and west of Newport News, VA. Moore wanted to show that most of the protected areas had no oysters and should be thrown open to planting. Moore did not map any oyster beds outside the Baylor Lines, even though some beds clearly went beyond them. Note the level of painstaking detail as well. From H. F. Moore, "Condition and Extent of the Oyster Beds of James River," USFC, *Report of the Commissioner of Fish and Fisheries* (1911).

they hoped their maps would pave the way for this, it never happened. Legal constraints forced Baylor to adopt procedures that designated large buffers around the natural beds. He codified traditional political compromises with straight-line maps that preserved tonger rights, in spite of his modernist ideals. Moore fixed this, but the state rejected his map because it was politically unacceptable to tongers.

Yates's Maryland Maps

Yates wanted his maps to change policy. At the outset of the survey he nailed a sign to the mast of his ship that read, "A survey that does not lead to legislation is a failure."[37] He believed that cartographic surveys not only clarified property rights but also revealed the true state of the fishery. He expected legislators and public opinion to respond rationally to the maps he provided. This was the educational ideal for modernist cartography. It assumed that rational actors would respond predictably to accurate information. The response Yates expected was expanded planting. This goal required mapping projects with detailed statistical picturing. They were the opposite of the populist straight-line maps Baylor produced. Even if Yates had wanted to create straight-line maps, this would have proved difficult in Maryland. Extensive dredging had spread the already expansive beds across vast regions; few places were entirely free of oysters.

Yates's survey was the most extensive natural bed mapping that occurred during this period and arguably remains the most painstaking oyster mapping effort in U.S. history. Taking seven years to complete (1906–1912), the result was a twenty-four hundred page document, with forty-three large maps. Its boundaries remained the legal boundaries for Maryland oysters, with minor modification, until 1983. Moore represented the USFC as an advisor, and the Maryland state government funded the project. Maryland legalized planting with the Haman act in 1906, and this required the state to map its natural beds so that leasing could proceed in other areas. Yates, who worked for the USCGS, carried out the survey while actively working on oyster legislation. He assisted with writing Maryland's most important planting laws, and Maryland shellfish commissioners and oyster navy captains were constantly requesting his advice.

Yates used methods developed by Caswell Grave, one of Maryland's oyster commissioners. Yates relied on the Goldsborough definition, but notes: "Before this definition could be of use in determining, accurately and scientifically, the status of an oyster ground, it was necessary to expand its central idea, 'livelihood,' into accurately determinable factors and to combine these factors into a practical scheme for investigating and determining the condition of the grounds under consideration."[38]

To do this, he split "livelihood" into constituent factors: income, price, oysters, time, and area. He adopted a low estimate of the income needed, which increased the area of natural beds. He does not explain how he arrived at an estimate of necessary wages. Yates asked oystermen and consulted weather records to see how long they spent at sea as a means of estimating the time it took to harvest the required quantity of oysters. He then took careful "grab" measurements. These estimated how many oysters one generally caught in the tongs, which allowed him to calibrate his sampling methods to the definition he was developing. Most of his figures come from work in the survey's starting point: Anne Arundel County. His report says nothing occurred in other counties to make him change the measures.[39]

Once he had established this economic definition, his next task was measuring the boundaries of natural beds. The survey vessel towed a cable. A person holding the cable onboard would detect hard objects on the bottom by the cable's vibration. When they detected hard objects, the crew would take samples to examine whether the objects were oysters. Measuring the density of the beds involved taking samples at regular intervals along a transect path and then counting the oysters taken from a standardized sampling technique. Yates then extrapolated these figures for the entire area of the oyster bed.

Yates always tried to give the tongers the benefit of the doubt, both while developing his measurement and during the actual mapping process. He knew that securing the acceptance of tongers was the only way they would allow planting. In line with this notion, Yates hired local tongers to operate the tongs efficiently. Tongers also helped him determine where to make examinations. Yates hoped their participation would create buy-in.[40]

Yates's team used several types of maps. Onboard they used "boat sheets" that showed areas that were thought to be oyster bars. They also brought projection maps that had the triangulation points, on which they plotted bars. Yates then published charts of the bars and stations, and the commission printed these and made these available to the public. There were also partially completed progress maps. The final products were leasing charts, which were published on or after 1912 (see figure 4).

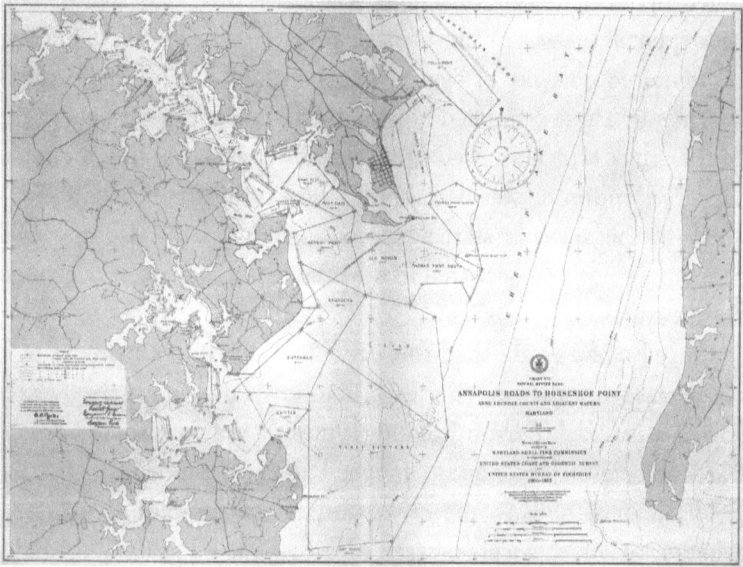

FIGURE 4. Detail from one of Yates's Maryland maps. This is the Annapolis Roads to Horseshoe Point map. The polygons, made by solid lines joining circles, contain oyster beds. Note the popular names for each bed/polygon. This section is roughly fourteen miles long. The author thanks the Special Collections at the University of Maryland for reproduction assistance. From Charles Yates, *Charts of Maryland Oyster Survey* (Washington, D.C.: USCGS).

Yates's mapping project failed to sway the opponents of the Haman act. The act never expanded leasing significantly because its opponents in the legislature weakened its provisions. The faith that accurate resource maps could change policy guided the two most detailed Progressive Era oyster maps. Both failed to have this effect.

CONCLUSION: MAPPING TRADITION

Cartographers created a new way of picturing nature and property. Maps contributed more rational, standardized, fixed, and quantitative measures to the previous understandings of natural bed locations. Natural beds were close to shore in shallow water, but their indistinct, shifting borders made them hard to map. More importantly, natural beds were a social construct. The courts and commissions divided beds into workable and unworkable areas based on an idea of livelihood, but there was no method that could reduce this to an objective measure. Cartographers developed two solutions and two kinds of maps to address this problem. Populist cartographers used straight-lines to map traditional compromises between planters and tongers. Modernist mappers use detailed techniques to show desirability for expanded planting.

Literature on the cultural history of cartography has drawn productively from social theory to read maps as texts and examine the meaning they embody.[41] This literature has shown how maps shape people's perceptions and guide their behavior, thereby empowering cartographers.[42] This interpretive framework fits the three Chesapeake modernist mapping projects. All three cartographers centralized knowledge, which produced new ways of seeing and valuing environments.[43] They sought to expand conservation, capitalism, and government control simultaneously. Moore especially used scientific cartography to legitimate expanded planting. Moore's and Yates's maps tried to create a more orderly and efficient management system, one that would further expand planting and decrease tonging as much as possible.

Straight-line maps sought to make tonger knowledge visible to the state. As with precision maps, they were graphic images of nature and property designed to prompt more orderly behavior. They also allocated space for capitalist expansion. The difference was in the way maps used cartographic methods to depict traditional political compromises. Straight-line maps sought to preserve and bureaucratize tonger property rights, whereas the modernist maps tried to radically recast property dispensation. Paradoxically, Moore and Yates's precision maps were less accurate in an important sense: they failed to depict real political compromises that favored erring on the side of preserving tonger rights. The simple, straight-line maps in Delaware Bay more accurately reflect this political tradition than Yates's twenty-four hundred pages. Straight-line maps preserve political complexity because they found a way to preserve tradition. Modernist maps explicitly tried to undermine these political compromises because their cartographers believed progress meant privatization.

CHAPTER 6

MAPPING PLANTERS' PROPERTY

Planters and packers needed maps depicting what no one could see. Cartographers came to their aid and produced a surprisingly varied array of maps. Cadastral maps encoded traditional planter property rights. Sanitary surveys mapped typhoid risk. Barren-bottom maps showed environmental conditions in southern states, which helped establish planting industries that would provide jobs for coastal communities. In mapping the featureless surfaces of bays, cartographers faced several challenges. They had to make visible unmarked planter property, as well as microbe concentrations that would indicate typhoid. Identifying oysters grown in low concentrations would make canned oysters appear safe to consumers, thereby supporting the packing industry. Marine cartographers made visible the invisible.

Pamela Gilbert's study of urban planning in Victorian Britain offers a persuasive interpretation of mapping for social reform. She notes, "Spaces were identified with their own protocols and good citizenship was aligned with a form of self-governance which involved adhering to those protocols."[1] Planners used maps "to remake the city into a structure more consonant with the planner's goals."[2] All three types of oyster maps intended to make the industry less chaotic and more productive. Cartographers sought to guide behavior. Most studies of nineteenth century cartography follow Henri Lefebvre and David Harvey in looking at the negative side of mapping.[3] They focus particularly on the way it aided the expansion of capitalism. As Gilbert puts it, the literature tends to depict mapping "as purely designed to suppress the freedom of the underclass."[4] However, early mapping also tried "to gesture toward utopian realization of the liberal narrative of progress."[5] This narrative could be modernist or populist, as seen in the last chapter. The three forms of maps in this chapter did aid capitalists. Lease maps produced Harvey's "abstract space" that made capitalist investment easier by standardizing leases and drawing marine property accurately. But maps helped an industry that bought tongers' seed oysters. Lease maps hurt no one. Sanitary maps improved public health and barren-bottom maps created jobs for coastal towns. Critiques of early state mapping that highlight the negative impact of capitalism paint an accurate but partial picture. The planter maps in this chapter benefitted coastal communities.

CADASTRAL SURVEYS AT SEA

"Chaotic Conditions": Early Lease Mapping in Rhode Island and Connecticut

Precommission lease mapping was a haphazard affair. The Rhode Island legislature made oyster grants to specific individuals for oyster planting in 1798, 1822, and 1827. Following the U.S. Supreme Court's ruling in *Martin v. Waddell*, Rhode Island passed its Oyster Act in 1844 and set up a commission to oversee leasing.[6] Planting and leasing expanded after this point. An 1864 law sought to improve the commission's administration, and the first extant report followed. The new commissioner, John P. Knowles, deplored the commission's "chaotic condition"[7]:

> The loose memoranda (not books) which came into my hands from my predecessors yield no information upon this point; nor, it may be added, any reliable information as to who of the leasees of oyster

beds had paid rents, or who were in default; or as to who were, in fact, the holders and owners of outstanding leases; or how many or which leases apparently outstanding in full force, had been, in an equitable view, surrendered or cancelled by the action or inaction of the Commissioners.[8]

Knowles granted twenty-nine new leases in 1864, bringing the total to one hundred and forty-two. He had trouble obtaining rent from some of the lease holders that he "suspected to be of the genus *skulker*, with whom, by the way, patience shall cease to be a virtue" (italics in the original).[9] Lessees were required to submit a report of their harvest to the commission. About half of them did, but many were unaware of this requirement. Others paid for leases but left them unused while they waited for starfish to die off. Rhode Island's next report (1881) attests to the commission's underfunding. Commissioners complained that there was nowhere to store lease maps. They had so little funding that they had to buy a desk for storage, which had to be portable because they had no office.[10]

One problem was the ad hoc landmarks used by planters. For example, two Connecticut towns set the borders of their planting ground at "a point whence the outer beacon bears halfway between the brick chimneys of Wheeler and Wilson's sewing-machine factory."[11] One of the first Rhode Island leases, granted in 1835, used six church steeples as landmarks. Only one remained when the commission began mapping in 1882. Rhode Island's commission complained that lease documents listed landmarks such as, "west by range of bunch of bushes on knoll over gate on land of the late George Ferris."[12]

Precommission paperwork was another source of vexation for commissioners. Connecticut commissioners searched town lease records to make their initial map, but these were often "defective and incomplete."[13] They listed a host of common problems: leases had separate names but were then transferred to one person (with the signatures all in one handwriting); signatures claiming to be from one person did not match; leases did not provide leaseholder names; leases failed to identify lease locations; or the acreage listed did not match the total designated on the lease. In other cases leaseholders complained that much of their designated area was unsuitable for planting, and thus they had not paid for it at all. One person leased almost eight thousand acres, of which he only paid for two thousand.[14] In both states, maps for precommission leases were often contradictory and poorly recorded. Planters hired their own surveyors who used no instruments and drew maps by hand. Towns would sometimes hire a surveyor to map a small area. When a planter applied for a lease, the town committee would go out and draw it on the map. A *Fishing Gazette* article describes the disorder of precommission lease mapping, "Before the Commission came into power it was no uncommon thing for an oysterman to get a designation and deed from a town and carry it in his pocket for years, often losing them. Many long and expensive lawsuits have been caused by carelessness. There are sections of oyster ground in the State jurisdiction under cultivation and taxes paid regularly where the party occupying the ground could not show any title. The Commission has always recognized those claims."[15]

Planters made matters worse by engaging in speculation and fraud. Once Connecticut established a commission, planters rushed to claim grounds in state waters. By the time the commissioners formed their board, planters had already claimed forty-five thousand acres.[16] The commissioners questioned the legality of many earlier leases, saying they were often permitted to "slip into the hands of a few favorites, contrary to the obvious spirit and intent of the law, and many of them at grossly inadequate prices." Their report lists the most questionable of these: Rowe, Connecticut's largest planter, received leases of one thousand, three hundred and fifty, eight hundred and fifty, and four hundred and fifty acres at fifty cents per acre.[17]

Rhode Island and Connecticut commissioners tried to avoid encroaching on tonger property as they mapped leases. Rhode Island's commission claimed it was as generous as possible to natural-bed tongers, which led them to exempt much area. They rejected six hundred acres of proposed leases in 1899, at a time when they had only leased around three thousand acres.[18] This ample protection expanded in 1901, when the legislature revised the law so that all land covered by less than four feet of water remained public, even though much of it was suitable for planting and never contained natural beds. Rhode Island could afford to adopt this generous definition in part because so much of Narraganset Bay was too deep for tonging. Planters had plenty of room. In addition, the success of deepwater cultivation in neighboring Connecticut led planters in Rhode Island to focus on deeper areas. Connecticut's commission also strove to maintain the older property dispensation. The commissioners' first task was determining the line that divided town from state jurisdiction. They held meetings with town selectmen, which they claimed went well. The 1881 act gave "considerable latitude for interpretation" to town jurisdiction, and the commissioners gave towns what they wanted to secure support.[19] Most tonging beds lay in town waters, and the commission maintained the older way of managing oysters by empowering town governments to protect tongers.

The Process of Cadastral Surveying

The Connecticut Shellfish Commission's first action was to hire surveyor James Bogart, whose "engineer's report" provides the most detailed record of lease mapping. The commissioners considered Bogart's triangulation survey to be "the most important and far-reaching... of all the work that has been imposed upon them."[20] He began by traveling to Washington, D.C., to get USCGS maps. These measured sixty-four feet long when placed end to end. He eventually traced all oyster leases onto the USCGS maps, which were reduced in scale and transferred to a master copy. Before surveying could begin, he had to establish baselines and fixed landmarks. Baseline surveys proved more time-consuming and expensive than plotting individual leases because he had to determine the landmark's latitude and longitude. He also had to raise signal markers in places without suitable landmarks. After completing the baseline survey, he began the slow process of surveying leases. The fundamental problem was the difficulty of marking fixed points on water, which has no landmarks of its own. Bogart accomplished this via triangulation. This method consisted of first sighting three fixed points on the land, whose exact location he knew. Then he measured the angles made by lines running from these to the boat. He also used a sextant to measure the declination of the sun, providing the known vertical point. This process allowed him to map a lease's location accurately on a featureless bay.

Bogart started surveying at New Haven and resurveyed leases as he went. Both lessees were present when their waters adjoined. He also set up thirty-five signal stations. These were made from four-by-six-inch wood planks and were sixteen to twenty-three feet high with a black-and-white marker on top. He explained that he was unsure how well the commission could maintain the position of the buoys marking the property lines. They swung around, leading to loss or gain of property when surveying. Deepwater beds also presented problems for accurate mapping. The distance from shore signal stations magnified interference from the boat's sway, and depth increased buoy movement.

In 1882, Bogart received funds to purchase better instruments. With the help of the USCGS, he set up and measured 118 more triangulation points that year. He could now draw accurate leases in all state waters from New York to the Connecticut River. While he placed 538 buoys, Bogart acknowledged that "a large number of lots remain to be located and buoyed."[21] The commission was able to lease almost 90,000 acres by the summer of 1883. Bogart built nineteen more signal stations, alongside another sixteen built by the USCGS. Despite the large number of stations, he continued to use "lighthouse towers, beacons, church spires, factory chimneys, [and] parts of buildings" to mark points during the surveying process.[22] The schooner *Palinurus* continued to assist him, and Rowe and other planters lent steamships to help place buoys.[23] Owners accepted the commission findings in all cases save one, although conflicts persisted between the owners of adjoining sites. Despite disagreements along borders, planters took pains to treat each other fairly and avoid litigation.

Bogart finished mapping all state waters in 1888. The commission reported few complaints, although adjacent owners continued to experience conflicts. By this time, the commission's engineering books added up to almost ten thousand double pages. In all he assembled forty-eight volumes of buoy books, sixteen volumes of buoy angles, five volumes of field records, six volumes of preliminary surveys, three volumes of signal records, twenty-four volumes of observational horizontal angles, four volumes of draft descriptions of all lots, eight volumes of Rhode Island boundary-line-survey notes, and one hundred and fifty maps. The sheer size of this undertaking illustrates that the commission made planter property more orderly and rational without simplifying it (see figure 5 for an example).

Cadastral surveys remained a fitful process throughout the Progressive Era. The Connecticut legislature cut all mapping funds after

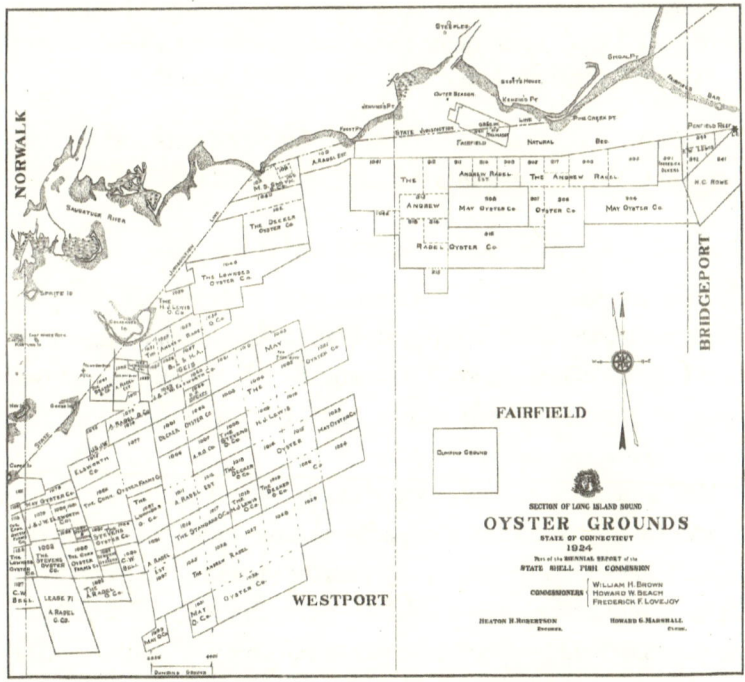

FIGURE 5. Connecticut planting lease map. The author thanks Mystic Seaport Museum for permission to publish. © Mystic Seaport Museum, G. W. Blunt Library, Mystic, CT #HFM 31.

Bogart completed his survey, apparently due to a political struggle over appointments to the commission. Although the commission lobbied for restored funding, the legislature did not fund surveys on an extensive scale again until 1920. The commission reported that boundary disputes arose constantly during this interim due to "obscure designations," "inaccurate location on the water," and the decay of shore landmarks and signal stations.[24] An 1896 *Fishing Gazette* article describes Connecticut mapping this way too. It explains that funds allocated for buoying were inadequate:

> The cry for the resetting of these buoys is constant, both from the oystermen who work the natural beds and from the owners of grounds adjacent thereto. The fact that the State does this work at all leads all parties to rely upon it, and the planters are less liable to keep their own buoys upon the natural bed boundaries, claiming, with considerable truth, that only the State buoys will be respected. Owing to the impossibility of keeping all the beds buoyed all the time, the Commission has been compelled to disregard many of the calls for the resetting of buoys and has only done what, in its judgment, the conditions most imperatively demanded.[25]

The case of Connecticut demonstrates the tenuousness and importance of the first cadastral surveys.

Small-Scale Cadastral Mapping in New York and New Jersey

Sources suggest small-scale commissions in New York and New Jersey encountered difficulties similar to Rhode Island and Connecticut state commissions. Towns and district commissions in New York and New Jersey mapped planting leases. According to the *New Jersey Courier*, a syndicate stood ready to buy all the leasing grounds in the Barnegat Bay at the onset of mapping in Ocean County.[26] The Ocean County district commissioners also claimed they needed to protect planters from "the depredations of the so-called 'free bottom' class."[27] The commission lacked adequate funds to do this. Many people told them that their task was impossible. Upon asking planters to identify the location of their oysters, the commission found "many applicants disregard the Commission's request altogether . . .

only a few comply."²⁸ Leases were small and irregular, which made them harder to locate. Faulty equipment forced the Ocean County District Commission to abandon all surveying one year. As late as 1912, the Atlantic County District Commission stated they had no funding for lease mapping and had stopped doing it altogether for two years.²⁹

Limiting Lease Mapping in Maryland

Maryland was unusual in that popular opposition limited leasing to a much greater extent than in any other state. Maryland passed one of the country's first planting laws in 1830. This so-called "one-acre law" gave riparian owners the right to plant oysters on up to one acre adjacent to their property. This law changed in 1865, when the state overhauled its oyster laws. The new "five-acre law" allowed riparian owners to plant up to five acres.³⁰ The biggest push to expand leasing came as harvests dropped in the early 1900s. Baltimore lawyer B. H. Haman championed planting-leasing legislation in the state and succeeded in passing the Haman Oyster Culture Law in 1906. The law was subject to a large public debate; at least thirty-five articles appeared on the issue in the *Baltimore Sun* between May 12, 1905 and April 11, 1906.³¹ The law allowed any Maryland citizen, rather than just riparian owners, to plant up to five acres of oysters, and it allowed them to do this in any location devoid of natural beds. Haman had to compromise to get support for the bill, and so it included provisions written by its opponents. These stipulations forced planters to use tongs and limited the period they could work on their leases to the same time as the natural-bed closed season. Ostensibly, these measures made it easier to stop illegal dredging, but these two provisions also decreased the efficiency of planting.

Caswell Grave, a Maryland fish commissioner stated that the opponents of the Haman act made sure planters would not have the rights they needed to farm oysters profitably. Tongers understood planters better than Haman.³² Grave also blamed the lack of organization and knowledge among planters. He said Maryland planters failed to properly support the act because they did not "recognize the natural division of labor which exists in oyster culture, and also failed to take into account the biological and physical conditions upon which these divisions depend."[33] As examples of this, Grave discussed how planters tried shelling under the five-acre law, but their riparian leases were usually upstream from natural beds so there was little set. Failure at shelling convinced oystermen that planting could not work. This became a widespread view. Many tongers believed that the real motivation of planters was to monopolize access to natural beds. Grave also referenced numerous cases in which planters placed too many oysters on too small an area. These oysters subsequently perished or stagnated for lack of food, which planters took to mean that cultivation on barren bottoms was impossible. As a scientist, Grave pointed out that cultivation on land was based on knowledge of what can be planted where, "but in the case of water territory, there seems to be a general feeling that its resources are unlimited."[34] He concluded that underwater conditions were harder to study and less well known in comparison to terrestrial farming.

The legislature agreed to fix the Haman act and passed the Price-Campbell act in 1912. This allowed for much larger leases: up to 100 acres in county waters and 500 acres in state waters, farther offshore. It also allowed planters to use dredges and work year-round. It reversed the measures of the Haman act that had hobbled planting. Leasing took off rapidly following the Price-Campbell act. By 1912, the state shellfish commission granted 141 leases covering 1,058.5 acres.[35] Applications for an additional 30,000 acres poured in the next year.[36] The commission issued 152 new leases covering 5,666 acres in 1913.[37] The new law drew immediate protest. Tongers demanded leases stop privatizing natural beds. The first major conflict sparked by lease mapping arose in the Patuxent River. In the summer of 1912, tongers showed the commission's engineer a natural bed in an area open for leasing. It was fifteen acres, but the Yates map overlooked it, making the commission powerless to prevent leasing this area.[38] The commission received numerous complaints like this, for which they identified several causes. First, many oystermen claimed that any place with a few shells or that once had oysters was still a natural bed, a sentiment contrary to the law. Second, new oysters were growing in some places that were absent during the initial survey. Third, most natural beds were not marked with buoys. Fourth, county authorities did not always recognize the importance of the Yates map, arguing that he was not directed by knowledgeable people. Fifth, many oystermen remained "violently opposed to oyster culture in any form."[39] By 1914 there were protests over lease applications covering 42,000 acres.[40] The commissioners bowed to tonger pressure and decided to delay leasing contested areas while also recommending that the legislature give them more discretion in granting leases. Further, they recommended charging protestors for resurvey if no beds were found, which would help limit the "indefinite" protests that "flooded" them.[41]

Opponents of leasing were also active in the legislature, and the contested acres gave them ammunition. In 1914 the legislature passed the Shepard act, again provoking public controversy.[42] It weakened the Haman and Price-Campbell acts by changing the designation of public beds so that any place oystermen found oysters in the last five years would be off-limits to planting. The testimony of any three oystermen in a circuit court was enough to establish the presence of oysters. Oystermen immediately filed into the courts and designated 54,000 acres of new natural beds. Planting leases stood at 5,666 acres in 1914 and slowly rose to about 9,000 acres in 1930. It remained roughly this size to the 1980s.[43] Maryland's Conservation Commission reflected on the Shepard act and said, "the oysterman has been his own worst enemy."[44] Tongers disagreed, arguing that limited planting was the only way to uphold tradition in Maryland.

Mapping Leases to Resolve Disputes in Virginia

Tongers accepted planting in Virginia, but the state had to overcome political obstacles to cadastral mapping. After the Civil War, northern planting investment declined and local planting increased.[45] Planters held leases through an irregular, ad hoc system.[46] Many hesitated to plant because it was easier for tongers to claim planted areas were on natural beds.[47] Despite these difficulties, over one thousand planters worked Virginia waters in 1880, and this led to property disputes among the state's numerous tongers.[48]

The Virginia legislatures passed a bill 1890 to lessen planter-tonger conflict. It required planters to have their ground surveyed prior to leasing. It also required a general survey of all natural beds. Tidewater representatives supported the bill and saw it as a workable compromise between planters and tongers. Both groups hoped the bill would settle their disputes. But Governor McKinney vetoed the bill. His major address on oysters stated that tidewater oystermen could not agree on what legislation was best and that opinions were split between planters, tongers, and dredgers.[49] He favored planting and felt that strictly enforcing the closed season would prevent the gathering of seed oysters in summer. He also felt that this shorter season would force tongers to plant, as they would have no other obligations in summer.[50] In an address at a major convention of planting advocates, he stated that "local prejudice [was] wearing out" and this would open room for "efficient legislation."[51]

A pamphlet entitled "A Defense of the Tidewater Oyster Industry" describes tidewater grievances and states that the region experienced heavy taxation and but neglect by the legislature. It describes an "oyster-industry mass meeting" in Mathews County on January 17, 1891, during which "ringing resolutions adopted demanding reform in the oyster law."[52] The mass meeting recommended defining natural beds, enforcing laws, surveying leases, allowing for fifteen-year leases, banning dredges, and creating a tax exemption for shelling. The legislature tried again, and the governor signed this bill into law in 1892. The new law balanced planter and tonger interests. It tried to end conflict between them by ordering a survey of natural beds (the Baylor survey) and by mapping planting leases.

The Virginia Board of Fisheries tried to modernize lease mapping under the new law. They reported a great deal of confusion and overlap between planters. According to one report, "The confusion caused by this is something that is hard to explain to one that has not seen the like."[53] McDonald Lee made much progress on cadastral mapping as fish commissioner from 1906 to 1912. Lee "broke up the pernicious 'permit' system" in the James River in 1906.[54] Under this system, planters would lease ground next to natural beds. They would sell written notes to tongers during the closed season stating these men were planters employees. Such tongers would illegally harvest on the natural beds and then move over to the planting leases when inspectors arrived on the scene. While judges wanted convictions for these violations, juries often sided with tongers. However, Lee was able to change public sentiment and get convictions. Even as he began to eradicate illegal practices in the James River, the same system emerged in the Rappahannock and Potomac Rivers. It remained difficult to achieve convictions there, and this cost Lee considerable time and effort. He felt that the natural-bed lines needed to be resurveyed everywhere, and he stressed that "*permanent markers should be placed when this is done*" (italics in the original).[55] Part of the difficulty stemmed from leases lacking uniformity or regular lines, which complicated accurate mapping.

The *Oysterman and Fisherman*, Virginia's main trade publication at the time, sheds light on the challenges the board of fisheries faced in mapping leases. A 1908 article claims that eight thousand men worked on planting grounds, most of them as hired hands. Planters and tongers still argued over space. Planters wanted a secure, stable seed supply and feared tongers would deplete beds because they saw oysters "much as the original settlers did" when wild game formerly abounded.[56] Two 1909 articles discuss a Chincoteague inspector. The first article says he was also a planter, which was illegal. He had assigned space designated as natural beds to planters, including areas he assigned to himself.[57] The second article, written by the inspector, refutes the first, claiming that his accuser harvested illegally. Another article claims that some planters paid for illegal seed to empty natural beds so that they might one day be opened for planting. The author worries that seed supply was not enough seed for all the planters actively working at that time.[58] Despite these difficulties, the board stated in 1913 that a "better feeling" had developed between planters and tongers. Both now had a better sense of their rights. Planting was no longer expanding, but planters leased 57,336 acres in 1913.[59] Virginia continued to slowly but successfully create accurate lease maps that settled disputes between tongers and planters.

SANITARY MAPS

Mapping Disease, Mapping Safety

Another type of map utilized scientific knowledge about the relationship between oysters and typhoid. Typhoid is caused by the bacterium *Salmonella typhi*.[60] This bacterium lives in the digestive tract and leaves the body via the stool. It is then spread by contaminated food or water. The typhoid infection causes high fever with potentially fatal complications. Sanitation maps greatly helped packers, much in the same way cadastral mapping helped planters. Neither needed to displace tongers to accomplish their objectives. No modernist version of sanitation mapping existed.

Efforts to reduce the spread of typhoid were part of larger efforts to address urban sanitation needs.[61] Typhoid rates closely tracked urban water quality in the United States. Typhoid declined in the Progressive Era as municipal water quality improved. Early sanitation efforts, however, hurt the oyster fishery. Most municipal sanitation officials believed in the dilution method of cleaning water, in which cities built sewers that dumped waste into bodies of water. They believed mixing sewage with water reduced sewage concentration to safe levels. This was the most common practice of treating sewage in 1880, and it was appealing to coastal cities.[62] It was cheap and had much scientific backing. As sanitation engineers improved municipal drinking water supplies by building underground sewer lines, cities used coastal bays more and more as sewage sinks. This led to typhoid outbreaks stemming from the consumption of contaminated oysters.

The bacteriological revolution in urban sanitation beginning in the 1880s required a new type of expert and a new form of knowledge production.[63] Sanitary scientists made disease and transmission patterns visible. Their first step was to identify the bacterium that caused typhoid, which they quickly accomplished. After this, scientists tried to increase the visibility of risk inherent in consuming oysters, which they did by establishing sanitary standards and conducting sanitary surveys. These surveys aimed to test oysters for contamination in bays and canneries. Sanitary conditions led to certification. Certification made safety visible to consumers. As the public increasingly purchased oysters from unfamiliar and distant sources, and as industrializing cities continued to release more invisible toxins, consumers needed ways to establish trust in the products they purchased. State agencies struggled against industry to make product safety visible to consumers through a certification process.[64] This was another instance of state invention to solve industrial problems in the Progressive Era.

Typhoid and Oysters

European scientists had long suspected that oysters could transmit typhoid. J. P. A. Pasquier's 1816 book *Oysters from a Medical Point of View* was the first scientific text to make this link. This text described an outbreak from oysters kept near a garrison's latrines. Occasional European accounts of outbreaks mentioned oysters, but the first investigation in a scientific paper originates from an Irish study conducted in 1880. The first U.S. investigation occurred after an outbreak in New Haven in 1886. Scientists tested the water supply and found it pure. They suspected oysters were the cause but they could not prove this.[65]

The first case to prove that oysters could carry typhoid followed an outbreak at Wesleyan University in 1894 that killed three students. Scientists at the college eliminated all other sources and traced the disease to raw oysters eaten at initiation dinners. All of the oysters came from the same dealer. The oysterman had grown them in Long Island Sound, but he had floated them near his house in a small creek about four hundred feet downstream from his sewer pipe. His wife and daughter grew ill with typhoid, and his wife died just before he sold the oysters. The *New York Times* followed this case closely, and subsequent scientific articles referred to it as the first time that anyone conclusively linked oysters and typhoid. The research methods of scientists involved simple detective work combined with microscopes and germ culture. They took samples from wells and milk supplies, cultured these, and then observed them under microscopes. As the scientists said in their articles, however, these measures were not necessary as they could reject these sources due to the pattern of contagion. Oysters were the only food all the victims ate. Once scientists focused on the oysters, they spoke to the dealer and established the obvious cause. Laboratory practices ultimately contributed little to this case.[66]

Consumers reacted to this outbreak by curtailing oyster purchases, establishing a pattern that would lower sales sporadically but steadily over the next three decades. Newspapers discussed a parallel belief that salt water killed typhoid, though it is difficult to judge how prevalent this was. This view appeared in articles periodically but declined in frequency as evidence accumulated to the contrary. At this point, recommendations also began appearing in newspapers advising consumers to cook oysters. A *New York Times* article titled "A lesson to housekeepers in the Middletown epidemic" provides an example. It addresses women primarily and stresses how hard it was to discern the origin of one's food, acknowledging, "probably only official inspection, backed by law, can protect us from impure food." The article advises women to cook oysters to kill microbes and it points out that the wife of the grower in the Wesleyan case died from typhoid too. It concludes with "it is most difficult to teach persons the great truth that there is duty beyond caring for the sick—that of protecting those who are well. In these days of enlightenment there is no excuse for this selfish ignorance."[67]

After the Wesleyan case, scientists began studying oysters from a sanitary perspective. These studies took two paths. One was a series of scientific studies in the laboratory and the field that produced knowledge on oyster bacteriology and focused on *S. typhi*. The other was a set of sanitary surveys.

As with artificial cultivation, oyster bacteriology originated in Europe. The 1880 Irish paper mentioned above inaugurated the modern bacteriology of the oyster. In 1889 V. de Giaxa studied how long *S. typhi* could live in saltwater. Since it could survive for several days, he concluded that closed oysters could transport the bacteria in the water within their shell. European scientists continued to study the problem, especially after the Wesleyan case. These early works culminated in H. T. Bulstrode's classic 1896 paper "Oysters Culture in Relation to Disease."[68]

United States scientists began studying oyster bacteriology more intensively after the Wesleyan case. Caleb Fuller's 1905 review summarizes American and European knowledge at the time.[69] Several studies demonstrated that placing oysters in a current of clean running water could displace the bacteria. This process is called depuration, and its more advanced form is widely acceptedfor cleaning oysters today. Several studies confirmed that cooking oysters did not eliminate all germs. Scientists established that *Escherichia coli* (*E. coli*) was not naturally found in oysters.[70] Scientists also found that neither *S. typhi* nor *E. coli* multiplied in oysters, although the bacteria could move into the oyster itself, and not just within the water inside the shell. *S. typhi* appeared to live about as long as *E. coli* in water. The first decade of studies established all the basic information needed to understand the link between typhoid and oysters. These studies also confirmed widely held and common-sense suspicions. In the 1910s scientists continued to study how temperature and time changed the concentration of *E. coli* in contaminated oysters and seawater. The other important topic remained, perfecting the methods used for detecting *S. typhi* in oysters.[71] Oyster bacteriology had grown into a mature field.[72]

Surveillance, Standards, and Certification
Typhoid surveys began in the 1890s and spread rapidly following the Wesleyan outbreak. These surveys are harder to trace through primary sources than property mapping. Many more agencies were

involved; there were at least four in New York City alone. Local government bodies with jurisdiction over sewage or local oyster inspectors often set standards, making these small-scale regulations difficult to unearth. Nonetheless, it is possible to recreate a general picture of what surveyors did and how this affected the development of regulations between the 1894 Wesleyan outbreak and the pivotal 1924–1925 outbreak. The latter remains America's largest typhoid outbreak caused by oysters; over one hundred people perished.

Sanitary surveys sought to discover the presence of *S. typhi* in oysters. *S. typhi* was difficult to detect, so scientists relied on *E. coli* as a surrogate. Both enter water via human waste, and the two are similar enough that if *S. typhi* is present the more common *E. coli* will be too. Scientists measured *E. coli* concentrations in water to map sewage pollution, which was a logical way of trying to gauge whether oysters might be carrying typhoid.

New York's first sanitary surveys began shortly after the Wesleyan case. The New York Fish Commission sponsored an investigation in 1895 by H. W. Conn and W. O. Atwater. Conn and Atwater recommended a ban on oysters floated near sewers. Floating was the practice of placing oysters in low salinity water near creeks. It made oysters plumper and caused them to expel sediment and kept them alive close to markets. Floating them near cities brought them in contact with sewage. The *New York Times* reported that floating caused much alarm and damaged the state's oyster industry. Following this study, the commission asked the state chief oyster inspector Joseph Mesereau to also investigate New York's floating industry. Mesereau called floating next to sewers a "reprehensible act, which I believe to be without precedent in the history of oyster culture."[73] He ordered a ban on floating oysters at Mill Creek, Staten Island, which in his opinion, was the only dangerous site in New York. The alarm caused by Conn and Atwater's study, plus the Wesleyan case, even led British dealers to cancel orders for New York's Blue Point oysters. The USFC became involved in New York too, surveying Great South Bay on Long Island, partly due to the declining sales of Blue Points.[74]

Despite the advent of surveys and floating bans, New York City unsurprisingly continued to experience some of the worst problems associated with sewage pollution. Jamaica Bay was hit the hardest. Most sewers from Brooklyn and Queens Counties drained into the shallow bay, where the barrier islands slowed circulation with the open ocean. Jamaica Bay was environmentally ill-suited to act as a sewage sink, but it was ideal for oysters. Scientists traced several serious outbreaks, including those of 1904 and 1911, back to Jamaica Bay oysters. After the 1904 case, George Soper, who was a sanitary engineer from the State Board of Health, investigated. He attributed twenty known cases to oysters from Rockaway, on Jamaica Bay. He estimated that these oysters may have caused hundreds, perhaps thousands, of typhoid cases. The *New York Times* quoted Soper saying, "it is only a matter of time before the waters of Jamaica Bay are excluded either the sewage or the edible shellfish."[75] The city passed a law in 1908 specifying that oysters could only be sold from locations certified as sanitary.[76]

Soper used small floating devices to study tides. Many believed that tides flushed the bays and river around the New York City clean each day, but Soper demonstrated otherwise. Soper believed oysters caused around fifteen percent of the city's typhoid cases.[77] Not everyone agreed. The efficacy of using the ocean to dilute sewage remained a subject for scientific debate. Walter Bensel, who also published on oyster sanitation, told the *New York Times* that tides in the Jamaica Bay washed away germs. A 1911 outbreak highlighted the growing dangers from Jamaica Bay oysters: After a fireman's dinner, seventeen people fell ill and one of died from eating raw Jamaica Bay oysters.[78]

Other states also began conducting surveys and passing sanitary oyster regulations. The Connecticut State Board of Health placed restrictions on the practice of floating in 1896.[79] New Jersey banned oysters from Atlantic City after a 1902 typhoid outbreak.[80] Atlantic City's increasing hotel development had rendered the water dangerously unhealthy. In his review of the field, Fuller commented that most of the more prominent growing and fattening areas in the United States and elsewhere had been examined in sanitary surveys by 1905.[81]

Fuller was a leader in the field, and his 1905 report provides the most comprehensive documentation of an early sanitation survey. For his PhD thesis at Brown, he surveyed sanitary conditions in Narragansett Bay. This survey served as a guide for many later studies. There was obvious sewage pollution in Narragansett Bay. Unfortunately, this was also Rhode Island's largest planting area. Unsurprisingly, the results of Fuller's surveys indicated that the Bay was seriously polluted with sewage. He produced a map that showed a general decrease in sewage concentrations as one receded from untreated sewage outfalls and associated urban areas. The state shellfish commission used his work to create three zones in Narragansett Bay. Oystermen could not grow or harvest oysters at all in the first zone. They could do both in the second, but their oysters had to pass an inspection. This second zone created the first U.S. system of oyster sanitary certification. The third zone had no restrictions. Surveying became more complicated when scientists discovered that oysters had much less sewage in them in the winter when they closed up, raising questions about when one could accurately sample. Of the state oyster commissions, Rhode Island's was the most involved in sanitation and published its first "sanitary report" in 1906.[82] They began issuing sanitary certificates in 1911.[83]

Problems of the Packing Industry: Self-Regulation and Consumer Confidence

Fear of contaminated oysters threatened the entire industry. Oystermen were well aware of this, and oyster packers and planters organized to shape public opinion. New York oyster packers and planters responded to public fears in 1897 by hiring their own scientist from the Carnegie Institute to test Blue Point oysters. He found them to be healthy and stated that seawater would kill any typhoid germs that might come into the bay. These planter-packers believed that rivals had started rumors about their product.[84] This example shows the two related problems oystermen faced: they needed outside scientists to help them establish the safety of their product to consumers, and they required unanimous cooperation because it took only one person to cause a problem.

In 1908 several prominent planters formed the Oyster Growers and Dealers Association (OGDA) to combat public fears associated with the consumption of their product. The bank panic of 1907 had hurt planting businesses too. Henry Rowe was the chief organizer. The OGDA held its first meeting in New York City in 1909, a year after the National Association of Shellfish Commissioners' meeting. The two organizations both had New York headquarters, and members of each attended the other's meetings. The OGDA's chief concern was "to educate the public about the wholesomeness of oysters."[85] Speeches at the first meetings depicted their disagreement with scientists on this issue. Their first president Azel Merrill said, "there seems to be an impassable gulf between scientific conclusions and the practical knowledge of the planter."[86] Despite this, they invited scientists such as H. F. Moore and Julius Nelson to speak. The OGDA also expressed the concern that competitors in the food packing business were spreading rumors exaggerating the safety risks of their product. The OGDA meetings drew from between one hundred and up to over three hundred people. Attendance dropped during World War I but then surged in 1925. A 1924–1925 typhoid outbreak, attributed to Raritan Bay oysters, killed one hundred and fifty people. Oyster sales plummeted. Baltimore dealers declared that five thousand people were out of work in the city due to cannery closures.[87] In 1927 the OGDA worked with the United States Public Health Service to create uniform standards for shucking, packing, and shipping oysters.

Packers also took steps to improve sanitary practices within their packing houses. Rhode Island planters led this effort. They formed the state Oyster Growers Association in 1908. This group complained to the state shellfish commission about pollution at a meeting in March 1910. They also expressed to the commission that they wanted the state to regulate packing houses. The commission was already using standards and certification on the oyster beds, and the planters association wanted this same process extended to their packing businesses. To this end, the association proposed a law to regulate their own packing house conditions. The commission reported they had toured packing houses twice during this general period and they found the sanitary conditions much improved. Almost all had installed steam-based or boiling sterilization systems. The association had also devised rules for opening oysters, and they had posted these in all packing houses. The state passed the packing house law in 1911. It stated that packing houses had to be well ventilated and cleaned every day. Shuckers had to open oysters in "proper containers," not on benches. They had to sterilize all utensils, wear gloves and aprons, leave work when they were sick, and refrain from spitting. The law set up an inspection system. The commission reported that all thirty-three houses obtained permits, and inspectors received no objections or complaints. A leading sanitation scientist described the packers' efforts: "They have cooperated nobly in the matter and have helped to bring about a complete revolution in their business, which has in many cases involved changes in methods which were as old as the industry itself."[88] This case illustrates how the association encouraged the state commission to translate their system into law. They wanted the state to help with enforcement to ensure total compliance. State certification also boosted consumer confidence.

BARREN-BOTTOM MAPS: SOUTHERN MAPS TO EXPAND PLANTING

In states south of Virginia, a different type of survey expanded planting. These surveys mapped environmental conditions on barren bottoms, or places without oysters, to highlight the best locations for initiating oyster aquaculture. The most important condition they mapped was bottom sediment. Oyster larvae cannot survive if they land on thick sediment. Muddy bottoms render planting pointless. These surveys also showed natural beds so planters could assess spat supply. The goal was to stimulate the planting industry and guide it in areas where it was in its infancy. The USFC conducted all barren-bottom surveys, sometimes working with state agencies, which fit with the USFC's goal of expanding economic development.

Francis Winslow wrote a number of letters about this type of survey. In a letter to Spencer Baird he explains that when he was in New Haven, Connecticut, he noticed the widespread impression among oystermen that the whole of Long Island Sound would be taken up for oyster farms. In Winslow's opinion, many people were taking up areas unsuitable for cultivation and were bound to lose money:

> No one along the Connecticut shore appears to realize that the food supply is one of the most important things to be considered; the general impression is that there is food enough for all the oysters that can be put in the water. I feel sure that the Connecticut people make a great mistake and this feeling is the cause for my calling your attention to the matter. It does not appear to me to be a difficult matter to investigate the character of the waters of the Sound . . . and ascertain the comparative richness of various localities.[89]

His ideal for this type of survey was to "indicate approximately the limits of oyster culture."[90] Winslow never conducted this work in Connecticut. He discussed doing so again in North Carolina so that he could "open new fields to the oyster growers, especially those of the Chesapeake Bay."[91] Baird instructed Winslow to "procure information desired as to location and extent of the oyster beds" in North Carolina in 1883.[92] Winslow completed a map of North Carolina natural beds and planting lots in 1887, but he never managed to map environmental conditions.[93]

The USFC's first true barren-bottom surveys began soon after in Georgia (1889-1890) and South Carolina (1890-1891).[94] Following a hiatus, Franklin Swift mapped bottom conditions in Saint Vincent Sound and Saint George Sound in Florida (1896).[95] Caswell Grave then mapped barren areas in North Carolina in 1899-1900.[96] Moore began working in Louisiana at this time.[97] He strengthened barren-bottom-survey methodology in an effort to create a standard model, employing techniques similar to those he developed in the James River. Moore began surveying southern states regularly in 1910. Moore failed to expand planting in the James River, but he found more fertile ground to the south. His work in Louisiana helped establish one be of the largest planting industries in the United States.[98]

CONCLUSION: VISIBILITY AND PROGRESSIVE REFORM

Progressive Era reform depended on making things visible. Law enforcement agencies used licenses and registration to see residency, commissioners collected all manner of data to present legislatures with overviews and advice, scientists delved into oyster biology to make the bivalve's inner workings known, and cartographers mapped property to end disputes. Maps symbolized this process. Dedicated public servants like Bogart and Fuller labored away creating pictures that never existed before. This chapter dwells at length on the slow progress of this fitful process because it was so fundamental. Bogart's minutely detailed sixty-four-foot map and Fuller's single-page sanitation chart are landmarks. Environmental reform requires visibility, which is precisely what those who oppose it fight against. The history of lead paint, to take but one prominent example, shows how powerful companies distorted science to silence critics.[99] They obscured an accurate picture of their product's harm.

Making things visible in marine space presented a special challenge. The bay surface was featureless and hard to mark. Stakes worked in shallow water, but storms knocked them over. Buoys could mark deeper water, but these too were impermanent. Water also lacked landmarks, so surveyors had to use ones constructed on land. The lack of permanent markings on the water's surface made it a difficult medium for property mapping, which in turn made state cadastral mapping laborious.

The detail seen in the resulting maps shows that cartographers did not simplify planter property rights in the process of making them more legible to a central authority. Property mapping bureaucratized traditional norms and practices. In Rhode Island, for example, the legislature ordered surveyors to protect tonger property in the "free fishery" and made generous allotments for them. Mapping helped expand planter's property by making investment less risky, and it kept it off public beds. Planter rights were a long-held norm in this fishery. Planters were capitalists and local people. Property maps made their rights more static and abstract. Connecticut's maps were an accurate rendering of property. State maps differed from the system that preceded them because they were more rational, orderly, and rigid. Most importantly, they made property visible to a central authority and fit it into a legal framework. These maps rationalized planter rights without simplifying them.

Sanitary maps made health risks visible. Packing house sanitation rules did the same thing. They solved the collective action problem of packers. Even one noncompliant packer could ruin everyone's reputation and business. Rhode Island packers solved this problem themselves, but this would have been much harder without state intervention. State knowledge production and police power assisted packers, and evidence from Rhode Island and the OGDA bears this out. Leadership among the packers and their associations was important to this process, as were crises that stimulated action. But packers desired state intervention for another reason: the state could employ scientists to certify the health of the product. This made safety visible to consumers. Sanitation scientists were part of a larger, ongoing effort to promote product certification for consumer protection. Industries that profited from pollution sought to limit or co-opt state certification, but sewage hurt packers. Their industry's interests aligned with public health. In cases like this, industries sought out certification. Patrick Joyce calls this state role the "omnipticon," or knowledge production that makes a subject visible to everyone, as opposed to making it visible for state surveillance only.[100] This chapter and the preceding one highlight the central role of visibility and mapping in progressive reform.

CONCLUSION

THE CHALLENGE OF COMPLEXITY

The challenge of complexity is alive and well in fisheries management. A vignette from Maine illustrates this point. At a public hearing, a couple with coastal property ask an oyster farmer questions about whether or not they will be able to sail around his proposed farm in Damariscotta Bay. The farmer shows them a nautical chart indicating his farm's intended location. A California resident who spends a few weeks here each summer asks whether noise from the farm will interfere with her rural reverie. The aquaculture farmer compares his equipment's volume to a lawn mower. Scenes like this are repeated all along Maine's coast each year as the aquaculture industry slowly grows. Public hearings for Maine's aquaculture lease can be bureaucratic, tedious, and contentious.

The mundane nature of the hearings makes it easy to miss what is actually happening. Landowners and aquaculture farmers participate in a complex social system. Many coastal landowners move here for the rugged coastline's scenic beauty. They suddenly find their picturesque, expensive view looks out on a shellfish farm. Aquaculture farmers, on the other hand, see a promising opportunity for local employment in sustainable food production. Reconciling these conflicting priorities is challenging, just as it is all across scenic areas where "amenity migrants" move into rural America. The public hearings of Maine's Department of Marine Resources serve as a place where landowners and farmers meet, often for the first time, to reconcile these priorities for marine space. They are generally able to do so. Farmers often agree to place conditions on their lease permits stipulating specific steps they will take to accommodate landowners' wishes. The result is a bottom-up process that allows the industry to adapt, on a farm-by-farm basis, to landowner perceptions. Any top-down regulation would be uniform and far less responsive. The hearings also bring the two sides together for face-to-face discussion, which builds trust, at least ideally. The priorities, traditions, and values of the two groups are multifaceted. Reconciling difference requires the flexibility of a bottom-up process.

Ninteenth-century oystermen also developed complex bottom-up solutions that reconciled their industry's conflicting priorities. Tongers and planters had different interests. Their management systems included diverse practices that varied with local conditions. They embodied the complex political compromises of local moral economies. There was a great deal of conflict and competition among oystermen, and conservation measures sought to preserve compromises over equity and access, while maximizing independence. Oystermen created one of the great early conservation achievements in U.S. history.

Industrialization disrupted this system. Packing houses in northern cities grew and expanded to Maryland, stressing local-scale conservation. Dredge boats multiplied, railroads expanded markets, urban populations grew, and demand rose. Oysters faced classic Progressive Era pressures, and states responded by founding new agencies. These agencies each faced a choice regarding oystermen's conservation system: should they take steps to shore up traditional conservation or should they replace it altogether? Oyster modernists simplified oystermen's complex goals down to maximizing productivity, replaced their common property rights with private leases, and forsook broader scientific goals for hatchery science. This book takes sides and critiques the modernists, but it is worth stepping back and acknowledging what they helped build. Both populists and modernists worked to create new institutions. Together, they built agencies that are indispensable to modern conservation. Oyster modernists deserve credit too.

The history of U.S. fisheries is replete with similar simplifications. The choice of fisheries managers to enshrine maximum sustainable yield as a management goal is the most obvious example. Carmel Finley argues that it gave fisheries managers "a false sense of security."[1] Scholars and fishermen have criticized this highly simplified, single-species management goal extensively.[2] It assumes fish stocks are homogenous, ignores geographically discreet substocks, and fails to calculate how removing fish affects the other species with which they interact.[3] Another similar simplification is top-down, broad-scale management that ignores the heterogeneity of local conditions.[4] Local comanaged institutions have emerged as a more complex process where fishermen are involved in setting goals and designing rules tailored to local places.[5] Ecosystem-based management is gaining a great deal of attention as a replacement for single-species management, and it provides an explicit response to past management's over-simplification.[6] The managers of fisheries are increasingly using fishermen's knowledge too. The primary fishery survey of scientists in the U.S. North Atlantic uses a random sampling method that provides a valuable standardized look at fish populations, and now has a longtime series of data, but it misses many important locations. The National Marine Fisheries Service has turned to fishermen's knowledge to supplement its survey.[7]

The more important lesson for fisheries is the larger context this book provides. The dilemma of progressives can help us see similarities between fisheries management and many other issues. Fire managers and trawl survey designers face the same pressures to deal with complex social-ecological systems. This book compares a wide range of simplifying solutions: Nancy Langston's forest fire eradication, Joseph Taylor's salmon hatcheries, Arthur McEvoy's fisheries privatization, and Donald Worster's water management. Historical conditions and cultural perceptions led environmental managers to simplify social-ecological systems in each of these cases. The forces pushing simplification in these cases, and in the present book, ranged from the scale of problems, the accelerating pace of change, the difficulty of acquiring knowledge, and colonial or technocratic views. The conviction driving this book is that environmental history can help people understand sustainability issues today by revealing larger patterns. We are wrestling with an "age of accelerations," as globalization, climate change, and the computer revolution reshape our lives.[8] Comparative histories can help us evaluate solutions for redirecting our turbulent, rapidly changing world. James Scott proposes a "litmus test" for an institution or enterprise whose success "depends on engaging the enthusiastic participation of its people."[9] He asks us to assess whether or not institutions incorporate the evolving, locally specific knowledge of the people engaged in them. At a minimum, these histories serve as a cautionary tale about the siren song of certainty, control, and simplification.

Today, oysters have captured the public's imagination. Elementary school students plant oyster reefs, and coastal hobby farmers set out oyster cages. Chefs like Barton Seaver promote local oysters as "fresh catch" sustainable seafood.[10] Oyster aquaculture brings jobs to economically depressed coastal communities. The role of oysters in ecological restoration also makes them an inspiring symbol. Chesapeake Bay's water quality improvements have enabled the oyster industry to expand once again, albeit slowly, and these commercial oyster farms in turn restore a crucial part of the bay's ecosystem.[11] Oyster aquaculture is a cornerstone for building a more sustainable relationship with our seafood. Maybe William Brooks was right about Chesapeake Bay after all. His millennial visions of oysters nurturing a great cradle of civilization may turn out to be prescient in a way we are only beginning to glimpse.

NOTES

INTRODUCTION: INSHORE FISHERIES, AQUACULTURE, AND COMPLEXITY IN ENVIRONMENTAL HISTORY

1. George Brown Goode, *The Fisheries and Fishery Industries of the United States, Section II: A Geographical Review of the Fisheries Industries and Fishing Communities for the Year 1880* (Washington, D.C.: Government Printing Office, 1882).
2. Clyde MacKenzie, "History of Oystering in the United States and Canada, Featuring Eight Great Oyster Estuaries," *Marine Fisheries Review* 58, no. 4 (1996): 1–78.
3. Ernest Ingersoll, *The Oyster-Industry* (Washington, D.C.: Government Printing Office, 1881).
4. Colin E. Nash, *The History of Aquaculture* (New York: Wiley-Blackwell, 2011).
5. Samuel P. Hays, *Conservation and the Gospel of Efficiency: The Progressive Conservation Movement, 1890–1920* (Pittsburgh: University of Pittsburgh Press, 1959).
6. John Chambers, *The Tyranny of Change: America in the Progressive Era, 1890–1920* (New York: St. Martin's Press, 1992); Robert H. Wiebe, *The Search for Order, 1877–1920* (Westport: Greenwood Press, 1967).
7. Richard W. Judd, *Common Lands, Common People: The Origins of Conservation in Northern New England* (Cambridge: Harvard University Press, 1997); Karl Jacoby, *Crimes against Nature: Squatters, Poachers, Thieves,*

and the Hidden History of American Conservation (Berkeley: University of California Press, 2001).

8. Nancy Langston, *Forest Dreams, Forest Nightmares: The Paradox of Old Growth in the Inland West* (Seattle: University of Washington Press, 1995).
9. Tony Davis, "The West's Hottest Question: How to Burn What's Bound to Burn," *High Country News*, June 5, 2000.
10. James C. Scott, *Seeing Like a State: How Certain Schemes to Improve the Human Condition Have Failed* (New Haven: Yale University Press, 1998).
11. Roderick Frazier Nash, *Wilderness and the American Mind* (New Haven: Yale University Press, 1967).
12. Hays, *Conservation and the Gospel of Efficiency*.
13. Scott, *Seeing Like a State*.
14. For an excellent example of this process in a nonenvironmental context, see Judith Merkle's study of Fredrick Taylor's "Scientific Management" movement, *Management and Ideology: The Legacy of the International Scientific Movement* (Los Angeles: University of California Press, 1980).
15. David B. Danbom, "The Agricultural Experiment Station and Professionalism: Scientists' Goals for Agriculture, 1887–1910," *Agricultural History* 60, no. 2 (1986): 246–55; David E. Hamilton, "Building the Associative State: The Department of Agriculture and American State Building," *Agricultural History* 64, no. 2 (1990): 207–18; Charles E. Rosenberg, "Science, Technology, and Economic Growth: The Case of the Agricultural Experiment Station Scientists, 1875–1914," *Agricultural History* 45, no. 1 (1971): 1–20.
16. Brian Balogh, "Reorganizing the Organizational Synthesis: Federal-Professional Relations in Modern America," *Studies in American Political Development* 5, no. 1 (1991): 119–72.
17. Thomas Princen, *The Logic of Sufficiency* (Cambridge: MIT Press, 2005).
18. Ibid., 64.
19. Ibid., 110.
20. Donald Worster, *Rivers of Empire: Water, Aridity, and the Growth of the American West* (New York: Oxford University Press, 1985), 5.
21. Karl A. Wittfogel, *Oriental Despotism: A Comparative Study of Total Power* (New Haven: Yale University Press, 1957).
22. Max Horkheimer and Theodor W. Adorno, *Dialectic of Enlightenment* (New York: Compendium Books, 1944).
23. Max Weber, *Economy and Society: An Outline of Interpretive Sociology* (Berkeley: University of California Press, 1977); Rogers Brubaker, *The Limits of Rationality: An Essay on the Social and Moral Thought of Max Weber* (London: George Allen & Unwin, 1984); Jürgen Habermas, *The Theory of Communicative Action, Volume I and II* (Boston: Beacon Press, 1984).

24. Michael Adas, *Machines as the Measure of Men: Science, Technology, and Ideologies of Western Dominance* (Ithaca: Cornell University Press, 1989).
25. Henry Nash Smith, *Virgin Land: The American West as Symbol and Myth* (Cambridge: Harvard University Press, 1970).
26. Raymond B. Craib, *Cartographic Mexico: A History of State Fixations and Fugitive Landscapes* (Durham: Duke University Press, 2004), 2.
27. Ibid., 12.
28. Ibid., 96.
29. Matthew H. Edney, *Mapping an Empire: The Geographical Construction of British India, 1765-1843* (Chicago: University of Chicago Press, 1997), 3.
30. Ibid., 340.
31. Scott Kirsch, "John Wesley Powell and the Mapping of the Colorado Plateau, 1869-1879: Survey Science, Geographical Solutions, and the Economy of Environmental Values," *Annals of the Association of American Geographers* 92, no. 3 (2002): 548-72.
32. Henri Lefebvre, *The Production of Space* (Oxford: Blackwell, 1974); David Harvey, *The Condition of Postmodernity: An Enquiry into the Origins of Cultural Change* (New York: Blackwell, 1991).
33. Thomas K. Rudel, *Defensive Environmentalists and the Dynamics of Environmental Reform* (Cambridge: Cambridge University Press, 2013).
34. W. Jeffrey Bolster, *The Mortal Sea: Fishing the Atlantic in the Age of Sail* (Cambridge: Harvard University Press, 2012).
35. Garrett Hardin, "The Tragedy of the Commons," *Science* 162, no. 3859 (1968): 1243-48.
36. Margaret Beattie Bogue, *Fishing the Great Lakes: An Environmental History, 1783-1933* (Madison: University of Wisconsin Press, 2000); Dean Bavington, *Managed Annihilation: An Unnatural History of the Newfoundland Cod Collapse* (Vancouver: University of British Columbia Press, 2010); Vera Schwach, "The Sea Around Norway: Science, Resource Management, and Environmental Concerns, 1860-1970," *Environmental History* 18, no. 1 (2013): 101-10; James R. McGoodwin, *Crisis in the World's Fisheries: People, Problems, and Policies* (Palo Alto: Stanford University Press, 1995); Callum Roberts, *An Unnatural History of the Sea* (Washington, D.C.: Island Press, 2008); Jeremy B. C. Jackson, *Shifting Baselines: The Past and Future of Ocean Fisheries* (Washington, D.C.: Island Press, 2011).
37. David F. Arnold, *The Fishermen's Frontier: People and Salmon in Southeast Alaska* (Seattle: University of Washington Press, 2008).
38. Connie Y. Chiang, *Shaping the Shoreline: Fisheries and Tourism on the Monterey Coast* (Seattle: University of Washington Press, 2008).
39. Brian J. Payne, *Fishing a Borderless Sea: Environmental Territorialism in the North Atlantic, 1818-1910* (East Lansing: Michigan State University Press, 2010).

40. See, for example, Theodore C. Bestor, *Tsujiki: The Fish Market at the Center of the World* (Berkeley: University of California Press, 2004).
41. James M. Acheson, *The Lobster Gangs of Maine* (Portland: University of New England Press, 1988).
42. Bonnie J. McCay and James M. Acheson, eds. *The Question of the Commons: The Culture and Ecology of Communal Resources* (Tucson: University of Arizona Press, 1987); Elinor Ostrom et al., eds. *The Drama of the Commons* (Washington, D.C.: National Research Council, 2002).
43. Payne, *Fishing a Borderless Sea*, xxiv.
44. Bonnie J. McCay, *Oyster Wars and the Public Trust: Property, Law, and Ecology in New Jersey History* (Tucson: University of Arizona Press, 1998).
45. Arthur F. McEvoy, *The Fishermen's Problem: Ecology and Law in the California Fisheries, 1850–1980* (Cambridge: Cambridge University Press, 1986).
46. Lawrence J. Taylor, *Dutchmen on the Bay: The Ethnohistory of a Contractual Community* (Philadelphia: University of Pennsylvania Press, 1985).
47. Christine Keiner, *The Oyster Question: Scientists, Watermen, and the Maryland Chesapeake Bay since 1880* (Athens: University of Georgia Press, 2009).
48. Mark Kurlansky, *The Big Oyster: History on the Half Shell* (New York: Random House, 2007); John R. Wennersten, *The Oyster Wars of Chesapeake Bay* (Centreville: Tidewater Publishers, 1981).
49. Joseph E. Taylor III, *Making Salmon: An Environmental History of the Northwest Fisheries Crisis* (Seattle: University of Washington Press, 1999).
50. Jerry C. Towle, "Authored Ecosystems: Livingston Stone and the Transformation of California Fisheries," *Environmental History* 5, no. 1 (2000): 54–74.
51. Darin Kinsey, "'Seeding the Waters as the Earth': The Epicenter and Peripheries of a Western Aquaculture Revolution," *Environmental History* 11, no. 3 (2006): 527–66.
52. Food and Agricultural Organization of the United Nations (FAO), *The State of the World Fisheries and Aquaculture: Contributing to Food Security and Nutrition for All* (Rome: United Nations, 2016).
53. Daniel Pauly et al., "Fishing down Marine Food Webs," *Science* 279, no. 5352 (1998): 860–63.
54. FAO, *State of the World Fisheries*.
55. Md Saidul Islam, *Confronting the Blue Revolution: Industrial Aquaculture and Sustainability in the Global South* (Toronto: University of Toronto Press, 2014).
56. Barry A. Costa-Pierce, ed., *Ecological Aquaculture: The Evolution of the Blue Revolution* (New York: Wiley-Blackwell, 2008).

CHAPTER 1: OYSTER MANAGEMENT BEFORE 1880

1. George Brown Goode, *The Fisheries and Fishery Industries of the United States, Section II: A Geographical Review of the Fisheries Industries and Fishing Communities for the Year 1880* (Washington, D.C.: Government Printing Office, 1882).
2. Clyde MacKenzie, "History of Oystering in the United States and Canada, Featuring Eight Great Oyster Estuaries," *Marine Fisheries Review* 58, no. 4 (1996): 1–78; V. S. Kennedy and L. L. Breisch, "Sixteen Decades of Political Management of the Oyster Fishery in Maryland's Chesapeake Bay," *Journal of Environmental Management* 16, no. 2 (1983): 153–71; National Research Council, *Nonnative Oysters in the Chesapeake Bay* (Washington, D.C.: National Academies Press, 2004).
3. Richard W. Judd, *Common Lands, Common People: The Origins of Conservation in Northern New England* (Cambridge: Harvard University Press, 1997); Bonnie J. McCay, *Oyster Wars and the Public Trust: Property, Law, and Ecology in New Jersey History* (Tucson: University of Arizona Press, 1998).
4. See for example Bonnie J. McCay and James M. Acheson, eds. *The Question of the Commons: The Culture and Ecology of Communal Resources* (Tucson: University of Arizona Press, 1987).
5. Bonnie J. McCay, "Sea Tenure and the Culture of the Commoners," in *A Sea of Small Boats*, ed. John Cordell (Cambridge: Cultural Survival, 1989).
6. Ernest Ingersoll, *The History and Present Condition of the Oyster Industry* (Washington, D.C.: Government Printing Office, 1882), 11–16.
7. Ibid., 21–22.
8. Michael A. Rice, *A Brief History of Aquaculture in Rhode Island* (Wakefield: Coastal Resources Management Council, 2006), 24.
9. McCay, *Oyster Wars*, 30.
10. Ingersoll, *Condition of the Oyster Industry*, 112. Brooklyn Daily Eagle, November 9, 1883; Mark Kurlansky, *The Big Oyster: History on the Half Shell* (New York: Random House, 2007).
11. Petition to the Virginia Legislature from citizens of Gloucester County, 1850.
12. Petition to the Virginia Legislature from citizens of Lancaster County, 1846.
13. Petition to the Virginia Legislature from citizens of Gloucester County, 1848.
14. Petition to the Virginia Legislature from citizens of Accomack County, 1818.
15. Petition to the Virginia Legislature from citizens of Northampton County, 1831.

16. Petition to the Virginia Legislature from the citizens of Gloucester County, 1845.
17. Petition to the Virginia Legislature from citizens of Lancaster County, 1832; Petition to the Virginia Legislature from citizens of Accomack County, 1852.
18. Petition to the Virginia Legislature from citizens of Isle of Wight County, 1851.
19. Petition to the Virginia Legislature from citizens of Nansemond County, 1849.
20. Petition to the Virginia Legislature from citizens of Northampton County, 1831.
21. Petition to the Virginia Legislature from citizens of Gloucester County, 1830.
22. Ingersoll, *Condition of the Oyster Industry*.
23. Petition to the Virginia Legislature from citizens of Essex County, 1847.
24. Petition to the Virginia Legislature from citizens of Northampton County, 1831.
25. Bonnie J. McCay, "The Culture of the Commoners: Historical Observations on Old World and East Coast U.S. Fisheries," in *Question of the Commons*, edited by McCay and Acheson.
26. *Charter of Rhode Island and Providence Plantations* (July 15, 1663), accessed April 2, 2017, from The Avalon Project at Yale Law School at http://avalon.law.yale.edu/17th_century/ri04.asp.
27. Ibid., 36–87.
28. Ibid., 46–87.
29. Ibid., 61. John M. Kochkiss, *Oystering from New York to Boston* (Middletown: Wesleyan University Press, 1974).
30. Ingersoll, *Condition of the Oyster Industry*, 61; P. de Broca, "On the Oyster Industry of the United States," *Report of the Commissioner of the United States Fish Commission* (Washington, D.C.: Government Printing Office, 1876 [1863]).
31. Ingersoll, *Condition of the Oyster Industry*, 61–67; Kochkiss, *Oystering from New York to Boston*, 15–24.
32. Ingersoll, *Condition of the Oyster Industry*, 63–70; Kochkiss, *Oystering from New York to Boston*, 15–24.
33. Ingersoll, *Condition of the Oyster Industry*, 80–81; Kochkiss, *Oystering from New York to Boston*, 132–33.
34. Ingersoll, *Condition of the Oyster Industry*, 86.
35. Eugene G. Blackford, "Report of the Work in an Oyster Investigation with the Steamer Lookout," in *Report of the Commissioner of the United States Fish Commission* (Washington, D.C.: Government Printing Office, 1885): 27–30.

36. New York City merchants shipped these oysters to Europe after 1870. Blue Points were the most popular variety in Europe, and packers placed these coveted oysters tightly and deep-side down to preserve their liquor. Shippers followed elaborate rules to protect live oysters in passage, including banning loud noises on board. Liverpool was the main destination for New York oysters. European inspectors tasted oysters at the dock to ensure they were actually the brand shippers claimed.
37. Ingersoll, *Condition of the Oyster Industry*, 98–107.
38. Ibid., 144–53.
39. Ingersoll, *Condition of the Oyster Industry*, 88–120; Blackford, "Oyster Investigation with the Steamer Lookout," 28.
40. McCay, *Oyster Wars and the Public Trust*, 105–6.
41. *New Jersey Courier*, April 3, 1873.
42. Ibid., 134–43; McCay, *Oyster Wars*.
43. Lawrence J. Taylor, *Dutchmen on the Bay: An Ethnohistory of a Contractual Community* (Philadelphia: University of Pennsylvania Press, 1985).
44. Ingersoll, *Condition of the Oyster Industry*, 145–53; Mary Emily Miller, *The Delaware Oyster Industry, Past and Present* (PhD diss., Boston University, 1962).
45. Ingersoll, *Condition of the Oyster Industry*, 66; John R. Wennersten, *The Oyster Wars of Chesapeake Bay* (Washington, D.C.: Eastern Branch Press, 13–16).
46. James Paxton, *Speech of James G. Paxton, esq., of Rockbridge, relative to the oyster fundum of Virginia* (Richmond: Ritchie and Dunnavant, 1858).
47. *Baltimore Sun*, October 27, 1853, 4.
48. *Baltimore Sun*, January 25, 1853, 4.
49. *Baltimore Sun*, December 24, 1859, 4, and December 26, 1859, 1.
50. In Virginia there was a provision allowing the sale of oysters to out of state vessels under certain sizes. The idea behind this was to allow the sale of of seed oysters to northern planters, without allowing dredging. Dredging required larger boats, so the size prohibition intended to allow the profitable trade many communities depended on while limiting destructive dredging. Dredging cut out tongers, so Virginians received no money for their oysters when northerners dredged them.
51. There was also an attempt to monopolize the oyster beds at this time. In 1860 a small group of Maryland legislators passed a little-noticed law granting six hundred thousand acres to a few individuals. Oystermen discovered their plan and had the law repealed, afterward calling a convention to fight monopolies.
52. *Baltimore Sun*, January 21, 1868.
53. *Baltimore Sun*, January 29, 1869.
54. Ingersoll, *Condition of the Oyster Industry*, 156–65.

55. Ingersoll, *Condition of the Oyster Industry*, 165–73; Wennersten, *Oyster Wars of Chesapeake Bay*.
56. Ibid., 156–73; Wennersten, *Oyster Wars of Chesapeake Bay*.
57. Ingersoll, *Condition of the Oyster Industry*, 165–73.
58. Wennersten, *Oyster Wars of Chesapeake Bay*, 18–28.
59. Goode, *Fisheries and Fishery Industries*.
60. Ibid., 188–204. Matthew Morse Booker, "Oyster Growers and Oyster Pirates in San Francisco Bay," *Pacific Historical Review* 75, no. 1 (2006): 63–88.
61. Brian Payne, "Local Economic Stewards: The Historiography of the Fishermen's Role in Resource Conservation," *Environmental History* 18, no. 1 (2013): 29–43.
62. Joyce Appleby, "Commercial Farming and the 'Agrarian Myth' in the Early Republic," *Journal of American History* 68, no. 4 (1982): 833–49.

CHAPTER 2: OYSTER LAW ENFORCEMENT

1. Karl Jacoby, *Crimes against Nature: Squatters, Poachers, Theives and the Hidden History of American Conservation* (Berkeley: University of California Press, 2001).
2. *Baltimore Sun*, November 14 and 16, 1868.
3. *Baltimore Sun*, June 11 and October 13, 1870.
4. *Baltimore Sun*, September 14, 1874.
5. *Baltimore Sun*, October 16, 187; Anonymous, *Correspondence of the Governor of Virginia with the Governor of Maryland and the Authorities of Accomac County, Va.* (Richmond: R. F. Walker, 1874).
6. Ibid.
7. *Baltimore Sun*, March 1, 3, and 14, 1883.
8. *Baltimore Sun*, March 1, 1883.
9. Virginia State Board of Fisheries, *Report of the State Board of Fisheries* (Richmond, 1907), 3.
10. Virginia State Board of Fisheries, *Report* (Richmond, 1906), 1–7.
11. Ibid., 20.
12. Hunter Davidson, *Report of the Oyster Resources of Maryland to the General Assembly* (Annapolis: W. Thompson, 1870).
13. Correspondences of Hunter Davidson, in Board of Commissioners of the State Oyster Police Force, Maryland State Papers, Scharf Collection, Maryland State Archive S1005 (1868–1880).
14. Davidson, *Report of the Oyster Resources*, 3.
15. Ibid., 3.
16. Ibid., 4.
17. Ibid., 4.

18. Ibid., 11.
19. Board of Commissioners of the State Oyster Police Force, Maryland State Papers, Scharf Collection, Maryland State Archive S1005 (1868–1880).
20. John Wennersten, *The Oyster Wars of Chesapeake Bay* (Washington, D.C.: Eastern Branch Press).
21. The person leading the grand jury was Judge William Goldsborough, who wrote an important definition of natural beds for oyster property mapping in 1882 (see chapter 5). Newspapers show he opposed Timmons.
22. *Baltimore Sun*, April 10 and 28, 1873.
23. *Baltimore Sun*, May 12, 1873.
24. Board of Commissioners of the State Oyster Police Force, Maryland State Papers, Scharf Collection, Maryland State Archive S1005 (1868–1880).
25. Starfish were a highly destructive oyster predator in northern waters. John K. Cowen, *The Maryland Oyster and His Political Enemies* (Baltimore, 1889).
26. Norman H. Plummer, *Maryland's Oyster Navy: The First Fifty Years* (Chesterton: Washington University Press, 1993), 17.
27. Cited in Plummer, *Maryland's Oyster Navy*, 10.
28. *Baltimore Sun*, May 25, 1868.
29. *Baltimore Sun*, February 3, 1869.
30. *Baltimore Sun*, February 3, 1869.
31. *Baltimore Sun*, February 13, 1869.
32. *Baltimore Sun*, April 18, 1874.
33. Plummer, *Maryland's Oyster Navy*, 10.
34. *Baltimore Sun*, January 6, 1876.
35. *Baltimore Sun*, February 2, 1878.
36. Wennersten, *Oyster Wars of Chesapeake Bay*, 43.
37. *Baltimore Sun*, November 28, 1882.
38. Wennersten, *Oyster Wars of Chesapeake Bay*.
39. *Baltimore Sun*, January 2, 1883.
40. *Baltimore Sun*, March 5, 1883.
41. *Baltimore Sun*, January 28, 1885.
42. *Baltimore Sun*, February 2 and 15, 1884.
43. Plummer, *Maryland's Oyster Navy*.
44. Wennersten, *Oyster Wars of Chesapeake Bay*, 76–82; *Baltimore Sun*, December 10 and 12, 1888. *New York Times*, November 28, December 8 and 12, 1888.
45. Cited in Plummer, *Maryland's Oyster Navy*, 10.
46. *New Jersey Courier*, March 6, 1902.
47. *New Jersey Courier*, February 27, 1902.
48. *New Jersey Courier*, November 2, 1902.
49. *New Jersey Courier*, January 24, 1904.
50. *New Jersey Courier*, April 3, 1873.

51. *New Jersey Courier*, December 10, 1874.
52. *New Jersey Courier*, March 25, 1875.
53. *New Jersey Courier*, February 20, 1874.
54. *New Jersey Courier*, April 17, 1873.
55. *New Jersey Courier*, February 28, 1871.
56. *New Jersey Courier*, April 3, 1873.
57. *New Jersey Courier*, February 8, 1871.
58. Eugene G. Blackford, "Report of the Work in an Oyster Investigation with the Steamer Lookout," in *Report of the Commissioner of the United States Fish Commission* (Washington, D.C.: Government Printing Office, 1885): 27–30.
59. *Fishing Gazette*, June 6, 1896.
60. Commissioners of Shell Fisheries, *Eighth Report of the Shell Fish Commissioners to the State of Connecticut* (Middletown: Pelton & King, 1889), 14.
61. *Peninsula Intelligence*, December 24, 1892.
62. New Jersey Bureau of Shell Fisheries, *Report of the Bureau of Shell Fisheries*, (Trenton, 1909).
63. *Peninsula Intelligence*, September 5, 1891.
64. Philip McKinney, *Special Message of the Governor of Virginia to the General Assembly Relative to Oysters* (Richmond, 1892).
65. Marshall McDonald, *Annual Report of the Fish Commissioner of the State of Virginia* (Richmond, 1878), 6.
66. *Fishing Gazette*, December 3, 1898.
67. *Peninsula Intelligence*, January 7, 1893.
68. *Peninsula Intelligence*, March 10, 1894.
69. Chief Oyster Inspector of Virginia, *Report of the Chief Inspector of Oysters of Virginia to the Auditor of Public Accounts* (Norfolk: Chas. W. Wilson & Co. 1870).
70. Letterbook of the Maryland Board of Public Works.
71. Letter from Thomas Howard to deputies of the Maryland State Fishery Force, November 10, 1910.
72. Letter from Howard to a deputy of the Maryland State Fishery Force, February 10, 1910.
73. Letter from Howard to a deputy of the Maryland State Fishery Force, n.d.
74. Letter from Howard to a deputy of the Maryland State Fishery Force, January 14, 1911.
75. Letters from Howard to oystermen, n.d. and September 9, 1910.
76. Board of Commissioners of the State Oyster Police Force, Maryland State Papers, Scharf Collection, Maryland State Archive S1005 (1868–1880).
77. Roderick P. Neumann, *Imposing Wilderness: Struggles over Livelihood and Nature Preservation in Africa* (Berkeley: University of California Press, 1998).

78. Jacoby, *Crimes against Nature*, 183.
79. Arthur F. McEvoy, *The Fishermen's Problem: Ecology and Law in the California Fisheries, 1850–1980* (Cambridge: Cambridge University Press, 1986).
80. Martin V. Melosi, *Garbage in the Cities: Refuse, Reform, and the Environment, 1880–1980* (College Station: University of Texas Press, 1981).

CHAPTER 3: SHELLFISH COMMISSIONS

1. E. P. Thompson, *The Making of the English Working Class* (New York: Penguin Books, 1968).
2. Robert H. Wiebe, *The Search for Order: 1877–1920* (Westport: Greenwood Press, 1967).
3. *Baltimore Sun*, November 17, 1883.
4. Samuel Lockwood, *The American Oyster, Fifth Annual Report of the Bureau of Statistics of Labor and Industries of the State of New Jersey* (Trenton, 1883); William Stainsby, *The Oyster Industry: A Historical Sketch* (Trenton, 1902).
5. Charles Townsend, *Report of Observations Respecting the Oyster Resources and Oyster Fishery of the Pacific Coast of the United States, Report of the Commissioner of Fish and Fisheries for the year 1889–1891* (Washington, D.C.: Government Printing Office, 1893); Charles Townsend, "Transplanting of Eastern Oysters to Willapa Bay, Washington, with Notes on the Native Oyster Industry," *Report of the Commissioner of Fish and Fisheries for the Year 1895* (Washington, D.C.: Government Printing Office, 1896); Ansley Hall, "Oyster Industries of New Jersey," *Report of the U.S. Commissioner of Fish and Fisheries for 1892* (Washington, D.C.: Government Printing Office, 1894); Charles Stevenson, "Oyster Industry of Maryland," *Bulletin of the U.S. Commission of Fish and Fisheries for 1892* (Washington, D.C.: Government Printing Office, 1894).
6. J. W. Collins, "Statistical Review of the Coast Fisheries of the United States," *Report of the Commissioner of Fish and Fisheries for the Year 1888* (Washington, D.C.: Government Printing Office, 1892), 92.
7. David Belding, *A Report on the Mollusk Fisheries of Massachusetts* (Boston: Wright and Potter, 1909), 6.
8. John Knowles, *Annual Report of the Commissioner of Shell Fisheries* (Providence, 1864), 7.
9. *Forest and Stream*, September 20, 1884.
10. Letter from Marshall McDonald to Eugene Blackford (January 3, 1890), U.S. Fish Commission archive, record group 22, National Archives.
11. Oyster Commissioners of Maryland, *Report of the Oyster Commission of the State of Maryland* (Annapolis: James Young, 1884).

12. Oyster Commissioners of Maryland, *Report*, 138.
13. *Baltimore Sun*, November 17, 1883.
14. *Baltimore Sun*, October 22, 1883.
15. Oyster Commissioners of Maryland, *Report*, 2.
16. *Baltimore Sun*, October 24, 1883.
17. Belding, *Report on the Mollusk Fisheries*, 5.
18. Knowles, *Annual Report of the Commissioner of Shell Fisheries*, 5.
19. T. B. Ferguson, *Report of T.B. Ferguson, a Commissioner of Fisheries of Maryland* (Annapolis: 1881), cxiv.
20. Virginia Fish Commissioners, *Annual Reports of the Fish Commissioners of the State of Virginia* (1878).
21. Virginia Board of Fisheries, *Report* (Richmond, 1902), 1.
22. Virginia Board of Fisheries, *Report* (Richmond, 1907), 6.
23. Connecticut Shellfish Commissioners, *Annual Report of the Shellfish Commissioners to the State of Connecticut* (1882), 73.
24. New Jersey Oyster Commission, *Report of the Oyster Commission* (1884), 17.
25. Eugene G. Blackford, *Second Report of the Oyster Investigations and Survey of the Oyster Territories*, New York State Fisheries Commission Second Annual Report (1886).
26. Virginia Fish Commissioners, *Annual Reports of the Fish Commissioners of the State of Virginia* (1878), 61.
27. Virginia Board of Fisheries, *Report* (Richmond, 1906), 20.
28. Connecticut Shellfish Commissioners, *Annual Report*, 73.
29. New Jersey Bureau of Shell Fisheries, *Report of the Bureau of Shell Fisheries* (1912), 25–26.
30. Connecticut Shellfish Commissioners, *Annual Report*, 73.
31. Connecticut Shellfish Commissioners, *Annual Report*, 53.
32. *Baltimore Sun*, June 18, 1883.
33. *Baltimore Sun*, September 22, 1883.
34. Belding, *Report on the Mollusk Fisheries*, 5.
35. Ibid., 8.
36. Oyster Commissioners of Maryland, *Report*, 133.
37. Ibid., 131.
38. Ibid., 139.
39. Ibid., 13.
40. Christine Keiner, *The Oyster Question: Scientists, Watermen, and the Chesapeake Bay since 1880* (Athens: University of Georgia Press, 2009).
41. Stevenson, "Oyster Industry of Maryland," 205.
42. Connecticut Shellfish Commissioners, *Annual Report* (1881), 21.
43. Ibid., 22.

44. Arthur McEvoy, *The Fishermen's Problem: Ecology and Law in the California Fisheries, 1850–1980* (Cambridge: Cambridge University Press, 1986).
45. Belding, *Report on the Mollusk Fisheries*, 5–6.
46. Garrett Hardin, "The Tragedy of the Commons" *Science* (December 13, 1968): 1243–1248.
47. Connecticut Shellfish Commissioners, *Annual Report* (1882), 44.
48. Connecticut Shellfish Commissioners, *Annual Report* (1884), 13.
49. New Jersey Bureau of Shell Fisheries, *Report of Shell Fisheries* (1904), 59.
50. Ibid., 60.
51. Quoted in Stevenson, "Oyster Industry of Maryland," 213.
52. Ibid., 206.
53. Ibid., 289.
54. Ibid., 290.
55. Michael Adas, *Machines as the Measure of Men: Science, Technology, and the Ideologies of Western Dominance* (Ithaca: Cornell University Press, 1989).
56. Thomas Princen, *The Logic of Sufficiency* (Cambridge: MIT Press, 2005).
57. New Jersey Oyster Commissioners, *Annual Report of the New Jersey State Oyster Commission* (1901), 21–22.
58. Ibid., 23.
59. Belding, *Report on the Mollusk Fisheries*, 5.
60. Ibid., 6.
61. Ibid., 132.
62. Blackford, *Second Report of the Oyster Investigations*, 7.
63. Ibid., 6.
64. Ibid., 5.
65. Knowles, *Annual Report of the Commissioner of Shell Fisheries*, 7.
66. David McDermott Hughes, *Whiteness in Zimbabwe: Race, Landscape, and the Problem of Belonging* (New York: Palgrave Macmillian, 2010).
67. Adas, *Machines as the Measure of Men*.
68. Knowles, *Annual Report of the Commissioner of Shell Fisheries*, 7.
69. Belding, *Report on the Mollusk Fisheries*, 6.
70. Ibid., 12.
71. New Jersey Oyster Commission, *Report* (1884), 17.
72. Ibid., 17.
73. Virginia Board of Fisheries, *Report of the State Board of Fisheries to the Governor of Virginia* (1907), 9.
74. Ibid., 10.
75. Ibid., 15; Virginia Board of Fisheries, *Report* (1908), xx.
76. Virginia Board of Fisheries, *Report* (1907), 10.
77. Ibid., 17.

78. Stevenson, *Oyster Industry of Maryland*, 234.
79. Ibid., 290.
80. Richard Kirkendall, "The Agricultural Colleges: Between Tradition and Modernization," *Agricultural History* 60, no. 2 (1986): 3–19.
81. Oyster Commissioners of Maryland, *Report*, 3.
82. Ibid., 8.
83. William K. Brooks, *The Oyster: A Popular Summary of a Scientific Study* (Baltimore: Johns Hopkins Press, 1891), 164.
84. Oyster Commissioners of Maryland, *Report*, 3.
85. Oyster Commissioners of Maryland, *Report*, 10–11.
86. Ibid., 11.
87. Ibid., 31.
88. Marshall McDonald, *Annual Report of the Fish Commissioner of the State of Virginia* (1878), 3.
89. McDonald, *Annual Report* (1883), 4.
90. Ibid., 5.
91. Connecticut Shellfish Commissioners, *Annual Report* (1887), 16.
92. Eugene G. Blackford, *Report of the Work in an Oyster Investigation with the Steamer Lookout* (1885), 68.
93. Blackford, *Second Report of the Oyster Investigation*, 5.
94. Maryland Commissioner of Fisheries, *Report of the Commissioner of Fisheries of Maryland* (1880), 160.
95. Virginia Fish Commissioners, *Annual Reports* (1878), 3.
96. Ibid., 16.
97. Belding, *Report on the Mollusk Fisheries*, 4.
98. Ferguson, *Report of T.B. Ferguson*, cv.
99. Oyster Commissioners of Maryland, *Report*, 8.
100. Stevenson, *Oyster Industry of Maryland*, 292.
101. Brian Balogh, "Reorganizing the Organizational Synthesis: Federal-Professional Relations in Modern America," *Studies in American Political Development* 5, no. 1 (1991): 119–72.
102. Charles Rosenberg, "Science, Technology, and Economic Growth: The Case of the Agricultural Experiment Station Scientists, 1875–1914" *Agricultural History* 45, no. 1 (1971): 1–20.
103. David E. Hamilton, "Building the Associative State: The Department of Agriculture and American State-Building" *Agricultural History* 64, no. 2 (1990): 207–18.
104. Melbourne Romaine Carriker, *Taming of the Oyster: A History of Evolving Shellfisheries and the National Shellfish Association* (Hanover: Sheridan Press, 2004), 9.
105. Ibid., 11.
106. Ibid., 19.

107. Ibid., 24.
108. Ibid., 29.
109. *New Jersey Courier*, May 22, 1902.
110. *New Jersey Courier*, January 29, 1903.
111. *New Jersey Courier*, February 12, 1903.
112. Spencer F. Baird Papers, National Archives, USFC collection, record group 22 (hereafter Baird Papers).
113. Cylde MacKenzie, "Bibliographic Memoir of Ernst Ingersoll: Naturalist, Shellfish Scientist, and Author," *Marine Fisheries Review* 53, no. 5 (1991): 23–29.
114. Baird Papers.
115. Daniel W. Schneider, "Local Knowledge, Environmental Politics, and the Founding of Ecology in the United States: Stephen Forbes and 'The Lake as a Microcosm' (1887)," *Isis* 91, no. 4 (2000): 681–705.
116. Henry Bryant Bigelow and William W. Welsh, *Fishes of the Gulf of Maine* (Washington, D.C.: Government Printing Office, 1925).
117. Charles Townsend, "The Distribution of Certain Whales as Shown by Logbook Records of American Whaleships," *Zoologica* 19, no. 1 (1935): 1–50.
118. R. Reeves, T. Smith, E. Josephson, P. Claphan, and G. Woolmer, "Historical Observations of Humpback and Blue Whales in the North Atlantic Ocean: Clues to Migratory Routes and Possibly Additional Feeding Grounds," *Marine Mammal Science* 20, no. 4 (2004): 774–86.
119. Bashford Dean, "Report on the European Methods of Oyster Culture," *Bulletin of the United States Fish Commission* (Washington, D.C.: Government Printing Office, 1891); Bashford Dean, "Japanese Oyster Culture," *Bulletin of the United States Fish Commission* (Washington, D.C.: Government Printing Office, 1902).
120. F. H. King, *Farmers of Forty Centuries, or Permanent Agriculture in China, Korea and Japan* (Emmaus: Rodale Press, 1911).
121. Samuel P. Hays, *Conservation and the Gospel of Efficiency: The Progressive Conservation Movement, 1890–1920* (Pittsburgh: University of Pittsburgh Press, 1959).
122. Richard Drayton, *Nature's Government: Science, Imperial Britain, and the 'Improvement' of the World* (New Haven: Yale University Press, 2000).
123. Raymond Williams, *The Country and the City* (New York City: Oxford University Press, 1973). Thompson, *Making of the English Working Class*.
124. Drayton, *Nature's Government*.
125. Adas, *Machines as the Measure of Men*.
126. McEvoy, *Fishermen's Problem*.
127. Nancy Langston, *Forest Dreams, Forest Nightmares: The Paradox of Old Growth in the Inland West* (Seattle: University of Washington Press, 1996).

CHAPTER 4: NATURAL SCIENCE

1. David L. Hull, *Science as a Process: An Evolutionary Account of the Social and Conceptual Development of Science* (Chicago: University of Chicago Press, 1990).
2. Andrew Abbott, *The System of Professions: An Essay on the Division of Expert Labor* (Chicago: University of Chicago Press, 1988).
3. Victor Coste, "Voyage d'Exploration sur le littoral de la France et de l'Italie (1851)," USFC, *Report of the Commissioner* (1883).
4. Darin S. Kinsey, "Seeding the Water as the Earth: The Epicenter and Peripheries of a Western Aquaculture Revolution," *Environmental History* 11, no. 3 (2006): 527–66.
5. Coste, "Voyage d'Exploration."
6. M. de Bon, "Report to Rear-Admiral the Marquis of Montaignac, Minister of Marine and the Colonies (1875)," USFC, *Report of the Commissioner* (1881).
7. M. de Bon, "Report to Rear-Admiral."
8. Ibid., 893.
9. M. de Bon, "Report to Rear-Admiral," 893.
10. Karl Möbius, "How Can the Cultivation of Oysters, Especially on the German Coasts, Be Made Permanently Profitable?" USFC, *Report of the Commissioner* (Washington, D.C.: Government Printing Office, 1880).
11. Ibid.
12. Karl Möbius, "The Oyster and Oyster Culture," USFC, *Report of the United States Commission of Fish and Fisheries* (Washington, D.C.: Government Printing Office, 1883).
13. William K. Brooks, "Abstract of Observations upon the Artificial Fertilization of Oyster Eggs, and on the Embryology of the American Oyster," *American Journal of Science*, (1879). Scientists now know Eastern Oysters can change sex with age and environmental conditions.
14. H. J. Rice, "Experiments in Oyster Propagation," *Forest and Stream* 21, no. 2 (August 9, 1883): 28–29.
15. William K. Brooks, *Chesapeake Zoological Laboratory: Report of the Director for its First Six Years, 1878–1883* (Baltimore: Johns Hopkins University, 1884).
16. USFC, *Report of the Commissioner* (Washington, D.C.: Government Printing Office, 1884).
17. Letter from Francis Winslow to Spencer Baird, March 29, 1882, Baird Papers.
18. Letters from Winslow to Baird, June 4 and June 28, 1882.
19. Letter from Winslow to Baird, June 4, 1882.

20. Letter from Winslow to Baird, June 28, 1882.
21. Ibid.
22. Letter from Winslow to Baird, August 5, 1882.
23. Letter from Henry Rowe to Spencer Baird, August 15, 1882, Baird Papers.
24. *Report upon the Station at St. Jerome's, Md., By the Committee of Inquiry, U S. Commission of Fish and Fisheries. Submitted Dec. 24th 1887*, Document in the National Archives, USFC Collection, record group no. 22.
25. USFC, *Report of the Commissioner* (1884).
26. USFC, *Report of the Commissioner* (1883).
27. USFC, *Report of the Commissioner* (1884).
28. John A. Ryder, "Notes on the Breeding, Food, and Cause of Green Color in Oysters," *Forest and Stream* 18, no. 1 (June 1, 1882): 349–51.
29. Ibid., 351.
30. USFC, *Report of the Commissioner* (1884); John A. Ryder, "Success in Oyster Culture," *Forest and Stream*, 19, no. 7 (September 14, 1882): 121.
31. Ryder, "Success in Oyster Culture."
32. Rice, "Experiments in Oyster Propagation," 28–29.
33. Letter from Winslow to Baird, August 3, 1883.
34. Ibid.
35. Letter from Winslow to Baird, September 13, 1883.
36. Letter from Winslow to Baird, August 3, 1883.
37. Letter form Francis Winslow to Theodore Gill, September 20, 1883, Baird Papers.
38. John A. Ryder, "Rearing Oysters from Artificially Fertilized Eggs, together with Notes on Pond Culture," *Bulletin of the USFC* 3 (1883): 281–94.
39. John A. Ryder, "The Oyster Problem Solved," *Forest and Stream* 21, no. 5 (August 30, 1883): 90.
40. USFC, *Report of the Commissioner* (1886).
41. John A. Ryder, "A New System of Oyster Culture," *Science* 6, no. 147 (1885): 465–67.
42. Ibid., 465.
43. John A. Ryder, "The Oyster Problem Actually Solved," *Forest and Stream* 25, no. 18 (October 22, 1885): 249–50.
44. USFC, *Report of the Commissioner* (1887).
45. USFC, *Report of the Commissioner* (1888).
46. *Report upon the Station at St. Jerome's, Md.*
47. Ibid.
48. Eugene G. Blackford, "The Propagation and Natural History of the American Oyster: Experiments at Cold Springs Harbor, L. I., by the New York State Fish Commission," *Fishing Gazette*, January 5, 1893.
49. USFC, *Report of the Commissioner* (1910).

50. Julius Nelson Papers, Rutgers University, Alexander Library Special Collections (hereafter Nelson Papers).
51. New Jersey Oyster Commission, *Report of the New Jersey State Oyster Commission* (1903).
52. Nelson Papers.
53. Abbott, *System of Professions*.
54. Marshall McDonald, *Report upon the Oysters and Fisheries of Tidewater Virginia* (Richmond: R. F. Walker, 1880), 7.
55. *Baltimore Sun*, November 15, 1883.
56. Joseph W. Collins, "Opening of the Oyster Season" *Fishing Gazette*, January 5, 1893.
57. McDonald, *Report upon the Oysters and Fisheries of Tidewater Virginia*.
58. James Taylor Ellyson, *Proceedings of a Convention Called to Consider and Discuss the Oyster Question* (Richmond, 1894), 28.
59. McDonald, *Oysters and Fisheries of Tidewater Virginia*.
60. New Jersey Oyster Commission, *Report of the New Jersey State Oyster Commission* (1903), 17.
61. Ellyson, *Proceedings of a Convention*, 30.
62. Ibid., 27.
63. *Baltimore Sun*, November, 15, 1883.
64. Letter from Marshall McDonald to Daniel Colt Gillman, n.d., Marshall McDonald Papers, Virginia Historical Society (hereafter McDonald Papers).
65. David L. Belding, *A Report upon the Mollusk Fisheries of Massachusetts*. Julius Nelson, Prince Edward Island study (1915), Nelson Papers.
66. William K. Brooks, *The Oyster: A Popular Summary of a Scientific Study* (Baltimore: Johns Hopkins Press, 1891), 127.
67. Belding, *Mollusk Fisheries of Massachusetts*.
68. Letter from Marshall McDonald, recipient and date unknown, USFC collection, National Archives.
69. Julius Nelson, Prince Edward Island study.
70. Letter from Winslow to Baird, July 18, 1882.
71. Ryder, "New System of Oyster Culture."
72. Ellyson, *Proceedings of a Convention*.
73. Nelson, Prince Edward Island study.
74. Letter from Marshall McDonald to J. B. Baylor, November 28, 1892, USFC collection, National Archives.
75. Letter from Marshall McDonald to Daniel Colt Gillman, n.d., McDonald Papers.
76. Ellyson, *Proceedings of a Convention*.
77. Ibid., 30.

78. Ellyson, *Proceedings of a Convention*, 31.
79. Jerry C. Towle, "Authored Ecosystems: Livingston Stone and the Transformation of California Fisheries," *Environmental History* 5, no. 1 (2000): 54–74; Matthew Evenden, "Locating Science, Locating Salmon: Institutions, Linkages, and Spatial Practices in Early British Columbia Fisheries Science," *Environment and Planning D: Society and Space* 22, no. 3 (2004): 355–72.
80. Ryder, "Green Color in Oysters."
81. New Jersey Oyster Commission, *Report of the New Jersey State Oyster Commission* (1903), 16.
82. Francis Winslow, "The North Carolina Oyster Industry," *Forest and Stream*, May 7, 1885, 292–93 and May 14, 1885, 332.
83. *Baltimore Sun*, October 22, 1884.
84. Ryder, "Green Color in Oysters."
85. *Baltimore Sun*, September 6, 1882.
86. Letter from Winslow to Baird, 1882.
87. *Baltimore Sun*, May 28, 1883.
88. Ellyson, *Proceedings of a Convention*, 37.
89. Ibid., 36.
90. Julius Nelson, *Oyster Interests of New Jersey, New Jersey Agricultural College Experiment Station. Special Bulletin E* (New Brunswick: Rutgers University, 1889), 37.
91. *New Jersey Courier*, October 15, 1903.
92. *New Jersey Courier*, November 5, 1903.
93. Julius Nelson, "A Half Century of Darwinism," "Sex and Health," and "Relation of Biology to Theology," n.d., Nelson Papers.
94. Nelson, "Relation of Biology to Theology."
95. Nelson, "Half Century of Darwinism."
96. Allen Harrison, "A Biographical Sketch of John Adam Ryder," *Proceedings of the Academy of Natural Sciences of Philadelphia* (Philadelphia: University of Pennsylvania, 1896), 232–33.
97. Ibid., 234.
98. Ibid., 236.
99. Letter from Marshall McDonald to Daniel Colt Gillman, n.d., McDonald Papers.
100. Letter from Marshall McDonald to George Brown Goode, May 11, 1889, USFC collection, National Archives.
101. Letter from Julius Nelson to Charles Bacon, September 3, 1903, Nelson Papers.
102. Letter from Nelson to Bacon, 1904.
103. Letters from Nelson to Bacon, 1905 and 1906.

104. Letter from Nelson to Bacon, 1907.
105. Letters from Nelson, 1908 and 1909, Nelson Papers.
106. Letter from Eugene Blackford to Marshall McDonald, Jan 7, 1888, USFC collection, National Archives.
107. Letter from Hugh Smith to Gilbert Grosvenor, October 27, 1915, USFC collection, National Archives.
108. Theodore M. Porter, *Trust in Numbers: The Pursuit of Objectivity in Science and Public Life* (Princeton: Princeton University Press, 1996).
109. Letter from Marshall McDonald to Spencer Baird, January 9, 1882, USFC collection, National Archives.
110. Letter from Marshall McDonald to William Brooks, May 19, 1892, USFC collection, National Archives.
111. Letter from Fred Mather to Marshall McDonald, January 26, 1892, USFC collection, National Archives.
112. Letter from Blackford to McDonald, January 26, 1892.
113. *New York Times*, February 15, 1900.
114. *Fishing Gazette*, April 12, 1894.
115. *Fishing Gazette*, January 5, 1893.
116. Letter from Mather to McDonald, January 26, 1892.
117. Ibid.
118. Letter from Blackford to McDonald, December 7, 1885.
119. Letter from Blackford to McDonald, January 5, 1891.
120. Letter from Blackford to McDonald, January 26, 1892.
121. Letter from Blackford to McDonald, January 28, 1893.
122. Letter from Blackford to McDonald, December 1, 1893.
123. Letter from Blackford to McDonald, October 15, 1887.
124. Letter from McDonald to Blackford, January 24, 1892; Letter from Blackford to McDonald, December 7, 1885.
125. Letter from John Ryder to Marshall McDonald, March 11, 1889, USFC collection, National Archives.
126. Letter from Marshall McDonald to John Ryder, March 18, 1892, USFC collection, National Archives.
127. Letter from Ryder to McDonald, August 14, 1892.
128. Letter from Blackford to McDonald, December 21, 1887.
129. Letter from Blackford to McDonald, August 4, 1888.
130. Letter from Lieut. Wood to W. E. Chandler, October 30, 1884, USFC collection, National Archives.
131. Letter from T. B. Ferguson to Spencer Baird, n.d., USFC collection, National Archives.
132. Dean E. Allard, *Spencer Baird and the U.S. Fish Commission* (New York: Arno Press, 1978); Carmel Finley, *All the Fish in the Sea: Maximum Sustainable Yield and the Failure of Fisheries Management* (Chicago:

University of Press, 2011); Michael L. Weber, *From Abundance to Scarcity: A History of U.S. Marine Fisheries Policy* (Washington, D.C.: Island Press, 2001).

133. Tim D. Smith, *Scaling Fisheries: The Science of Measuring the Effects of Fishing, 1855–1955* (Cambridge: Cambridge University Press, 1994).
134. Hull, *Science as a Process*.
135. Joseph E. Taylor III, *Making Salmon: An Environmental History of the Northwest Fisheries Crisis* (Seattle: University of Washington Press, 1999), 76.
136. Jennifer Hubbard, "Mediating the North Atlantic Environment: Fisheries Biologists, Technology, and Marine Spaces," *Environmental History* 18, no. 1 (2013): 88–100.

CHAPTER 5: MAPPING NATURAL BEDS

1. C. C. Yates, *Survey of Oyster Bars* (1912), 127.
2. Connecticut Shell-Fisheries Commissioners, *Report of the Commissioners of Shell-Fisheries of Connecticut* (1882), 9.
3. Connecticut Shell-Fisheries Commissioners, *Shell-Fisheries of Connecticut* (1883), 9–10.
4. Connecticut Shell-Fisheries Commissioners, *Shell-Fisheries of Connecticut* (1885), 6.
5. Ibid., 11.
6. Connecticut Shell-Fisheries Commissioners, *Shell-Fisheries of Connecticut* (1886), 15–16.
7. New Jersey Oyster Commission, *Annual Report of the New Jersey State Oyster Commission* (1900), 7.
8. New Jersey Oyster Commission, *Annual Report* (1901), 3.
9. Ocean County District Oyster Commission, *Annual Report of the State Oyster Commission for the District of Ocean County, New Jersey* (1904), 49.
10. Towns mapped natural beds in New York.
11. Ocean County District Oyster Commission, *Annual Report* (1903).
12. Ocean County District Oyster Commission, *Annual Report* (1905).
13. *The Oysterman and Fisherman*, October 1908.
14. *New Jersey Courier*, February 27, 1902.
15. James B. Baylor, *Survey of the Oyster Grounds of Virginia: Report of J. B. Baylor to the Governor of Virginia* (Richmond, 1895).
16. James Bowen Baylor Papers, University of Virginia, Small Library Special Collections (hereafter Baylor Papers).
17. Baylor Papers.
18. James Taylor Ellyson, *Proceedings of the Convention Called to Consider and Discuss the Oyster Question* (Richmond, 1894), 19.

19. Letter from William Ellinger to J. B. Baylor, December 19, 1892, Baylor Papers.
20. Letter from Ellinger to J. B. Baylor, May 30, 1893.
21. Letter from B. Howard Haman to J. B. Baylor, October 27, 1905, Baylor Papers.
22. Baylor, *Survey of the Oyster Grounds*, 6.
23. *Richmond Times*, December 4, 1892.
24. *Richmond Times*, December 18, 1892.
25. *Richmond Times*, January 28, 1893.
26. *Fishing Gazette*, July 22, 1899.
27. Ibid.
28. *Fishing Gazette*, July 22, 1899.
29. Ibid.
30. *Fishing Gazette*, July 22, 1899.
31. H. F. Moore, "Condition and Extent of the Oyster Beds of James River, Virginia, 1909," USFC, *Report of the Commissioner of Fish and Fisheries* (1911).
32. Ibid., 58–59.
33. Ibid., 80.
34. Ibid., 13.
35. Ibid., 57.
36. Ibid., 82.
37. Ibid., 20.
38. Maryland Shell Fish Commission, *Fourth Report of the Shell Fish Commission of Maryland* (1912), 49.
39. Ibid., 49–51.
40. Ibid., 83.
41. J. B. Harley, *The New Nature of Maps: Essays in the History of Cartography* (Baltimore: Johns Hopkins Press, 2001).
42. Ruben Rose-Redwood, "Governmentality and the Geo-Coded World," *Progress in Human Geography* 30, no. 4 (2012): 469–86.
43. Scott Kirsch, "John Wesley Powell and the Mapping of the Colorado Plateau, 1869–1879: Survey Science, geographical Solutions and the Economy of Environmental Values" *Annals of the Association of American Geographers* 92, no. 3 (2002): 548–72.

CHAPTER 6: MAPPING PLANTERS' PROPERTY

1. Pamela K. Gilbert, *Mapping the Victorian Social Body* (Albany: State University of New York Press, 2004), 5.
2. Ibid., 6.

3. Henri Lefebvre, *The Production of Space* (Oxford: Blackwell, 1974); David Harvey, *The Condition of Postmodernity: An Enquiry into the Origins of Cultural Change* (New York: Wiley-Blackwell, 1991).
4. Gilbert, *Mapping the Victorian Social Body*, 7.
5. Ibid., 7.
6. Michael A. Rice, "A Brief History of Oyster Aquaculture in Rhode Island" *Aquaculture in Rhode Island: Annual Report 2006* (Rhode Island Coastal Resources Management Council, 2006), 24–38.
7. John P. Knowles, *Annual Report of the Commissioner of Shell Fisheries* (Rhode Island, 1864), 1.
8. Ibid., 2.
9. Knowles, *Annual Report*, 2.
10. Rhode Island Shell Fish Commission, *Annual Report of the Commissioners of Shell Fisheries* (1882).
11. Ibid., 39.
12. Ibid., 91.
13. Connecticut Shell-Fisheries Commission, *Report of the Commissioners of Shell-Fisheries of Connecticut* (1882), 53.
14. Ibid., xx.
15. *Fishing Gazette*, December 3, 1898.
16. Ibid., 47.
17. Ibid., 48.
18. Rhode Island Shell Fish Commission, *Annual Report of the Commissioners of Shell Fisheries* (1890).
19. Connecticut Shell-Fisheries Commission, *Report of the Commissioners of Shell-Fisheries of Connecticut* (1882), 7.
20. Connecticut Shell-Fisheries Commission, *Report* (1883), 4.
21. Ibid., 5.
22. Connecticut Shell-Fisheries Commission, *Report* (1884), 25.
23. By 1884 all of the 1881 deeds were drawn, all but 20 from 1882 were drawn, and about half of 1883's were drawn. There were 118 triangulation points, 35 of which were markers; 347 buoys had been set, and 431 old buoys surveyed and reset as needed. They expected that every town would be given a map by 1885. The New Haven map was the first completed in 1885.
24. Connecticut Shell-Fisheries Commission, *Report* (1889).
25. *Fishing Gazette*, June 20, 1896.
26. *New Jersey Courier*, October 7, 1902.
27. Ocean County Oyster Commission, *Annual Report of the State Oyster Commission for the District of Ocean County, New Jersey* (1903), 36.
28. Ibid., 36.
29. Ocean County District Oyster Commission, *Annual Report* (1912).

30. Caswell Grave, "The History of Oyster Production in Maryland," Maryland Shell Fish Commission, *Fourth Report of the Oyster Commission of the State of Maryland* (1912), 291.
31. Christine Keiner, *The Oyster Question: Scientists, Watermen, and the Maryland Chesapeake Bay since 1880* (Athens: University of Georgia Press, 2009).
32. Maryland Shell Fish Commission, *Fourth Report* (1912), 289.
33. Ibid., 291.
34. Ibid., 291–93.
35. Maryland Shell Fish Commission, *Fourth Report* (1912), 253–56.
36. Maryland Shell Fish Commission, *Sixth Report* (1913).
37. Ibid., 26–27.
38. Ibid., 7–8.
39. Ibid., 9.
40. Ibid., 12.
41. Ibid., 13. For some reason about three-fourths of the protested acres were in Dorchester County.
42. Keiner, *Oyster Question*.
43. Victor S. Kennedy and Linda L. Breisch, "Sixteen Decades of Political Management of the Oyster Fishery in Maryland's Chesapeake Bay," *Journal of Environmental Management* 16, no. 2 (1983): 153–71.
44. Maryland Conservation Commission, *First Annual Report of the Conservation Commission of Maryland* (1916), 6.
45. Laws in the 1870s gave exclusive planting rights to landowners who held both banks of streams, and said that shore owners could ask for planting rights in areas adjoining their property. Planters had to stake their claims and have an inspector verify it or others could take up the area. In cases where multiple persons applied for planting grants, the area was auctioned. Northern planting was diminishing, and the law restricted nonresidents to bedding during the open season. The General Assembly could revoke any planting lease.
46. Marshall McDonald, *Report upon the Oysters and Fisheries of Tidewater Virginia* (Richmond: Superintendent of Public Printing, 1880).
47. W. N. Armstrong, *Notes on the Oyster Industry of Virginia* (Hampton, 1879).
48. Lynnhaven, Hampton, and Chincoteague were major planting areas, as were the Rappahannock and Potomac Rivers. Ingersoll estimated the latter two areas had roughly 1,000 planters, about 5,000 employed, and around 400,000 bushels planted annually.
49. McKinney also mentioned that a special act in 1888 gave 3,000 acres to one person for 20 years and only $.20/acre (the act was repealed the next year).

50. Philip W. McKinney, *The Oyster Question* (Norfolk, 1892).
51. McKinney quoted in James Taylor Ellyson, *Proceedings of a Convention Called to Consider and Discuss the Oyster Question*.
52. James Stubbs, *A Defense of the Tidewater Oyster Industry* (Richmond: Everett and Waddel Co., 1891).
53. Virginia Board of Fisheries, *Report of the Board of Fisheries* (1901), 22.
54. Virginia Board of Fisheries, *Report* (1906), 7.
55. Virginia Board of Fisheries, *Report* (1907), 18.
56. *The Oysterman and Fisherman*, November 1908.
57. *Oysterman and Fisherman*, January 1909.
58. *Oysterman and Fisherman*, May 1909.
59. Virginia Board of Fisheries, *Report* (1913).
60. *S. typhi* was known as *B. thypus* during the time period covered in this study.
61. Martin V. Melosi, *The Sanitary City: Urban Infrastructure in America from Colonial Times to the Present* (Baltimore: Johns Hopkins Press, 2001).
62. Ibid., 163.
63. Ibid., 138.
64. Gerald Markowitz and David Rosner, *Deceit and Denial: The Deadly Politics of Industrial Pollution* (Berkeley: University of California Press, 2002).
65. *New York Times*, November 15, 1886.
66. Caleb Fuller, "The Distribution of Sewage in the Waters of Narragansett Bay, with Especial Reference to the Contamination of the Oyster Beds" USFC, *Report of the Commissioner of Fish and Fisheries* (Washington, D.C.: Government Printing Office, 1905).
67. *New York Times*, November 1, 1894.
68. Fuller, "Distribution of Sewage."
69. Ibid.
70. *E. coli* was known as *B. coli* during this time period.
71. Stephen Gage, "Methods of Testing Shellfish for Pollution," *Science* 2, no. 31 (1910): 548–49.
72. Paul Galtsoff, *Bibliography of Oysters and Other Marine Organisms Associated with Oyster Bottoms and Estuarine Ecology* (Boston: G. K. Hall, 1972).
73. *New York Times*, January 5, 1895.
74. *New York Times*, January 25, 1895.
75. *New York Times*, March 5, 1905.
76. *New York Times*, May 11, 1908.
77. *New York Times*, March 15, 1911.
78. *New York Times*, September 16, 1911.
79. *New York Times*, February 14, 1896.
80. New Jersey Oyster Commission, *Annual Report of the New Jersey State Oyster Commission* (1903).

81. Fuller, "Distribution of Sewage."
82. Rhode Island Commissioners of Shell Fisheries, *Annual Report of the Commissioners of Shell Fisheries* (1906). Providence also established the first municipal public health laboratory in 1888.
83. Rhode Island Commissioners of Shell Fisheries, *Annual Report* (1912).
84. *New York Times*, January 31, 1897.
85. Melbourne Romaine Carriker, *Taming of the Oyster: A History of Evolving Shellfisheries and the National Shellfisheries Association* (Hanover: Sheridan Press, 2004), 5.
86. Ibid., 15.
87. *New York Times*, January 25, 1925.
88. Frederic P. Gorham, "The Sanitary Regulation of the Oyster Industry," *American Journal of Public Health* 2 (1912): 77–85.
89. Letter from Francis Winslow to Spencer Baird, August 5, 1882, Baird Papers.
90. Ibid.
91. Letter from Winslow to Baird, July 18, 1882, Baird Papers.
92. Letter from Baird to Winslow, February 19, 1883, Baird Papers.
93. Francis Winslow, "Report of the Sounds and Estuaries of North Carolina, with Reference to Oyster Culture," *USCGS Bulletin* no. 10 (1887): 136.
94. Francis Winslow, "On the Sounds and Estuaries of Georgia, with Reference to Oyster Culture," *USCGS Bulletin* no. 19 (1890); Francis Winslow, "An Investigation of the Coast Waters of South Carolina with Reference to Oyster Culture," *USFC Bulletin* no. 10 (1890).
95. Franklin Swift, "The Oyster Grounds of the West Florida Coast: Their Extent, Condition, and Peculiarities," *USFC Bulletin* no. 17 (1897).
96. Caswell Grave, "Investigations for the Promotion of the Oyster Industry of North Carolina," *USFC Report of the Commissioner of Fish and Fisheries* (1905).
97. H. F. Moore, "Report on the Oyster Beds of Louisiana," *USFC Report of the Commissioner of Fish and Fisheries* (1899).
98. Moore ran into problems mapping property rights around the Mississippi Delta. It was too flat to have any landmarks, and hurricanes and shifting channels quickly wiped out signal stations. The environment was so dynamic that even if a lease was accurately marked somehow, it could be covered with sediment and quickly become land. He overcame these problems and contributed to Louisiana's continued growth.
99. Markowitz and Rosner, *Deceit and Denial*.
100. Patrick Joyce, *The Rule of Freedom: Liberalism and the Modern City* (London: Verso, 2003).

CONCLUSION: THE CHALLENGE OF COMPLEXITY

1. Carmel Finley, *All the Fish in the Sea: Maximum Sustainable Yield and the Failure of Fisheries Management* (Chicago: University of Press, 2011).
2. Donald Ludwig, Roy Hilborn, and Carl Walters, "Uncertainty, Resource Exploitation, and Conservation: Lessons from History," *Ecological Applications* 3, no. 4 (1993): 548–49.
3. P. A. Larkin, "An Epitaph for the Concept of Maximum Sustained Yield," *Transactions of the American Fisheries Society* 106, no. 1 (1977): 1–11.
4. Kevin St. Martin, "Making Space for Community Resource Management in Fisheries," *Annals of the Association of American Geographers* 91, no. 1 (2001): 122–42.
5. Svein Jentoft, Bonnie J. McCay, and Douglas C. Wilson, "Social Theory and Fisheries Co-Management," *Marine Policy* 22, no. 4–5 (1998): 423–36.
6. Ellen K. Pikitch et al., "Ecosystem-Based Fishery Management," *Science* 305, no. 5682 (2004): 346–47.
7. Teresa R. Johnson and Bonnie J. McCay, "Trading Expertise: The Rise and Demise of an Industry/Government Committee on Survey Trawl Design," *Maritime Studies* 11, no. 1 (2012): 14–38.
8. Thomas L. Friedman, *Thank You for Being Late: An Optimist's Guide to Thriving in the Age of Accelerations* (New York: Farrar, Straus and Giroux, 2016).
9. James C. Scott, *Seeing Like a State: How Certain Schemes to Improve the Human Condition Have Failed* (New Haven: Yale University Press, 1998), 356.
10. Barton Seaver, *American Seafood: Heritage, Culture and Cookery from Sea to Shining Sea* (New York: Sterling Epicure, 2017).
11. Chesapeake Bay Foundation, "2016: State of the Bay."

INDEX

Page numbers in italics denote illustrations.

Abbott, Andrew, 97, 112, 132
abstract space, 13, 156
acceleration, age of, 183
access: common-property rights vs., 115; competing ideas of, 54–55; equity concerns and, 30; local traditions on, 22, 43; modernist solutions and, 87; for the poor, 2, 22, 24, 30–31, 46, 73; privilege protection vs., 55–57; sustainability vs., 22, 34–35; tongers' value on, 8, 22, 54–55; Virginia legislative petitions on, 29, 43–44
Acheson, James, 15
Adas, Michael, 11, 80–81, 94
Adorno, Theodor, 10
African Americans, 42, 82–83
agriculture: *Farmers of Forty Centuries* on, 93; Jeffersonian ideals of, 83; modernists on, 8, 79; planting as, 118; public-private partnerships in, 89; in the South, 143
Alaskan fisheries, 14
American Field, 128
American West, water resources in, 9–10

Anne Arundel County, Maryland, 151
applied science, 97, 124–25, 132
aquaculture: colonial studies and, 11; employment in, 183; expansion of, 119, 131, 143, 144, 150, 153–54; as farming, 118; French research in, 97–103; growth of, 16–17; history of, 2, 28; industrialization and, 3, 17; in Maine, 180–81; modernists on, 64, 70, 77–80; multitrophic, 17; pollution from, 17; pond culture system of, 100–101, 107, 109–10, 111, 117, 118; privatization and, 22, 70; pros and cons of, 16–17, 28; in Rhode Island, 63; shellfish commissions and, 63; as the solution for overharvesting, 16; spat collectors for, 98–99, 100, 101; sustainability and, 17, 183. *See also* aquaculture leases; hatcheries; oyster science; planting
aquaculture leases: for barren bottoms, 78–79, 176–78; cartographers on, 141; common-property rights vs., 181; in Connecticut, 79, 157–62, *161*, 207n23; in Delaware Bay, 139; Haman act on, 144; hatcheries and, 84;

213

aquaculture leases (*continued*) in Long Island Sound, 35; in Maryland, 163–65, 208n41; in the mid-Atlantic region, 39; in New Jersey, 39, 162–63; in New York, 39, 162–63; opposition to, 163, 165, 208n41; perpetual, 72–73; precommission, 156–58; protests against, 165, 208n41; in Rhode Island, 156–59; shellfish commissions on, 72–74; town jurisdiction over, 28–29; in Virginia, 79, 165–68. *See also* lease maps; privatization
armed conflict, 47, 51–52, 53–54, 61
Arnold, David, 14
artificial cultivation, 130–32; artificial fertilization for, 103–6, 109, 111; as the oyster decline solution, 116–23; promise of, 132; pure science research vs., 124–25; scientific research from 1878–1885 on, 103–11; scientific research post-1885 on, 111–12; scientists' preference for, 130–32; seawater for, 103–4, 105, 108. *See also* hatcheries
artificial fertilization, 103–6, 109, 111
assassination attempt, 52
Atlantic City, New Jersey, 173
Atlantic County, New Jersey, 140
Atlantic County District Commission (New Jersey), 163
attachment stage, 24, 106, 107, 108–9, 111
Atwater, W. O., 172

Bacon, Charles, 89, 90–91, 124–25
bacteriology, 168–69, 170, 171
Baird, Spencer: Ferguson and, 130; on hatcheries, 87; Mather on, 127; McDonald and, 126; Taylor on, 132; USFC survey and, 91–92; Winslow and, 106, 177
Baltimore, Maryland: dredge boats from, 41, 46; packing industry in, 2, 41–42, 68, 175
Baltimore Sun: on the decline of oyster beds, 53; on dredgers, 46–47; 48, 51–52; on the Haman act, 163; on the oyster decline, 68, 113
bank panic of 1907, 175
Barnegat Bay, 55, 57, 62, 139–41, 162
barren bottom cultivation, 164
barren bottom leases, 78–79
barren bottom maps, 13, 135, 138, 155, 176–78, 210n98
Baylor, James, 141–45, 148–49, 150
Baylor Line maps, 141–45, 148–49, 149, 150
beds, natural. *See* natural oyster beds
Belding, David: characterization of tongers by, 81; on common-property rights, 72; on existing legislation, 69; investigative surveys by, 65, 66; on monopolies, 73; on natural oyster beds, 115; optimistic statements by, 87–88; on the oyster decline, 67, 74; on privatization, 79; solutions held by, 93–94
Bensel, Walter, 173
Bigelow, Erastus, 92
bioconone, 102
Blackford, Eugene: attachment stage research and, 108; correspondence of, 125, 127, 128–30; on existing legislation, 70, 71; on Ferguson, 129–30; investigative surveys by, 65–66; on local traditions, 93; on Mather, 127; McDonald and, 129; on oyster decline, 67, 79–80; on science, 86
Blue Mountains, 4–5, 95
Blue Point oysters, 38, 172, 174, 191n36
Board of the Chesapeake, 51
boats. *See* vessels
boat sheets, 152
Bogart, James, 159–62, 178, 207n23
Bolster, Jeffrey, 14
bottom sediment, 110, 176, 210n98
bottom-up processes, 181
boundary lines, 47, 49, 142, 161
bounties, on starfish, 86
brands, of oysters, 38, 191n36
British India, 12

INDEX   215

Brooklyn Oyster Protective Association, 58
Brooks, William: artificial fertilization and, 103–6, 111; attachment stage research and, 108–9; correspondence with, 126–27; on education, 117; on existing legislation, 69; on farming, 118; on hatcheries, 84–85; on leasing, 72–73; as a modernist, 66; optimistic statements by, 88, 119, 120, 183; *The Oyster*, 84; on the oyster decline, 68, 112–13, 115; solutions held by, 93–94
Bulstrode, H. T., 171
buoys, 160, 178, 207n23
Bureau of Statistics of Labor and Industries of the State of New Jersey, 66

cadastral maps. *See* lease maps
California, 14, 16, 61, 74
Canada, 115–16
canneries. *See* packing industry
capitalism: abstract space and, 13; commodification and, 9–10; expansion of, 153–54, 156; maps and, 156, 179; pre-1880, 44; "Thirty Years Reminiscences of a Veteran Oyster Planter" on, 140–41
capture fisheries, 3–4, 16
Carnegie Institute, 174
carp, 85, 118
cartographers: goal of, 156; Mexican, 12; modernist, 12–13, 133, 141–53, 154; populist, 12–13, 133, 141, 153. *See also* maps and mapping
Cartographic Mexico (Craib), 11–12
certificates, sanitary, 169, 174, 176, 179
Chesapeake Bay: armed conflict in, 51–52, 53–54, 61; Baylor Line maps of, 141–45, 148–49, *149*, 150; boundary lines of, 47, 49; Brooks on, 120; exclusion in, 61–62; Goldsborough definition for, 135; illegal dredgers in, 40–41, 49–55; law enforcement in, 45, 46, 55; maps of, 141–53, *149*;

Moore's 1909 resurvey of, 146–50, *149*; natural oyster beds in, 73, 135–36, 141–53; New Haven packing houses and, 36; Nile River comparison to, 120; opposition to planting in, 119; overharvesting in, 17; oyster decline in, 113; oyster navies in, 46–55; pre-1880 production in, 21; residency laws and, 27; seed from, 40; Southern Trade and, 2, 40–43; water quality improvements in, 183; Yates's 1906–1912 survey of, 150–53, *152*, 164, 165. *See also* Maryland; Virginia
Chester River, 53–54, 62
Chiang, Connie, 14
Chincoteague Island, 29, 167, 208n48
Choptank River, 51, 52
civil disobedience, 15, 39
Civil War, 41, 46, 143
clam beds, 140
class conflict, 36, 40, 49–50
closed seasons: in France, 101; home consumption during, 24; legislation on, 23, 34, 163; Moore on, 146; purpose of, 23, 34; reproduction and, 23, 71; shellfish commissions on, 70; Virginia legislative petitions on, 30
coastal landowners, 180–81
codes of conduct, locally defined, 15
Cold Springs Harbor, 111, 127, 128
collective action, 14, 74–77, 179
Collins, Joseph, 113, 129
colonial grants, 27
colonialism, 11, 12, 77, 80–81, 94
commissions. *See* shellfish commissions
common-property rights: access and, 115; characterization of tongers and, 81; farming metaphors for, 79; in France, 101; for inshore fisheries, 22; leases vs., 181; local traditions and, 6; maps and, 12; modernists on, 70, 72–74, 144–45; overharvesting and, 14; oyster decline and, 72, 74–77, 113, 116; populists on, 73, 75;

common-property rights (*continued*)
privatization vs., 87; progress and, 77–78, 94; property incentives and, 74–77; starfish and, 75
commons, tragedy of, 74
complexity: challenge of, 1, 180–83; conservation practices and, 22, 43–44, 181–82; of ecological systems, 3–4, 5, 43–44, 132; of local traditions, 22, 43–44, 181; shellfish commissions and, 95; of social systems, 17; substantive rationality and, 10
compromises: bottom-up process for, 181; Chesapeake Bay maps and, 136; complexity of, 43–44; Goldsborough definition and, 134; law enforcement and, 45; local traditions and, 22, 43, 153; modernist maps and, 154; populist maps and, 153; straight-line maps and, 150, 154; Virginia legislators on, 166
Conn, H. W., 172
Connecticut: aquaculture history in, 2, 131; aquaculture leases in, 79, 157–62, *161*, 207n23; canning in, 2; deepwater cultivation and, 37; definition of natural beds in, 137–38; on enclosures, 33; law enforcement in, 58; lease maps of, 137, 157–58, 159–62, *161*, 207n23; Moore on, 147; oyster wars and, 37; packing industry in, 35–36, 40–43; planting industry in, 78, 119; productivity in, 88; property rights disputes in, 37–38; residency laws in, 27; sanitary maps of, 173; straight-line maps of, 137–39
Connecticut Shellfish Commission: on common-property rights, 74–75; on existing legislation, 70–71; founding of, 66; law enforcement and, 58; lease maps by, 159–62, *161*, 207n23; mapping surveys by, 137–39; on privatization, 73–74; on science, 86; structure of, 65

Connecticut State Board of Health, 173
conservation law enforcement. *See* law enforcement
conservation practices: banning of dredges and, 24–26; closed seasons for, 23, 34; complexity and, 22, 43–44, 181–82; cull laws for, 24, 34; harvest limits as, 23–24; legislative petitions and, 29–34, 43–44; lime laws and, 23, 34; modern, 44; in northern New England, 22; pre-1880, 2–3, 21–44; pre-industrial, 15; preservationist management vs., 7–8; residency laws for, 26–27; simplification of, 1; size limits for, 24; in small-scale fisheries, 15; sustainability and, 43, 44. *See also* ecological systems; local traditions
cooking oysters, 170, 171
cooperative organizations, 115
coots, 86
Costa-Pierce, Barry, 17
Coste, Jean Victor: failure by, 120; Kinsey on, 16; Page on, 87; pioneering work of, 96; praise for, 118, 119, 132; research by, 97–103; short-term results from, 131
Craib, Raymond, 11–12
Crimes against Nature (Jacoby), 45–46
criminal negligence, 50–51
Crisfield, John, 42
Crisfield, Maryland, 42, 68, 104
cross-border fisheries, 15
crown fires, 5
cull laws: collective action and, 75–76; law enforcement for, 61; local traditions and, 44; Moore on, 146; purpose of, 24, 34; shellfish commissions and, 75–76
customary rights, 56. *See also* local traditions

Dabney, Charles, 142
Damariscotta Bay, 180
dams, 9–10, 34

Darwinism, 121, 122–23
Davidson, Hunter, 49–50, 51, 52, 61
Deal's Island, 41, 60–61
Dean, Bashford, 92–93
de Bon, M., 98–99
deepwater cultivation, 36–38, 40, 58, 159, 160
"Defense of the Tidewater Oyster Industry, A" (pamphlet), 166
Delaware Bay, 39–40, 56–57, 139–41, 154
Delaware fish commissions, 66–67
Democratic Party, 50–51, 68
Department of Marine Resources (Maine), 181
depuration, 171
Dialectics of Enlightenment (Horkheimer and Adorno), 10
dispossession, 12, 13, 77, 80, 83, 94
Dorchester County, Maryland, 208n41
Drayton, Richard, 94
dredgers, 26; banning of, 24–26, 27, 29, 41, 115; class conflict with, 49–50; deepwater cultivation and, 37; definition of, 2; expansion of beds by, 31–32; natural bed definition and, 135; overharvesting by, 52, 69; residency requirements for, 41; vessel size limits and, 191n50; Virginia legislative petitions on, 31. *See also* illegal dredging
drinking water supplies, 168
drum fish, 56
Drummond, Henry, 121
Dutch immigrants, 16, 39–40
Dutchmen on the Bay (Taylor), 39–40

Eastern Oysters, sex of, 103, 200n13
Eastern Shore railroad, 42
Easton Ledger, 71
E. coli. See *Escherichia coli*
ecological systems: complexity of, 3–4, 5, 43–44, 132; efficiency and, 3–4; local traditions and, 43; in the mid-Atlantic region, 38–39; simplification and, 1, 3–4, 182; spatial planning and, 38; state agencies on, 4. *See also* social-ecological systems
Economy and Society (Weber), 10–11
Edney, Matthew, 12
education, 117–18, 131, 142–43
"Education and Production" (Dabney), 142
efficiency: definition of, 8; ecological systems and, 3–4; goal of, 9; Hays's gospel of, 64; modernists on, 64; populists on, 7, 64; productivity and, 9; progress and, 94–95; property maps and, 18; public good and, 8; shellfish commissions and, 18; simplification and, 3–4, 95; two gospels of, 3–4, 7–8, 18, 95
Ellinger, William, 144
emancipation movement, 33
employment, 21, 36, 42–43, 167, 175, 183
enclosures, 33–34, 77–78, 94
entrepreneurs, 8, 89
environmental conditions: barren bottom maps and, 155, 176–77; Eastern Oysters' sex and, 200n13; hatcheries and, 132; knowledge of, 131; variations in, 71, 108, 113; visibility and, 178
environmental history, 2–3, 4–5, 9–10, 183
equity: access and, 30; goal of, 22; harvest limits for, 23; local traditions on, 8, 43; modernist solutions and, 87; Virginia legislative petitions on, 30–31
Escherichia coli (*E. coli*), 171, 209n70
ethics, 15, 78, 87
Europe: Blue Points to, 38, 191n36; as a model of progress, 118–19; oyster decline in, 74–75, 100; oyster science in, 18, 96–97; productivity in, 142; typhoid research in, 169, 171; USFC report on, 92–93
even-age forests, 7
evolutionary theory, 117, 122–23
exclusion, 48, 55–58, 61–62, 72
Exclusive Economic Zone, 13–14

Fairfield, Connecticut, 139
family consumption. *See* home consumption
farmers, Jeffersonian ideals of, 83
Farmers of Forty Centuries (King), 93
farming. *See* agriculture
"Farming the Waters" (Smith), 125
fattening (floating), 27–28, 97, 172, 173–74
federal government, 91, 125–30. *See also* United States Fish Commission
Ferguson, T. B., 88, 110, 127, 129–30
fines, for illegal dredgers, 49, 50
finfish fisheries, 3, 14
Finley, Carmel, 182
fire cycle, simplification of, 5, 182
fish and game legislation, 55
fish and game poaching, 45–46
fish commissions, 66–67. *See also* shellfish commissions
fisheries: Alaskan, 14; in California, 74; capture, 3–4, 16; cross-border, 15; finfish, 3, 14; inshore, 15, 22; offshore, 15; small-scale, 15; USFC survey of, 91–92; wild, 3, 16, 17. *See also* natural oyster beds
fisheries conservation. *See* conservation practices
fisheries history, 1–2, 14–19, 182
Fishes of the Gulf of Maine (Bigelow), 92
fish farms. *See* aquaculture
fish hatcheries, 118, 120
Fish Hawk (ship), 110, 130
Fishing Bay, 53
Fishing Gazette, 113, 158, 162
fishways, 34, 85
five-acre law of 1865 (Maryland), 163, 164
floating. *See* fattening
Florida, 43, 177
food supplies, for oyster larvae, 105, 106, 107–8
Forest and Stream, 109, 128
Forest Dreams, Forest Nightmares (Langston), 4–5

forest management, 4–5, 6–7, 22, 95, 182
formal rationality, 10–11
Frankfurt School, 10
French oyster science: labor-intensive nature of, 93; as a model of progress, 118–19; pond culture system and, 100–101, 107, 109–10; productivity and, 142; research in, 97–103, 117
frontier analogies, 77–78, 80, 83, 144–45
Fuller, Caleb, 171, 173–74, 178
Fulton Street market experiments, 108, 111, 127
funding, for oyster science, 124

game wardens, 55
genetically modified–farmed fish, 17
Georgia, 177
German carp, 118
German forestry, 7
Giaxa, V. de, 171
Gilbert, Pamela, 155
goals, simplification and, 8–9
Goldsborough, Charles, 134–35
Goldsborough, William, 193n21
Goldsborough definition, 134–35, 136, 137–38, 148, 151
Goode, George, 124
government agencies. *See* federal government; shellfish commissions; state agencies
grab measures, 151
Graduate Record Examinations (GRE), 5–6
grand jury, 51, 193n21
Grave, Caswell, 151, 163–64, 177
GRE. *See* Graduate Record Examinations
Great Bay, Long Island, 16, 140
great pond ordinance (Massachusetts), 79
Great South Bay, 38–39, 172, 191n36
Green, Seth, 128
Griffith ("Licensed Tongmen"), 50
Grosvenor, Gilbert, 125

ground fires, 5
Gulf of Maine, 28

"Half Century of Darwinism, A" (Nelson), 121, 122
Haman, B. H., 163
Haman Oyster Culture Law of 1906 (Maryland), 144, 150, 153, 163–64, 165
Hardin, Garrett, 14, 74
harvest limits, pre-1880, 23–24
Harvey, David, 13, 156
hatcheries: artificial fertilization for, 103–6; fish, 118, 120; modernists on, 8, 87; Moore on, 146; Nelson on, 120–21; privatization and, 87, 123, 131; profitability of, 121; progress and, 131; pure science research vs., 124–25; scientific research from 1878–1885 on, 103–11; scientific research post-1885 on, 111–12; scientists' preference for, 116–23, 130–32, 181; seawater for, 103–4, 105, 108; shellfish commissions on, 84–87; as the solution to the oyster decline, 116–23; state agencies on, 4, 131; USFC and, 96
Hays, Samuel, 3, 8, 64, 93
hedges, 34
hermaphrodites, 103
High Country News, 5
home consumption, 24, 27
Honga River, 53
Horkheimer, Max, 10
Howard, Thomas, 54, 60–61
Hubbard, Jennifer, 132
Hull, David, 96, 131
hunting clubs, 55
Huntington, L. D., 128–29
hydraulic societies, 10

illegal dredging: armed conflict and, 53–54; captured vessels and, 40–41; in the Chesapeake Bay, 40–41, 49–55; fines for, 49, 50; Haman Oyster Culture Law on, 163; methods of, 52–53; by out-of-state vessels, 29, 51; oyster decline and, 115; protective associations and, 57–58; reduction in, 62; shellfish commissions on, 70; Virginia oyster navies and, 46–48
immigrants, 16, 39–40, 81
independence, 8–9, 22, 43, 83
individual transferable quotas (ITQs), 14
industrial education, 143
industrialization: aquaculture and, 3, 17; history of, 2–3, 11, 181; modernists on, 11; overharvesting and, 14–16, 17; wild fisheries and, 3. *See also* packing industry
infusoria, 105, 106, 108
Ingersoll, Ernest, 28, 35, 39, 91–92, 208n48
inshore fisheries, 15, 22
inspections, 60, 176
instrumental rationality, 9–11, 18
international politics, 15
interventionists, 3, 64, 101
Ireland, 169, 171
irrigation studies, 9–10
ITQs. *See* individual transferable quotas

Jackson, Elihu Emory, 53
Jacoby, Karl, 3, 15, 45–46, 61
Jamaica Bay, 38, 58, 173
James River: permit system for, 167; survey of 1909, 136, 147–49, *149*, 178
Japan, 93
Jeffersonian ideals, 11, 83
Joyce, Patrick, 179
Judd, Richard, 3, 15, 22, 44
judge-appointed tongers, 141
juvenile oysters, 23, 34

Keiner, Christine, 16
King, F. H., 93
Kinsey, Darin, 16
knowledge: of complex systems, 95; of environmental conditions, 131; of fishermen, 182; lack of, 5, 119, 123,

knowledge (*continued*)
131, 132; locally specific, 22, 43, 71, 91–92, 154, 183
knowledge production, 179
Knowles, John P.: characterization of tongers by, 81; on existing legislation, 69; frontier analogies by, 80; on oyster decline, 67; on the shellfish commission, 156–57; solutions held by, 93–94

labor-saving machines, 142, 143
Lake Fusaro, Italy, 98
Lancaster County, Virginia, 30
Langston, Nancy, 4–5, 95, 182
larvae. *See* oyster larvae
law enforcement, 45–62; armed conflict with, 47, 51–52, 53–54; in the Chesapeake Bay, 45, 46–55; in Connecticut, 58; corrupt, 45, 50; lack of, 31, 42; local traditions and, 17, 45–46, 57–58; in Maryland, 49–55, 60–61; moral economies and, 61–62; in New Jersey, 45, 55–58; in New York, 45; for privilege or protection, 55–57, 62; resistance to, 45–46; in Rhode Island, 58; the Riggin affair and, 47; shellfish commissions on, 70; slavery and, 32–33; in Virginia, 46–48
lead paint, 178
lease maps, 155–68; capitalism and, 156, 179; of Connecticut, 137, 157–62, *161*, 207n23; of Maryland, 163–65, 208n41; of New Jersey, 162–63; of New York, 162–63; precommission, 156–58; of Rhode Island, 156–59; of Virginia, 165–68
Lee, McDonald, 82–83, 166–67
Lefebvre, Henri, 13, 156
Legg, Henry, 66, 68, 73
legislation: on aquaculture leases, 28–29, 39; Baylor on, 145; on closed seasons, 23, 34, 163; on cull laws, 24, 34, 44, 75–76, 146; on the definition of natural beds, 137–38; on dredgers, 24–26, 41, 191n50; on enclosures, 33–34; existing precommission laws, 69–72; fish and game, 55; five-acre law of 1865 (Maryland), 163, 164; Haman Oyster Culture Law of 1906 (Maryland), 144, 150, 153, 163–64, 165; on harvest limits, 23–24; on inspections, 176; on lime laws, 23, 34, 44; local (place-specific), 30, 69; on monopolies, 191n51; one-acre law of 1830 (Maryland), 163; Oyster Act of 1844 (Rhode Island), 156; on packing houses, 176; on planters' rights (1870s), 208n45; on planting, 27–29; pre-1880, 23–29; Price-Campbell act of 1912 (Maryland), 164–65; on residency requirements, 26–27; Shepard act of 1914 (Maryland), 165; on size limits, 24; special act of 1888 (Virginia), 208n49; town vs. state, 70–71, 159; on vessel restrictions, 26; Yates and, 150–51
legislative petitions, in Virginia, 29–34, 43–44, 46
Leila (boat), 49–55
"Licensed Tongmen" (Griffith), 50
licensing, 58–61
lime laws, 23, 34, 44
livelihood, 6, 83, 135, 148, 151, 153
lobster fishery, 15
local (place-specific) legislation, 30, 69
local knowledge, 22, 43, 71, 91–92, 154, 183
local traditions: on access, 22, 43; codes of conduct and, 15; common-property rights and, 6; complexity of, 22, 43–44, 181; customary rights and, 56; definition of natural beds and, 134–36; on equity, 8, 43; German forestry and, 7; goals of, 8–9, 22; heterogeneity of, 182; law enforcement and, 17, 45–46, 57–58; maps and, 133, 134, 139, 179; populists and, 8, 64, 70–72, 93, 133; pre-1880 conservation practices and, 21–22; scientists on, 114–15; "Thirty Years Reminiscences of a Veteran Oyster Planter" on, 141

INDEX 221

Lockwood, William, 37
Logic of Sufficiency (Princen), 8–9
Long Island Sound, 27, 34–35, 36–38, 48, 67
long-term results, vs. short-term success, 5
Louisiana, 43, 142, 177, 178, 210n98

machines, labor-saving, 142, 143
Machines as the Measure of Men (Adas), 11
Maine, 15, 28, 92, 180–81
Making Salmon (Taylor), 132
Maltby, Caleb, 42
maps and mapping, 133–55; barren bottom, 13, 135, 138, 155, 176–78, 210n98; Baylor Line maps, 141–45, 148–49, *149*, 150; boat sheets, 152; common-property rights and, 12; of Connecticut, 137–39, 157–58, 159–62, *161*, 179, 207n23; cultural history of, 153; James River 1909 survey, 136, 147–49, *149*; local traditions and, 133, 134, 139; of Maryland, 163–65, 208n41; by modernists, 12, 141–53; Moore's 1909 resurvey, 146–50, *149*; of New Jersey, 139–41, 162–63, 172–73; of New York, 162–63; populists and, 141; precision maps, 136; progress maps, 152, 156; projection maps, 152; of Rhode Island, 136–37, 138, 139, 156–59; role of, 11–14, 18, 142; for social reform, 155; straight-line maps, 133–34, 136–45, 148–49, *149*, 150, 154; types of, 18; of Virginia, 141–45, 148–49, *149*, 150, 165–68; visibility and, 155, 178–79; Yates's 1906–1912 survey, 150–53, *152*, 164, 165. *See also* cartographers; lease maps; sanitary maps
marine space: modernists on, 64, 70; simplification of, 3; territorialization of, 13–14; visibility of, 178. *See also* compromises; maps and mapping
Martin v. Waddell, 156
Maryland: artificial propagation experiments by, 107; barren bottoms in, 79; Board of Public Works, 60–61; Brooks on, 119; characterization of tongers in, 83; common-property rights in, 78; cull laws in, 76; definition of natural beds in, 134–35; dredging ban in, 41; employment in, 21; five-acre law of 1865, 163, 164; Haman Oyster Culture Law of 1906, 144, 150, 153, 163–64, 165; illegal dredging and, 40–41, 46–48, 49–55; law enforcement in, 49–55, 60–61; lease maps of, 163–65, 208n41; on monopolies, 191n51; one-acre law of 1830, 163; overharvesting in, 17; oyster decline in, 67; oyster navies in, 49–55, 60–61, 68; packing houses in, 41–42; packing industry in, 2, 41–42, 68, 175; peak oyster harvests in, 53; planting laws in, 28; politics in, 16; Price-Campbell act of 1912, 164–65; residency laws in, 27; Shepard act of 1914, 165; State Oyster Police Force, 47; Stevenson's report on, 73; Virginia boundary line with, 47, 49; Yates's 1906–1912 survey of, 136, 150–53, *152*, 164, 165. *See also* Chesapeake Bay
Maryland Fish Commission, 66
"Maryland Oyster and His Political Enemies" (pamphlet), 51
Maryland's Conservation Commission, 165
Maryland Shellfish Commission: corruption in, 129–30; 1884 report of, 68–69; on existing legislation, 69, 71; first commissioner of, 63; on the oyster decline, 68–69; scientific findings of, 86–87; structure of, 66. *See also* Brooks, William; Waddell, James
Massachusetts: Baylor on, 142; closed seasons law in, 23; on enclosures, 33–34; great pond ordinance in, 79; lime laws in, 23; oyster decline in, 67; residency laws in, 27
Massachusetts Fish Commission, 66

Massachusetts Shellfish Commission, 65, 69, 87–88
materialism, 130
Mather, Fred, 127–28, 130
Mathews County, Virginia, 166
Maurice River Cove, 139–41
maximum sustainable yield, 182
McCay, Bonnie, 15–16, 22, 39
McDonald, Marshall: on artificial cultivation, 107, 108; Blackford and, 129; correspondence of, 126–28, 129; on farming, 118; on hatcheries, 85; on local traditions, 114; on natural oyster beds, 115; on oyster decline, 112, 113; on progress, 117; on pure science, 124
McEvoy, Arthur, 15, 61, 74, 94, 182
McKinney, Philip, 59–60, 166, 208n49
McLane (ship), 54
Merrill, Azel, 175
Mesereau, Joseph, 172
Mexican cartographers, 12
mid-Atlantic region, 38–40
Middletown typhoid outbreak, 170
Miles River, 52
militia, Virginia, 48
Mill Creek, Staten Island, 172
Ministry of the Marine (France), 99, 101
Mississippi Delta, 210n98
Möbius, Karl, 96–97, 101–3, 119, 120, 131
modernism, high, 6–7
modernists: on agriculture, 8, 79; on aquaculture, 64, 70, 77–80; as cartographers, 12–13, 133, 141–53, 154; characterization of tongers by, 80–83; on common-property rights, 70, 72–74, 144–45; contradictory, 124–30; critique of, 181–82; on education, 143; on efficiency, 64; on existing legislation, 69, 70, 72; frontier analogies by, 77–78, 80; on hatcheries, 8, 87; historical narratives by, 77, 80; on industrialization, 11; maps by, 12, 141–53; on marine space, 64, 70; OGDA and, 89; optimistic statements by, 88, 93–94; on overharvesting, 67, 77; on oyster decline, 115–16; on planting, 64, 72, 87–88, 94; populists vs., 7–9, 65; on privatization, 7–8, 11, 64, 72–73, 94; on property incentives, 74–77; pure science and, 124–25; as scientists, 84–85, 88, 96, 123, 125–30; simplification and, 78; solutions held by, 93–95
monoculture, 4, 37
monopolies, 30–31, 73, 144, 191n51
Moore, H. F.: barren bottom maps and, 177–78, 210n98; Chesapeake Bay 1909 survey by, 146–50, *149*; Goldsborough definition and, 135; James River survey of 1909 and, 178; maps and, 142, 145, 153; natural bed dispersion and, 136; OGDA and, 175; pond culture system and, 111–12
moral economies, 45, 50, 58, 61–62, 64, 181

Narragansett Bay, 34–35, 36, 137, 159, 174
National Association of Shellfish Commissioners (NASC), 89–90, 175
National Geographic Society, 125
National Marine Fisheries Service, 182
Native Americans, 23, 28
natural history, 104, 112
natural law, 7, 72, 121–22
Natural Laws in the Spiritual World (Drummond), 121
natural oyster bed decline. *See* oyster decline
natural oyster beds: barren, 78–79, 176–77; buffers around, 150; in Chesapeake Bay, 73, 135–36, 141–53; Civil War impact on, 41; common-property rights for, 115; in Connecticut, 137–39; definition of, 29, 134–36, 137, 193n21; dispersed by dredging, 135–36; exhausted,

135, 138; expansion of, 31–32; in France, 100, 102–3; Goldsborough definition of, 134–35, 136, 137–38, 148, 151; lease maps and, 158–59; in Long Island Sound, 35; modernists on, 141–53; Moore's 1909 resurvey of, 146–50, *149*; in New Jersey, 139–41; populists on, 88; Price-Campbell act on, 164; public, 22, 165; reduced pressure on, 58; in Rhode Island, 136–37, 138, 139; shifting borders of, 153; as social constructs, 133, 153; straight-line maps and, 141–45, 148–49, *149*, 150; Virginia legislative petitions on, 31–32. *See also* maps and mapping; overharvesting

natural resource management: centralized control of, 9; complexity and, 95; efficiency and, 3–4; evolution of, 113, 114; influence of maps on, 13; local traditions and, 114–15; preservationist vs. conservationist, 7–8; Southern Trade and, 36. *See also* conservation practices

Nelson, Julius: artificial cultivation and, 111, 112, 114; correspondence of, 124–25; on education, 117; on natural oyster beds, 115; OGDA and, 175; optimistic statements by, 120–21; personality of, 121; on pond culture, 118; on Prince Edward Island, 115–16; religious views of, 121–22

New England, northern, 22, 44

New Haven, Connecticut, 35–36, 40–43, 169, 207n23

New Jersey: aquaculture history in, 2; aquaculture leases in, 39, 162–63; Atlantic County District Commission, 163; closed seasons law in, 23; cull laws in, 24; fisheries history of, 15; law enforcement in, 45, 55–58; lease maps of, 162–63; licensing in, 59; lime laws in, 23; maps of, 139–41, 162–63, 172–73; nineteenth-century politics in, 22; Ocean County District Commission, 90–91, 140, 162–63; planting laws in, 28; protective associations in, 57; residency laws in, 27; sanitary maps of, 172–73; spatial divisions in, 39; straight-line maps of, 139–41; typhoid outbreaks in, 173

New Jersey Commission for the Investigation of the Oyster Conditions, 90–91

New Jersey Courier, 55, 56, 90, 121, 162

New Jersey District Commission, 140

New Jersey Fish Commission, 66

New Jersey Shellfish Commission: characterization of tongers by, 81–82; on cull laws, 75–76; on existing legislation, 70, 71; lease maps by, 162–63; on leasing barren bottoms, 78–79; mapping surveys by, 139–41; Nelson's correspondence with, 124–25; scientific findings of, 86–87; structure of, 65, 66

Newtonian principles, 123

New York: aquaculture history in, 2; aquaculture leases in, 39, 162–63; Blue Point oysters from, 38, 172, 174, 191n36; closed seasons law in, 23; law enforcement in, 45; lease maps of, 162–63; lime laws in, 23; packing industry in, 2, 174; planting laws in, 28; protective associations in, 57–58; residency laws in, 27

New York Fish Commission, 66, 172

New York Shellfish Commission: investigative surveys by, 65–66; lease maps by, 162–63; on oyster decline, 67; political patronage and, 128; on science, 86; structure of, 65. *See also* Blackford, Eugene

New York Times, 170, 172, 173

night operations, 32–33, 52

North Carolina, 43, 177

northerners: Baylor on, 145; corruption of slaves by, 32–33; packing industry and, 29, 35–36; as planters, 40, 165, 191n50, 208n45; seed

northerners (*continued*)
  oysters for, 40, 191n50; Virginia planters' rights laws and, 29, 165, 208n45. *See also* outsiders

Ocean County District Commission (New Jersey), 90–91, 140, 162–63
offshore fisheries, 15
OGDA. *See* Oyster Growers and Dealers Association
one-acre law of 1830 (Maryland), 163
Oriental Despotism (Wittfogel), 10
outsiders, 22, 26–27, 29, 46. *See also* northerners
overharvesting: aquaculture for, 16; collective action and, 74–75, 76–77; commons model of, 14; by dredgers, 52, 69; formal rationality and, 10; industrialization and, 14–16, 17; modernists on, 67, 77; oyster decline and, 113, 115–16; populists on, 8, 67, 77; post–Civil War, 48; shellfish commissions on, 67–69; simplification of, 10; solutions to, 17–18, 132; state agencies on, 3–4
oversimplification. *See* simplification
Oyster, The (Brooks), 84
Oyster Act of 1844 (Rhode Island), 156
oyster brands, 38, 191n36
oyster commissions. *See* shellfish commissions
oyster conservation practices. *See* conservation practices
oyster decline: Blackford on, 67, 79–80; common-property rights and, 72, 74–77, 113, 116; in Europe, 74–75, 100; fear of, 53; hatcheries as the solution to, 116–23; the inevitable decline problem and, 112–16; modernists on, 115–16; post–Civil War, 48; shellfish commissions on, 67–69; temporary vs. permanent, 68; Virginia legislative petitions on, 31. *See also* overharvesting
oyster farms. *See* aquaculture

Oyster Growers and Dealers Association (OGDA), 89, 91, 175, 179
Oyster Growers Association (Rhode Island), 175–76
oyster harvests, in the 1880s, 53
oyster hatcheries. *See* hatcheries
oyster larvae: attachment stage and, 106, 107, 108–9; cull laws for, 24; food supplies for, 105, 106, 107–8; growth of, 106; in laboratories, 103–11; spat collectors for, 98–99, 100
Oysterman and Fisherman, 167
oyster mapping. *See* maps and mapping
oystermen. *See* tongers
oyster navies, 42, 46–55, 60–61, 68
oyster police force (Connecticut), 58
"Oyster Problem Solved, The" (Ryder), 109, 110
oyster science, 103–11, 116–23; in Europe, 18, 96–97; evolution of, 96–97; French research in, 97–103; funding for, 124; history of, 16–17; the inevitable decline problem and, 112–16; modernists and, 88; NASC and, 90; political patronage and, 97; populists and, 86–87, 125; productivity and, 84, 88, 97; role for, 86, 127; scientific research from 1878–1885 on, 103–11; scientific research post-1885 on, 111–12; shellfish commissions and, 84–87, 93; USFC and, 67, 91. *See also* scientists
"Oysters Culture in Relation to Disease" (Bulstrode), 171
Oysters from a Medical Point of View (Pasquier), 169
oyster shells, 23, 24, 42
Oyster Wars and the Public Trust (McCay), 22

packing industry: on access, 54–55; in Connecticut, 35–36, 40–43; definition of, 2; employment in,

36, 42–43, 175; history of, 2; law enforcement and, 45; legislation on, 176; local traditions and, 181; in Maryland, 2, 41–42, 68, 175; in New York, 2, 174; northerner-owned, 29, 35–36; organized labor in, 14; Philadelphia Ring and, 57; pre-1880, 35–36; in Rhode Island, 175–76, 179; sanitary maps and, 13, 155, 168; sanitary practices in, 174–76, 179; typhoid outbreaks and, 91, 174–76
Page, J. R., 87
Palinurus (schooner), 160
park-based conservation, 45, 61
Pasquier, J. P. A., 169
patrol boats, gasoline-powered, 48
Patuxent River, 164
Payne, Brian, 14–15, 44
permit system, 167
perpetual leases, 72–73
Philadelphia, Pennsylvania, 40–41, 57
phylogeny, dynamics of, 122
piracy, 54
place-specific (local) legislation, 30, 69
planters: capitalistic, 153–54; characterization of, 80; definition of, 2; employment by, 167; Haman Oyster Culture Law of 1906 on, 163–64; hatcheries and, 87; motivation of, 164; northern, 40, 165, 191n50, 208n45; on the Ocean County District Commission, 90–91; property rights and, 37–38, 62; rights of, 165, 208n45; sanitary maps and, 13; special act of 1888 (Virginia) on, 208n49; speculation by, 158; Virginia legislative petitions on, 31
planter-tonger relationships. *See* tonger-planter relationships
planting: armed guards for, 45; Baylor Line maps and, 141; deepwater cultivation for, 36–38, 40, 58, 159, 160; education on, 117; expansion of, 119, 131, 143, 144, 150, 153–54; as farming, 118; French research on, 97–103; history of, 28; legislation on, 27–29; in Long Island Sound, 35; modernists on, 64, 72, 87–88, 94; optimistic statements on, 87–88, 119–20; populists on, 88; profitability of, 115; as progress, 131, 147; pros and cons of, 16–17, 28; in San Francisco Bay, 43; seed oysters for, 40, 191n50; spatial divisions for, 38. *See also* aquaculture; aquaculture leases; hatcheries; lease maps; oyster science
planting beds, definition of, 134
poaching, 45–46
Pocomoke (schooner), 46
Pocomoke Sound, 47
political activism, by tongers, 39
political compromises. *See* compromises
political patronage, 50–51, 97, 125–30, 132
pollution: from aquaculture, 17; sewage, 172, 173, 174–75, 179
pollution reform, 62
polyculture, vs. monoculture, 4
pond culture system, 100–101, 107, 109–10, 111, 117, 118
ponderosa forests, 5
the poor, access for, 2, 22, 24, 30–31, 73
populists: as cartographers, 12–13, 133, 141, 153; cautious statements by, 88; collective action and, 76; on common-property rights, 73, 75; on efficiency, 7, 64; on existing legislation, 69, 70–71; investigative surveys by, 66; local traditions and, 8, 64, 70–72, 93, 133; modernists vs., 7–9, 65; on overharvesting, 8, 67, 77; on oyster science, 86–87, 125; on planting, 88; on progress, 79–80; role of, 182; solutions held by, 93; on tongers, 8, 70–72, 83
Porter, Theodore, 126
Port Norris, New Jersey, 139
Potomac River, 47, 107, 167, 208n48

poverty, 80, 81–82, 142, 143, 145
precommission lease maps, 156–58
pre-industrial conservation practices, 15
preservationist resource management, 7–8
Price-Campbell act of 1912 (Maryland), 164–65
prices: cull laws and, 61; foreign vs. domestic, 93, 100, 101; livelihood and, 135, 148; overharvesting and, 52; size limits and, 24
Prince Edward Island, 115–16
Princen, Thomas, 8–9
Princess Anne Herald, 46
privatization: aquaculture and, 22, 70; of barren bottoms, 78–79; Baylor on, 145; common-property rights vs., 87; frontier analogies of, 80; hatcheries and, 87, 123, 131; maps and, 18; for maximization of production, 11, 118, 147; modernists on, 7–8, 11, 64, 72–73, 94; monopolies and, 73; Moore on, 146–47; pond culture system and, 117; Price-Campbell act on, 164; progress and, 77–78, 84–85, 94, 113–14, 147, 154; property incentives and, 74–77; public rights vs., 22; simplification and, 74, 182; state agencies on, 4
privilege, vs. protection, 55–57, 62
productivity: education and, 142–43; efficiency defined as, 9; moral economies vs., 64; privatization and, 11, 118, 147; for the public good, 7–8, 11; science and, 84, 88, 97; simplification and, 11, 78, 181
professions, 97, 112, 132
profitability: deepwater cultivation and, 36–37; Haman act and, 163; of hatcheries, 121; of illegal dredging, 41; of planting, 115; from pollution, 179; size limits and, 191n50
progress: common-property rights and, 77–78, 94; efficiency and, 94–95; enclosures and, 94; in Europe, 118–19; frontier analogies of, 80; hatcheries and, 131; maps and, 152, 156; modernists on, 77, 80; Moore on, 147; planting as, 131, 147; populists on, 79–80; privatization and, 77–78, 84–85, 94, 113–14, 147, 154; in the South, 143; tradition vs., 114–115; visibility and, 118, 179
Progressive Era reform: cartography and, 11–14; efficiency and, 3–4; interventionists of, 64; policy solutions promoted by, 7–8; pressures of, 181; simplification in, 1; Taylorist approach to, 78, 94–95; theoretical lens on, 19; visibility and, 178–79
progress maps, 152
projection maps, 152
property maps. *See* maps and mapping
property rights: in Connecticut, 37–38; maps and, 11–13, 133, 154; modernists on, 11; planters and, 37–38; planting laws and, 28–29; public, 22, 72, 83, 135, 145, 165; science and, 84; simplification of, 1; as social constructs, 133; state agencies on, 4; territorialization of space and, 13–14; tonger-planter division and, 62. *See also* common-property rights; privatization
protection, vs. privilege, 55–57, 62
protective associations, 57–58
Providence, Rhode Island, 210n82
Providence River, 35
public good, 8, 11, 77, 126
public health, 168–71, 179
public health laboratories, 210n82
public opinion, 144–45, 146, 147, 150
public-private partnerships, 89
public property rights, 22, 72, 83, 135, 145, 165
pure science, 97, 124–25, 132

"raccoon" oysters, 43
racial prejudice, 82–83
railroads, 42, 44
Rappahannock River, 167
Raritan Bay, 38, 175

rationality: formal vs. substantive, 10–11; instrumental, 9–10, 18
Ravenel, William, 109–10
regional interactions: deepwater cultivation and, 36–38; impact of, 2; in the mid-Atlantic region, 38–40; New Haven packing houses and, 35–36, 40–43; pre-1880, 21–22, 34–43, 44
registration of vessels, 58, 59, 60
"Relation of Biology to Theology" (Nelson), 121
religion, science and, 121–22
reproduction: artificial cultivation and, 98, 103–11; artificial fertilization and, 103–6, 109, 111; closed seasons and, 23, 71; cull laws and, 24; impact of dredging on, 32; overharvesting and, 77. *See also* hatcheries
residency requirements, 26–27, 30, 41, 58–59, 82
resource management. *See* natural resource management
restocking, 98, 99, 101, 103, 118
Rhode Island: aquaculture in, 63; boundary-line surveys for, 161; closed seasons law in, 23; cull laws in, 24; definition of public land in, 159; expansion of planting in, 119; law enforcement in, 58; lease maps of, 156–59; lime laws in, 23; natural oyster beds in, 136–37, 138, 139; Oyster Act of 1844, 156; oyster decline in, 67; packing industry in, 175–76, 179; planting laws in, 28; residency laws in, 27; sanitary practices in, 179; sanitary surveys of, 174, 210n82; straight-line maps of, 136–37, 138, 139
Rhode Island Fish Commission, 66
Rhode Island Shellfish Commission: on existing legislation, 69; first commissioner of, 63; funding for, 157; Knowles on, 156–57; mapping surveys by, 136–37, 138, 139, 179; packing industry and, 175–76; sanitary maps and, 174, 210n82; structure of, 65

Rice, Gus, 53–54
Rice, H. J., 104, 108, 109
Richmond Chamber of Commerce, 142
Richmond County Oyster Protective Association, 57–58
Richmond Times, 144–45
Riggin, John, 47, 49
Rivers of Empire (Worster), 9–10
Roanoke, Virginia, 59
Rowe, Henry: deepwater cultivation and, 36, 37; leases for, 158; OGDA and, 91, 175; packing industry and, 42; Winslow and, 107
Ryder, John: on Blackford, 129; correspondence of, 129; on French oyster science, 118; optimistic statements by, 119, 122–23; oyster science research by, 107–10; on pond culture, 117

salmon, 16, 118, 128, 182
Salmonella typhi, 168, 170, 172, 209n60
San Francisco Bay, 15, 43
sanitary certificates, 169, 174, 176, 179
sanitary maps, 168–76; of Connecticut, 173; of New Jersey, 172–73; public health and, 168–69, 179; of Rhode Island, 174, 210n82; typhoid outbreaks and, 13, 155, 168, 171–74; visibility and, 178
sanitary practices, in the packing industry, 174–76, 179
Sayville, New York, 39–40
science: productivity and, 84, 88, 97; property rights and, 84; for the public good, 126; pure vs. applied, 97, 124–25, 132; religion and, 121–22; simplification of, 18. *See also* oyster science
scientists: contradictory views of, 124–30, 132; correspondence of, 124–25; on hatcheries as the solution, 116–23, 130–32, 181; the inevitable decline problem and, 112–16; intellectual lineages and, 96; on local traditions, 114–15;

scientists (*continued*)
  modernists as, 84–85, 88, 96, 123, 125–30; optimistic statements by, 87–88, 93–94, 119–21, 122–23, 131; personalities of, 121–23; on political patronage, 125–30, 132; sanitation, 179; social reform and, 122; "system of professions" model for, 97
Scott, James, 6–7, 19, 63–64, 183
Seaver, Barton, 183
seawater, for hatcheries, 103–4, 105, 108
seed oysters, 40, 98–99, 137, 191n50
Seeing Like a State (Scott), 6–7, 19, 63–64
seiners, 56
Seth, Joseph, 76
sewage: pollution from, 172, 173, 174–75, 179; sanitary surveys of, 174; treatment of, 168
"Sex and Health" (Nelson), 121
sexes, 103, 104, 200n13
sextants, 147, 160
shad, 34, 85, 118
shellfish commissions, 63–95; aquaculture and, 63; characterization of tongers by, 80–83; on common-property rights, 72–74; on cull laws, 75–76; efficiency and, 18; establishment of, 18; on existing legislation, 69–72; historical narratives by, 77–80; licensing by, 58–61; maps by, 134; optimistic statements by, 87–88; organizations and alliances for, 88–91; on overharvesting, 67–69; permanent, 65; political patronage and, 125–30; on privatization, 64; on property incentives, 74–77; reports and surveys by, 64–66; science and, 84–87, 93; simplification by, 18, 95; structure of, 65–67; temporary, 65–66; on the two solutions, 93–95. *See also specific state commissions*
shells. *See* oyster shells
Shepard act of 1914 (Maryland), 165
short-term success, vs. long-term results, 5
shucking, 35, 42–43, 175

signal stations, 160, 162, 210n98
simplification: challenge of, 18–19; choice of, 132; for control, 63–64; ecological systems and, 1, 3–4, 182; efficiency and, 3–4, 95; in fisheries history, 182; of forest management, 4–5, 95, 182; goals and, 8–9; McCay on, 15; modernists and, 78; of overharvesting, 10; privatization and, 74, 182; for production maximization, 11, 78, 181; of property rights, 1; public good and, 11; of science, 18; by shellfish commissions, 18, 95; of social-ecological systems, 4, 6–7, 63–64, 183; of social systems, 3–4, 5–6; solutions and, 182–83; top-down regulation and, 182
size limits, 24, 44, 101
slavery, 32–33
small-scale fisheries, 15
Smith, Hugh, 125
Smith, Tim, 131
social-ecological systems: definition of, 4; in Europe, 18; simplification of, 4, 6–7, 63–64, 183
social law, 77–78, 93, 94–95, 143
social reform, 122, 155
social systems, 3–4, 5–6, 17, 180–81
Soper, George, 173
Southern Trade, 2, 35–36, 40–43
space, 12, 13–14, 156. *See also* marine space; spatial planning
spat, artificial cultivation of, 116–17
spat collectors, 98–99, 100, 101
spatial planning, 14, 19, 38–39, 134, 155
spawning, 23, 98, 99
sperm, 105
starfish, 37, 74, 75, 86
state agencies: efficiency and, 3–4; modernist vs. populist, 7–9; political patronage and, 125–30; simplification by, 63–64; town jurisdiction vs., 70–71, 159. *See also* shellfish commissions
state legislatures, 65, 70–71, 89, 131, 159. *See also* legislation
steamships, 26, 37, 44, 54
Stevenson, Charles, 73, 76–77, 83, 93

St. Jerome Creek experiments, 107, 109, 110–11
St. Michael's Comet, 51
straight-line maps, 133–34; Baylor Line, 141–45, 148–49, 149, 150; in Connecticut and Rhode Island, 136–45
Stratford, Connecticut, 139
substantive rationality, 10–11
surveillance, 45–46, 62
surveys. *See* maps and mapping
sustainability: access and, 22, 34–35; complex systems and, 17; environmental history and, 183; maximum sustainable yield and, 182; simplification and, 18–19; traditional conservation practices and, 43, 44
Swift, Franklin, 177
System of Professions (Abbott), 132
"system of professions" model, 97, 132

Tangier (schooner), 46
Tangier Sound, 60
taxes, 58, 59–60, 147
Taylor, Joseph, 16, 78, 94–95, 132, 182
Taylor, Lawrence, 16, 39–40
technocracy, 10, 183
telegraph, 53
Tennessee, 142
territorialization of space, 13–14
territorial use rights for fishing (TURFs), 14
Texas, 143
"Thirty Years Reminiscences of a Veteran Oyster Planter," 140–41
Thompson, E. P., 64, 94
tides, study of, 173
Timmons, William, 50–51, 53, 134, 193n21
tonger-planter relationships: compromises in, 22, 43–44, 134, 136, 153, 166; employment and, 167; property rights and, 62; in Sayville, 39–40; Virginia legislation and, 166
tongers: on access, 8, 22, 54–55; as anachronisms, 11; characterization of, 80–83; class conflict with, 49–50; definition of, 2; education for, 117–18; Ellinger on, 144; on equity, 8; greed of, 75, 76; independence of, 8–9, 22, 43, 83; judge-appointed, 141; lease maps and, 158–59; limiting, 142, 153; livelihood of, 6, 83, 135, 148, 151; Moore's 1909 resurvey and, 150; murder of, 141; opinions of, 71–72; on the oyster decline, 68; on planter's motivations, 164; political activism by, 39; populists on, 8, 70–72, 83; property rights and, 62; stereotypes of, 83; Yates's 1906–1912 survey and, 151–52. *See also* local traditions
tongs, 25, 148, 152, 163
top-down regulation, 181, 182
tourism, 14
Towle, Jerry, 16
towns: aquaculture leases by, 39; lease maps by, 158; residency laws and, 27; state jurisdiction vs., 70–71, 159. *See also* local traditions
Townsend, Charles, 92
traditional customs. *See* local traditions
triangulation surveys, 159
Tuckerton Bay, 140
TURFs. *See* territorial use rights for fishing
typhoid: bacteriology of, 168–69, 170, 171; cause of, 168, 169, 209n60; outbreaks of, 169–70, 172, 173, 175; packing industry and, 91, 174–76; sanitary maps for, 13, 155, 168, 171–74; transmission of, 169–71

United States Coastal and Geological Survey (USCGS), 141, 142, 147, 150, 160
United States Fish Commission (USFC): applied science and, 125; artificial propagation experiments by, 107; barren bottom maps by, 177–78; Baylor Line maps and, 141; Blackford's letters to, 125; 1880 survey by, 91–92; 1893 report by, 73;

United States Fish Commission (*continued*)
Ferguson and, 129; letter archives of, 125–30; Möbius's research and, 102; Moore's 1909 resurvey and, 147; oyster science and, 18, 67; report on European practices, 92–93; research on hatcheries by, 96; sanitary surveys and, 172; St. Jerome Creek experiments and, 110–11; Taylor on, 132
United States Public Health Service, 175
United States Supreme Court, 156
USCGS. *See* United States Coastal and Geological Survey
USFC. *See* United States Fish Commission
utilitarianism, 130

Verrill, Addison, 106–7, 127
vessels: captured, 40–41; illegal dredging by, 29, 46–48, 51; registration of, 58, 59, 60; restrictions on, 26, 32–33; size limits on, 191n50. *See also* oyster navies
Virginia: aquaculture leases in, 79, 165–68; Baylor Line maps of, 141–45, 148–49, *149*, 150; boundary line with Maryland, 47, 49; Brooks on, 119; closed seasons in, 23, 30; employment in, 21; on enclosures, 34; illegal dredgers in, 40–41; law enforcement in, 46–48; lease maps of, 165–68; legislative petitions in, 29–34, 43–44, 46; licensing tax in, 59–60; lime laws in, 23; Moore's 1909 resurvey of, 146–50, *149*; number of planters in (1880), 208n48; overharvesting in, 17; oyster decline in, 67; oyster navies of, 46–48; planters' rights in, 28, 165, 208n45; residency requirements in, 27, 30; seed oysters and, 40, 191n50; special act of 1888, 208n49. *See also* Chesapeake Bay
Virginia Board of Fisheries, 48, 166

Virginia Fish Commission, 66, 67, 69–70, 82–83, 86–87
visibility: increasing, 6–7; maps and, 155, 178–79; progress and, 118, 179; Progressive Era reform and, 178–79; spatial planning and, 19

Waddell, James: on existing legislation, 69; on hatcheries, 84–85; on leasing, 72–73; as a modernist, 66; optimistic statements by, 88; on oyster decline, 68; telegraph system used by, 53
wages, 39, 40, 142, 151
wasted space, 12
water resources, 9–10, 182
Weber, Max, 10–11
Weibe, Robert, 64
weirs, 33–34
Wesleyan University typhoid outbreak, 169–70, 171, 172
West Creek, New Jersey, 39, 56
whale biogeography, 92
Whyte, William, 52
wild fisheries, 3, 16, 17
Williams, Raymond, 94
Winslow, Francis: attachment stage research and, 108–9; on barren bottom maps, 177; on French oyster science, 118–19; optimistic statements by, 119; on oyster science, 116; oyster science research by, 104–7; on tongers, 117
Wittfogel, Karl, 10
Wood, W. M., 130
Wood, Frank, 89
World Wide Law, A (Dabney), 142
Worster, Donald, 9–10, 18, 182

Yates, Charles: Chesapeake Bay 1906–1912 survey by, 150–53, *152*, 164, 165; Goldsborough definition and, 135; modernist plans and, 142; natural bed dispersion and, 136
yeoman ideal, 144

zoning ordinances, 13–14

SAMUEL P. HANES was born in Austin, Texas. He graduated from the University of Texas and obtained his MA and PhD in geography from Rutgers University. He is an assistant professor teaching geography and environmental courses at the University of Maine. His previous writing has appeared in *Sustainability Science, Renewable Agriculture and Food Systems, Geographical Review, Journal of Cultural Geography*, and other journals. He lives in Old Town, Maine, with his wife and daughter.

www.ingramcontent.com/pod-product-compliance
Lightning Source LLC
Chambersburg PA
CBHW030135240426
43672CB00005B/135